# LightFoot Guide
# to the
# Via Francigena
# Edition 6

## Vercelli
## to
## St Peter's Square
## Rome
## 848 kilometres

The authors have done their best to ensure the accuracy and currency of the information in this LightFoot Guide to the Via Francigena, however they can accept no responsibility for any loss, injury or inconvenience sustained by any traveller as a result of information contained in the guide. Changes will inevitably occur within the lifespan of this edition and the authors welcome notification of such changes and any other feedback that will enable them to enhance the quality of the guide.

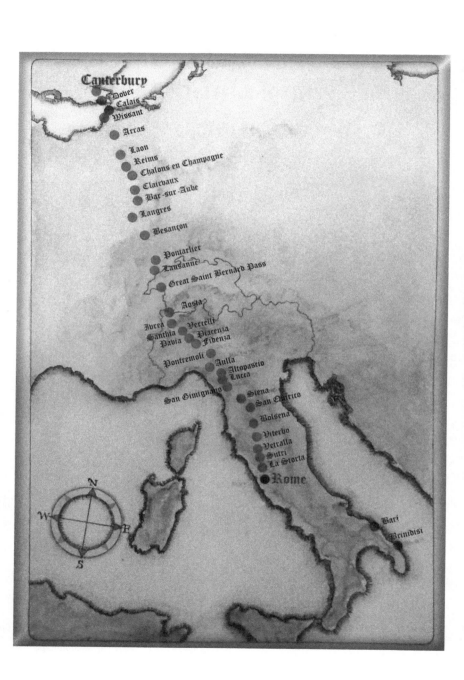

The Lightfoot Guide to the Via Francigena, written by Paul Chinn and Babette Gallard presents, in great detail, the official routes for cyclists, walkers and horse riders.

The European Association of Via Francigena (EAVF), founded in 2001, is the custodian of the Cultural Route Via Francigena. In 2006 it became the official body recognised by the Council of Europe for supporting, promoting and developing the route.

In France, the Association Via Francigena France (associated to the EAVF) manages the co-ordination of regional walking groups and liaison with other national organisations.

For more information and for downloading the Italian route see : www.viefrancigene.org"

VIA FRANCIGENA
EUROPEAN ASSOCIATION
of the Francigena Ways

Massimo Tedeschi
President
European Association of Francigena Ways

## About the Authors

We are two very ordinary people who quit the world of business and stumbled on the St James Way during our search for a more viable, rewarding alternative to our previous lifestyle. Since then we have completed four pilgrimages, one of which was particularly tough and finally prompted us to create Pilgrimage Publications and the LightFoot guide series. We have no religious beliefs, but share a 'wanderlust' and need to know about and contribute to the world we occupy.

Pilgrimage Publications is a not-for-profit organisation dedicated to the identification and mapping of pilgrim routes all over the world, regardless of religion or belief. Any revenue derived from the sale of guides or related activities is used to further enhance the service and support provided to pilgrims.

The ethos of Pilgrimage Publications has 4 very basic aims:
To enable walkers, cyclists and riders to follow pilgrim routes all over the world.
To ensure LightFoot guides are as current and accurate as possible, using pilgrim feedback as a major source of information.
To use eco-friendly materials and methods for the publication of LightFoot guides and Travel Books.
To promote eco-friendly travel.

Also by LightFoot Guides
Riding the Milky Way
Riding the Roman Way
LightFoot Guide to the via Francigena - Besançon to Vercelli
LightFoot Guide to the via Francigena - Vercelli to Rome
LightFoot Companion to the via Francigena
LightFoot Guide to the Three Saints Way - Winchester to Mont St Michel
LightFoot Guide to the Three Saints Way - Mont St Michel to St Jean d'Angely
LightFoot Guide to Foraging - a guide to over 130 of the most common edible and medicinal plants in Western Europe
LightFoot Companion to the via Domitia- Arles to Rome
Your Camino - information, maps for Camino routes in France and Spain
Camino Lingo - 'cheats' guide to speaking Spanish on the Camino
Slackpacking the Camino Frances - provides all the information and advice you'll need to plan your perfect Camino.

LightFoot Guides are designed to enable everyone to meet their personal goals and enjoy the best, whilst avoiding the worst, of following ancient pilgrimage routes. Written for Walkers, Cyclists (mountain bikes) and Horse Riders, every section of this LightFoot guide provides specific information for each group.

The authors would like to emphasise that they have made great efforts to use only public footpaths and to respect private property. Historically, pilgrims may not have been so severely restricted by ownership rights and the pressures of expanding populations, but unfortunately this is no longer the case. Today, even the most free- spirited traveller must adhere to commonly accepted routes. Failure to do so will only antagonise local residents, encourage the closure of routes and inhibit pilgrims following on behind.

Please let us know about any changes to the route or inaccuracies within this guide book. mail@pilgrimagepublications.com

## *Our special thanks go to:*

We would like to thank François Louviot and all the members of the Association Via Francigena France for their commitment to sign posting.
Adelaide Trezzini for her contribution to the development and mapping of the via Francigena route. http://www.francigena-international.org/

Openstreetmap: The maps in this book are derived from data (c) Openstreetmap (http://www.openstreetmap.org) and its contributors and are made available under the Creative Commons agreement http://creativecommons.org/licenses/by-sa/2.0/

Maperitive for the creation of an indispensable tool used in the drawing of our maps. http://igorbrejc.net/about

# Contents

## *Your LightFoot Guide to the via Francigena*

This book traces the Via Francigena from Canterbury to Besançon. You will find an introductory section followed by ?? chapters, each of which covers a segment of the route.

Each chapter contains:

- A Route Summary
- Detailed instructions
- Map
- Altitude profile
- Addresses and contact information for accommodation and other facilities

### Layout

The entire distance has been divided into manageable sections of approximately 22 kilometres, but accommodation (where it exists) is listed for the entire length of the section so that is up to you and your body where you decide to stop.

### Instructions

The entire route has been GPS traced and logged using way point co-ordinates. On this basis, it should be possible to navigate the route using only the written instructions, though a map is provided for additional support and general orientation. Use of a compass is recommended.

### Each instruction sheet provides

- Detailed directions corresponding to GPS way point numbers on the map - GPS waypoint data can be downloaded from www.pilgrimagepublications.com
- Verification Point - additional verification of current position
- Distance (in metres) between each way point
- Cross Reference to GPS and Compass direction to next waypoint

### Each map provides:

- A north/south visual representation of the route with way point numbers
- Altitude Profile for the section
- Icons indicating facilities en route (see Map symbols)
- A map scale bar. The scale differs from map to map.

### Accommodation Listings:

The price banding is based on the least expensive option for two people in each establishment - accurate at the time of entry, but subject to change. For simplicity, the listing is divided into 3 price bands:

**A** = (€/£) 70+   **B** = (€/£) 35 - 70   **C** = (€/£) 0 - 35   **D** = Donation

There are no listings above 80£/€ per night, unless nothing else is available in the area. Accommodation is listed in ascending order (i.e. cheapest first). Prices may or may not include breakfast and some establishments charge a tariff for dogs. In general, dogs are not welcome in Youth or Religious Hostels. Similarly, the general rule for accommodation in Religious Houses is that reservations must be made 24 hours ahead of arrival. Note: **Donation** means just that, you are expected to give what you can and think the accommodations warrants.

## *Accommodation is classified as follows:*

### Pilgrim Hostel
Hostel that specifically offers accommodation to via Francigena pilgrims. Usually with dormitory accommodation, kitchen facilities and shared bathrooms. The hostels may be run by commercial, municipal or religious authorities.

### Religious Hostel
A facility with accommodation managed by a religious group which may have space for via Francigena pilgrims. Usually with dormitory accommodation, kitchen facilities or the possibility of prepared meals and shared bathrooms.

### Church or Religious Organisation
Places where limited, basic accommodation or assistance may be offered.

### Commercial Hostel
Commercial or municipal hostel including gîte d'etape in France. Usually with dormitory accommodation, kitchen facilities and shared bathrooms.

### Hotel and Bed and Breakfast
More expensive commercial accommodation including chambres d'hôtes in France and Agriturismos in Italy. Usually double or family sized rooms with the possibility of a private bathroom. Hotels normally are priced by room while bed and breakfast and chambres d'hôtes may charge by room or by person. Bed and Breakfasts and Agriturismos may be isolated from shops and restaurants. Often dinner can be provided if requested in advance. Kitchen access may be possible. Where there is a choice of room types the price band is given for the room type with the lowest price. In some situations there may be seasonal premiums.

## *Following the route :*

In Italy signposting has been undertaken at a national, regional and community level as well as by many volunteer groups. As a result you will find many types of signpost with some pointing in conflicting directions. You will encounter the large brown via Francigena road signs with with 2 hikers indicating a walking route, but also bike and car symbols for other groups. This is supplemented by smaller pilgrim signs on a yellow and brown background. In areas the signs have become the target of vandalism and trophy hunting.

A volunteer group have supplemented the official signs with painted signs showing red and white stripes with a small black pilgrim. These have often proved more durable.

Each year route numerous small modifications are proposed in Italy to improve safety or increase amenity of the route. We endeavour to keep up to date with these changes in each edition of the books, but there can be a lag in the authorities adapting the signposts to the changes.

Where we describe the « Official Route » then this is the route agreed by the national managing authority and where signposting should be most complete.

## The Basics in Italy

Currency:
Euro.  Standard banking Hours: 08.30–13.30 and 14.30-16.00, Monday to Friday.  Closed on Sundays.

Post Offices
 Standard Opening Hours: 08.30-19.30 and 13.45-18.30, Monday to Friday.  Branches in smaller towns and villages close for an hour, 13.00-14.00.
Phone booths that still accept coins are hard find. If you're planning to use a public phone purchase of a telephone card is recommended.
Numbers beginning with 800 are free.
170 - English-speaking operator.
176 - International Directory Enquires.
 12 - Telephone Directory Assistance Number
112 - Carabinieri (national-level police who also perform military police duties)
113 - Emergency Police Help Number (also ambulance and fire)
115 - Fire Department
116 - A.C.I. (Italian Automobile Club) road assistance.
118 - Medical Emergencies

**Note:**  Italian telephone numbers can include 4, 5, 6, 7, or even 8 digits, so don't automatically assume you have the wrong number if it looks strange.   Since December 1998, calls to land lines in most cities, but not all, and all other points in Italy must include a leading '0' regardless of whether the call originates within or outside of Italy. However, the leading '0' is not required with mobile phones.
Letters can be sent **poste restante** to any Italian post office by addressing them "Fermo Posta" followed by the name of the town; your surname should be double-underlined for easier identification, when picking items up take your passport, and – in case of difficulty – make sure they also check under your middle names and initials.

Basic Business Hours
08.00-13.00 and 16.00-19.00, Monday to Friday. Shops in smaller towns may close on Saturday afternoons and Monday mornings.

Visiting churches and religious sites.
Most churches are open in the early morning for Mass and close around noon, opening up again at 16.00 and closing at 19.00 or 20.00.  In some remote places, churches only open for early morning and evening services.  Opening hours for museums are generally Tuesday to Saturday, 09.00 to 19.00 with a midday break.

## Health Care
All EU citizens are eligible for free health care in Italy, if they have the correct documentation. Non EU Citizens must arrange personal health insurance.

## Food
Pizza is now a worldwide phenomenon, but Italy remains the best place to eat it. Italian ice cream (gelato) is justifiably famous and available in every conceivable flavour. Traditionally Italian food consists of lunch (pranzo) and dinner (cena) starting with antipasto (literally before the meal), a course consisting of cold meats, seafood and vegetables. The next course, primo, involves soup, risotto or pasta, followed by secondo - the meat or fish course, usually served alone. Vegetables - contorni - are ordered and served separately.

## Public Holidays
August, particularly during the weeks either side of Ferragosto (August 15) is a difficult time for travellers, because many towns are deserted, with shops, bars, hotels and restaurants shut.

## Accommodation
Italian **hotels** fall into a number of categories, though the difference between each is gradually decreasing. Virtually all hostels (excepting Religious Hostels) are members of the International Youth Hostel Association and you'll need to be a member.
**Agritourismo** - basically an upmarket B&B in a rural area and usually a working farm (see Travel tips for more information)
Camping in Italy is popular and the sites are generally well equipped.

## *Useful Links*

www.Pilgrimstales.com
PILGRIM TALES publishing is passionate about inspiring others with the possibility of discovery, understanding and peace through travel.

www.pilgrimstorome.org.uk
Practical information for the pilgrimage to Rome.

www.theexpeditioner.com
THE EXPEDITIONER popular travel-themed webzine featuring articles about travel, music and film.

www.eurovia.tv/
EUROVIA serves as a platform made by pilgrims, for pilgrims. Everybody is welcome to share their experiences withothers, and to contribute their views and opinions. Other pilgrims are always grateful to receive useful tips.

http://www.viefrancigene.org/ –
Multilingual site containing: maps, GPS traces and accommodation information for the route in Italy sponsored by the European Association of the Via Francigena

http://www.francigena-international.org/
Multilingual site providing credentials, news and maps for the route in Switzerland and Italy

http://www.viefrancigene.it/ –
Italian language site with integrated Google translation providing news, credentials, maps, GPS data and accommodation throughout the route.

http://www.movimentolento.it/ – Italian language site providing information on pilgrim routes throughout Italy

http://www.regione.toscana.it/via-francigena – Italian language site with extensive information on the route in Tuscany

http://www.francigenalazio.it/ - multilingual site with extensive information on the route in Tuscany

http://pilgrim.peterrobins.co.uk/ – English language site with information on pilgrim routes throughout Europe

http://www.urcamino.com/ – English language site with accommodation information

## Facebook groups:
Via Francigena – multilingual group for all with a valid interest in the route
Via Francigena España – Spanish language group


## Recommended Reading

| | |
|---|---|
| The Art of Pilgrimage | Phil Cousineau |
| Have Saddle Will Travel | Don West |
| The Essential Walker's Journal | Leslie Sansone |
| The Pilgrim's France - A Travel Guide to the Saints | Jonathan Sumption |
| Along the Templar Trail | Brandon Wilson |
| Rome: a pilgrim's companion | David Baldwin |
| The Age of Pilgrimage: The Medieval Journey to God | Jonathan Sumption |
| In Search of a Way: two journeys of spiritual discovery | Gerard Hughes |
| The Via Francigena Canterbury to Rome | Alison Raju |
| Traveling Souls: Contemporary Pilgrimage Stories | Brian Bouldrey (Editor) |

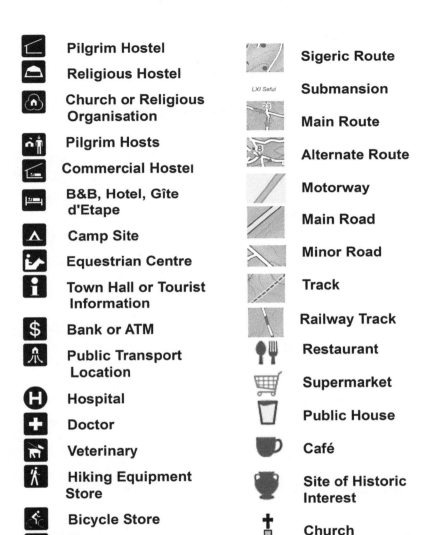

Pilgrim Hostel

Religious Hostel

Church or Religious Organisation

Pilgrim Hosts

Commercial Hostel

B&B, Hotel, Gîte d'Etape

Camp Site

Equestrian Centre

Town Hall or Tourist Information

Bank or ATM

Public Transport Location

Hospital

Doctor

Veterinary

Hiking Equipment Store

Bicycle Store

Farrier

Railway Station

Sigeric Route

Submansion

Main Route

Alternate Route

Motorway

Main Road

Minor Road

Track

Railway Track

Restaurant

Supermarket

Public House

Café

Site of Historic Interest

Church

View-point

# Vercelli to
# St Peter's Square
# Rome
# 848 kilometres

*Let your mind start a journey thru a strange new world. Leave all thoughts of the world you knew before. Let your soul take you where you long to be... Close your eyes let your spirit start to soar, and you'll live as you've never lived before.*

Erich Fromm

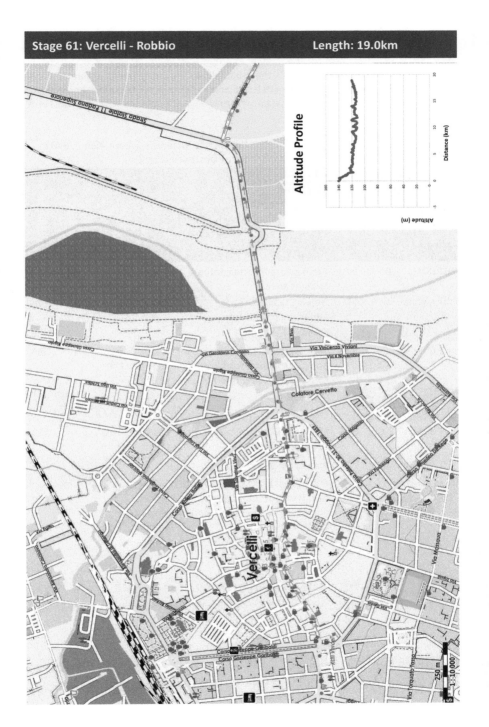

8

Stage Summary: after leaving Vercelli the route follows the argine (embankment) beside the river Sesia to Palestro. Between Palestro and Robbio the route continues on farms tracks and minor roads, but intensive farming may have affected some of the tracks and signs.

Distance from Vercelli: 0km             Distance to St Peter's Square, Rome: 848km
Stage Ascent: 90m                       Stage Descent: 111m

| Waypoint | Distance between waypoints | Total km | Directions | Verification Point | Compass | Altitude m |
|---|---|---|---|---|---|---|
| 61.001 | 0 | 0.0 | From piazza Paietta continue straight ahead | Corso Libertà | NE | 140 |
| 61.002 | 300 | 0.3 | After passing the kiosk, turn left on via Camillo Benso Cavour | Towards the arches | N | 138 |
| 61.003 | 50 | 0.4 | Turn right into piazza Cavour and go straight ahead keeping to the right side of the piazza | Statue in the centre of the piazza | E | 138 |
| 61.004 | 90 | 0.5 | Bear right on via Francesco Crispi | Paved road | E | 139 |
| 61.005 | 30 | 0.5 | In the small piazza, turn right, towards the tower | Remain on via Crispi | S | 139 |
| 61.006 | 40 | 0.5 | At the end of the road turn left in piazza San Paolo | Corso Libertà | E | 139 |
| 61.007 | 500 | 1.0 | At the mini-roundabout at the end of Corso Libertà continue straight ahead | Piazza Modesto Cugnolio, via Francigena sign beside the kiosk ahead | E | 130 |
| 61.008 | 140 | 1.1 | At the roundabout continue straight ahead, direction Pavia | Cross bridge over waterway | E | 129 |
| 61.009 | 300 | 1.4 | At the next roundabout go straight ahead, direction Pavia (SS11) | Cross over the Sesia river bridge | E | 126 |
| 61.010 | 1000 | 2.4 | After the bend to the left on the main road, turn right on the small road Strada del Boarone | Via Francigena sign | SE | 123 |

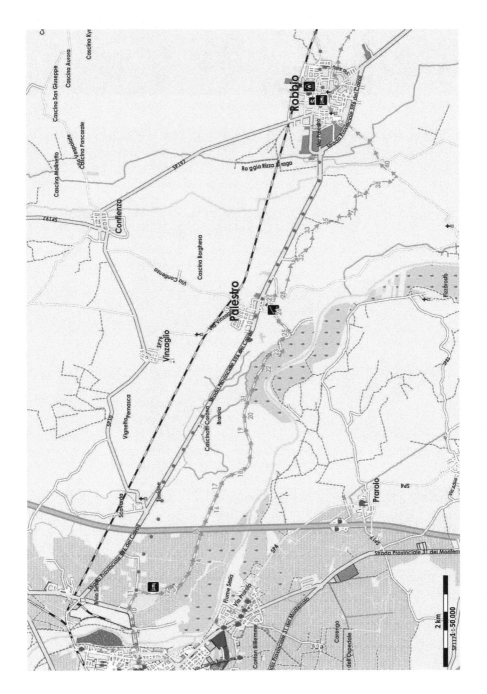

| Waypoint | Distance between waypoints | Total km | Directions | Verification Point | Compass | Altitude m |
|---|---|---|---|---|---|---|
| 61.011 | 400 | 2.8 | At the fork, bear right towards the river | VF sign | S | 121 |
| 61.012 | 600 | 3.4 | At the fork, keep right, and then bear left | Pass the farm house on your right | S | 119 |
| 61.013 | 500 | 3.9 | Cross the bridge and turn left on the embankment | Pass a house on the left | SE | 119 |
| 61.014 | 700 | 4.6 | At the crossroads in the track, continue straight ahead | | E | 119 |
| 61.015 | 700 | 5.3 | Continue straight ahead | Under the Autostrada bridge | E | 120 |
| 61.016 | 500 | 5.7 | At the crossroads in the track, continue straight ahead on the embankment | | SE | 118 |
| 61.017 | 600 | 6.4 | At the crossroads in the track, continue straight ahead | | SE | 117 |
| 61.018 | 400 | 6.8 | Continue straight ahead | Avoid the turning towards the farm on the left | E | 119 |
| 61.019 | 1200 | 8.0 | At the crossroads in the track, continue straight ahead | Fields to the left woods on the right | E | 114 |
| 61.020 | 300 | 8.3 | Continue straight ahead and right on the embankment | Ignore the track on the left and right | E | 114 |
| 61.021 | 400 | 8.7 | At the crossroads in the track, continue straight ahead | | SE | 116 |
| 61.022 | 700 | 9.4 | At the junction in the tracks, bear left | | SE | 115 |
| 61.023 | 700 | 10.1 | Turn left | Wooden bridge | E | 112 |
| 61.024 | 250 | 10.3 | At the T-junction in the tracks, turn right | | SE | 116 |

| Waypoint | Distance between waypoints | Total km | Directions | Verification Point | Compass | Altitude m |
|---|---|---|---|---|---|---|
| 61.025 | 300 | 10.7 | At the T-junction, turn left, towards the village of Palestro | VF sign | NE | 113 |
| 61.026 | 600 | 11.3 | At the Stop sign in Palestro, turn right on the SP56 - via Garibaldi | VF sign | E | 117 |
| 61.027 | 300 | 11.6 | Cross the bridge and proceed straight ahead at the next Stop sign | VF sign | SE | 118 |
| 61.028 | 80 | 11.7 | Turn right direction Rosasco on via Rosasco | VF sign | SW | 117 |
| 61.029 | 150 | 11.8 | Immediately before crossing the irrigation channel, turn left on the broad track | Trees on your right | E | 113 |
| 61.030 | 800 | 12.6 | Turn right | Cross the irrigation channel | SE | 116 |
| 61.031 | 230 | 12.8 | Follow the sign to the left | | NE | 116 |
| 61.032 | 60 | 12.9 | Turn right on the track | Beside the trees | SE | 116 |
| 61.033 | 800 | 13.6 | Bear right | Trees to the right | SE | 115 |
| 61.034 | 230 | 13.9 | At the end of the path beside the trees turn right on the track | | S | 117 |
| 61.035 | 230 | 14.1 | Follow the sign to the left and immediately turn right | Track zigzags around fields | SE | 117 |
| 61.036 | 1300 | 15.4 | Turn right towards the farm | VF sign | S | 115 |
| 61.037 | 180 | 15.6 | At the farm turn left | | SE | 113 |
| 61.038 | 250 | 15.8 | At the crossroads continue straight ahead | | S | 113 |
| 61.039 | 600 | 16.4 | At the T-junction with the tarmac road turn left on the road | VF sign | NE | 114 |
| 61.040 | 500 | 16.9 | At the road junction, continue straight ahead | Direction Robbio | NE | 114 |

| Waypoint | Distance between waypoints | Total km | Directions | Verification Point | Compass | Altitude m |
|---|---|---|---|---|---|---|
| 61.041 | 1200 | 18.0 | At the crossroads with the SS596 proceed straight ahead | Towards Robbio centre | N | 117 |
| 61.042 | 290 | 18.3 | At the crossroads, after passing the building material yard, turn right | VF sign, via Rosasco | E | 117 |
| 61.043 | 500 | 18.8 | At the crossroads, proceed straight ahead | VF sign, direction Mortara | E | 119 |
| 61.044 | 200 | 19.0 | Arrive at Robbio centre beside the trafffic lights | Church of San Pietro and a small park on your left | | 120 |

**Accommodation & Facilities .... Vercelli - Robbio**

La Torre Merlata,Via Vodano, 5,27030 Palestro(PV),Italy; Tel:+39 3497 909044; +39 3341 835360

Parrocchia di S.Stefano,Via Santo Stefano, 2,27038 Robbio(PV),Italy; Tel:+39 0384 670436; +39 3401 539929; Price:D

Hotel Valsesia,Via Galileo Ferraris, 104,13100 Vercelli(VC),Italy; Tel:+39 0161 250842; +39 3493 942427; Email:hotelvalsesia@gmail.com; Web-site:www. hotelvalsesia.wordpress.com; Price:B

Hotel Restorante il Giardinetto,Via Luigi Sereno, 3,13100 Vercelli(VC),Italy; Tel:+39 0161 257230; Email:giardi.dan@libero.it; Web-site:www.ilgiardinettovercelli.com; Price:A

B&B Cascina Erbade,(Carola Gräfin von Hardenberg ),Strada Boarone,13100 Vercelli(VC),Italy; Tel:+39 0161 213656; +39 3280 149335; Email:hardenberg@ tiscali.it; Web-site:www.bedandbreakfastineurope.com/cascinaerbade; Price:A

Vercelli Palace Hotel,Via Tavallini, 29 ,13100 Vercelli(VC),Italy; Tel:+39 0161 300900; Email:reservation@vercellipalacehotel.it ; Web-site:www.vercellipalacehotel.it; Price:A

Hotel Moderno,Via Mazzini, 5,27038 Robbio(PV),Italy; Tel:+39 0384 670367; Price:B

Tourist Office,Corso Giuseppe Garibaldi, 90,13100 Vercelli(VC),Italy; Tel:+39 0161 257899; Web-site:www.atlvalsesiavercelli.it

Banca Sella SPA,Via Castelnuovo delle Lanze, 2,13100 Vercelli(VC),Italy; Tel:+39 0161 211397; Web-site:www.sella.it

## Accommodation & Facilities  ....  Vercelli - Robbio

**$** Biverbanca Cassa di Risparmio,Corso Mario Abbiate, 21,13100 Vercelli(VC),Italy; Tel:+39 0161 210627; Web-site:www.biverbanca.it

**$** Banca Popolare di Novara,Via Vittorio Veneto, 15/17,27038 Robbio(PV),Italy; Tel:+39 0384 670407

**A** Stazione Ferrovie,Piazza Roma, 18,13100 Vercelli(VC),Italy; Tel:+39 06 6847 5475; Web-site:www.renitalia.it

**H** Ospedali Riuniti,Corso Mario Abbiate, 21,13100 Vercelli(VC),Italy; Tel:+39 0161 5931

**+** Salamano - Medico Generico,Piazza Solferino,13100 Vercelli(VC),Italy; Tel:+39 0161 260527

**🐕** Clinica Veterinaria Sant'Andrea,Viale Rimembranza, 105,13100 Vercelli(VC),Italy; Tel:+39 0161 503331

**🚶** Decathlon,Corso Torino,13100 Vercelli(VC),Italy; Tel:+39 0161 393687

**🚲** Bike Shop di Minola Violino Manuel,Via Francesco Crispi, 22,13100 Vercelli(VC),Italy; Tel:+39 0161 503188

**📍** D'Agostino Carmelo,Via Pinerolo, 100,10067 Vigone(TO),Italy; Tel:+39 3488 718200

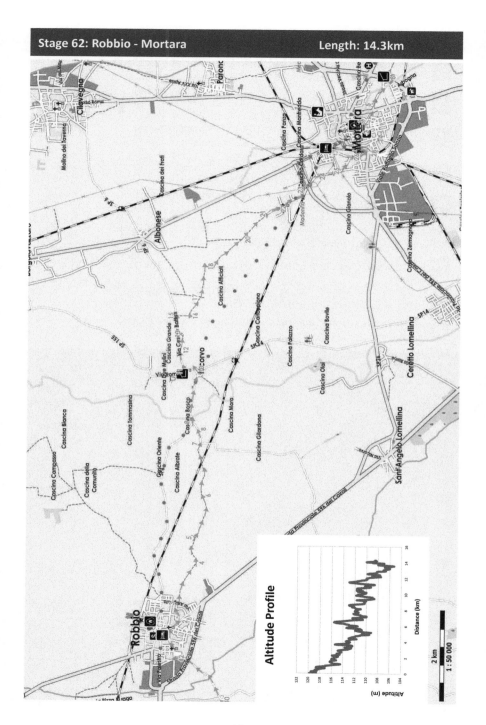

Altitude Profile

Altitude (m)

Distance (km)

2 km

1 : 50 000

15

Stage Summary: this short section of the route continues on level farm tracks between rice fields, with only short stretches on minor roads. Mortara offers abroad range of facilities.

Distance from Vercelli: 19km                    Distance to St Peter's Square, Rome: 829km
Stage Ascent: 57m                              Stage Descent: 68m

| Waypoint | Distance between waypoints | Total km | Directions | Verification Point | Compass | Altitude m |
|---|---|---|---|---|---|---|
| 62.001 | 0 | 0.0 | At the traffic lights beside the park, Giardini San Pietro, bear right, direction Mortara | Via Mortara, pass the church on the left | SE | 119 |
| 62.002 | 260 | 0.3 | Turn left onto via Roggetta | VF sign | E | 119 |
| 62.003 | 400 | 0.7 | At the crossroads with a major road, continue straight ahead beside the sports ground | VF sign, tarmac road becomes a gravel track | SE | 117 |
| 62.004 | 1000 | 1.7 | Bear left after crossing a small bridge | VF sign | E | 115 |
| 62.005 | 600 | 2.3 | Fork right passing a large concrete barn on the right | VF sign | E | 115 |
| 62.006 | 1000 | 3.3 | Fork right | VF sign | E | 113 |
| 62.007 | 1200 | 4.5 | At the junction with road bear left | VF sign, irrigation ditch on the right | E | 112 |
| 62.008 | 400 | 4.9 | Take the left fork over the small bridge | VF sign | NE | 111 |
| 62.009 | 200 | 5.1 | At the T-junction, turn right, direction Nicorvo, SP6 | VF sign, towards mobile-phone mast | E | 110 |
| 62.010 | 1200 | 6.3 | At the T-junction in Nicorvo, turn left | Direction Cilavegna | N | 113 |
| 62.011 | 240 | 6.5 | In the centre of Nicorvo with the bell tower on the left, turn right, direction Mortara | VF sign, via Albonese | E | 115 |

| Waypoint | Distance between waypoints | Total km | Directions | Verification Point | Compass | Altitude m |
|---|---|---|---|---|---|---|
| 62.012 | 500 | 7.0 | Bear right onto the track. Note:- the route will return to the road 400m ahead | | E | 112 |
| 62.013 | 400 | 7.4 | Turn left | Towards the road | N | 111 |
| 62.014 | 110 | 7.5 | Rejoin the road and turn right | | E | 112 |
| 62.015 | 400 | 7.9 | Turn right onto the part grassed track between rice fields | VF sign | S | 112 |
| 62.016 | 270 | 8.1 | At the T-junction, turn left | VF sign | SE | 111 |
| 62.017 | 500 | 8.6 | Cross the gravel track and continue on the grass track | Large red farm building on the right | E | 113 |
| 62.018 | 700 | 9.4 | Turn right to cross over concrete bridge | VF sign | SE | 110 |
| 62.019 | 400 | 9.8 | At the crossroads in the track, continue straight ahead | VF sign | SE | 110 |
| 62.020 | 700 | 10.4 | Bear right at the T-junction in track | VF sign | SE | 110 |
| 62.021 | 800 | 11.3 | Bear right at T-junction in track | | SE | 108 |
| 62.022 | 210 | 11.5 | Proceed straight ahead and pass through the village of Madonna del Campo | Walled gardens on both sides of the road | SE | 112 |
| 62.023 | 800 | 12.3 | Continue straight ahead across the railway tracks. Note:- the route ahead includes a subway under the main railway line. Riders are recommended to bear left at this point and then turn right at the junction with the main road into the centre of the Mortara and the end of the section | VF sign, towards apartment buildings on the horizon | SE | 107 |

| Waypoint | Distance between waypoints | Total km | Directions | Verification Point | Compass | Altitude m |
|---|---|---|---|---|---|---|
| 62.024 | 400 | 12.6 | At the junction, continue straight ahead | Concrete barn on the left | S | 109 |
| 62.025 | 600 | 13.2 | At the junction bear left towards the railway and the prominent apartment block | Via de Cantiano | SE | 106 |
| 62.026 | 400 | 13.6 | At the rear of the railway sidings turn right | Railway on the left | S | 105 |
| 62.027 | 170 | 13.8 | In the square beside a water-tower continue straight ahead into the No Through Road | Railway close on the left | S | 107 |
| 62.028 | 230 | 14.0 | Take the pedestrian subway under the railway and continue straight ahead on the far side | | NE | 108 |
| 62.029 | 300 | 14.3 | Arrive at Mortara centre in front of the railway station | Beside fountain | | 108 |

**Accommodation & Facilities  ....  Robbio - Mortara**

Casa Parrocchilae,Piazza Libertà, 2,27020 Nicorvo(PV),Italy; +39 3383 785706; +39 3396 005229; Email:nicorvofrancigena@libero.it

Abbazia Saint Albino,Via Tiziano Vecellio,27036 Mortara(PV),Italy; Tel:+39 0384 295327; +39 3477 194503; Price:C

Parrocchia San Lorenzo - Casa Parrocchiale,Contrada San Dionigi, 1,27036 Mortara(PV),Italy; Tel:+39 0384 99772; Price:C

Albergo Bel Sit,Viale Capettini Arturo e Casare, 58,27036 Mortara(PV),Italy; Tel:+39 0384 295954; +39 0384 98169; Price:B

Hotel della Torre,Contrada Torre, 7,27036 Mortara(PV),Italy; Tel:+39 0384 90775; Price:B

Centro Ippico Mortara,Via Parona Cassola, 433,27036 Mortara(PV),Italy; Tel:+39 0384 295988

Centro Ippico Mortara,Via Parona Cassola, 433,27036 Mortara(PV),Italy; Tel:+39 0384 295988; Web-site:www.centroippicomortara.it/

Municipio di Mortara,Piazza Martiri della Libertà, 21,27036 Mortara(PV),Italy; Tel:+39 0384 256411

Banca Popolare di Sondrio,Via Roma, 23,27036 Mortara(PV), Italy; Tel:+39 0384 295744; Web-site:www.popso.it/FixedPages/Common/DoveSiamoFiliali.php/L/IT

## Accommodation & Facilities .... Robbio - Mortara

**$** Credito Artigiano,Corso Cavour, 18,27036 Mortara(PV),Italy; Tel:+39 0384 090101; Web-site:www.creval.it

**🚉** Stazione Ferrovie,Piazza Guglielmo Marconi, 12,27036 Mortara(PV),Italy; Tel:+39 06 6847 5475; Web-site:www.renitalia.it

**H** Ospedale Asilo,Strada Pavese, 1125,27036 Mortara(PV),Italy; Tel:+39 0348 2041

**✚** Casale Protti - Studio Medico,Via Goia Luigi, 24,27036 Mortara(PV),Italy; Tel:+39 0384 98640

**🐾** Clinica Veterinaria Citta' di Mortara,Strada Per Cascina Cassagalla,27036 Mortara(PV),Italy; Tel:+39 0384 93330

19

## Altitude Profile

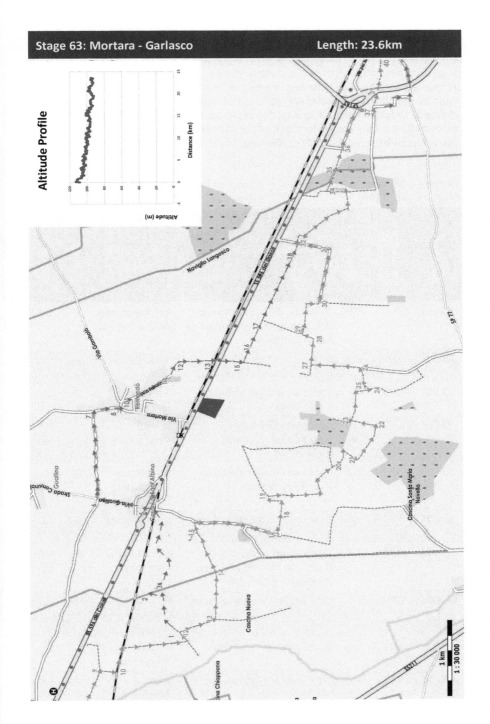

Stage Summary: after Mortara the route continues to meander through the rice fields. The route passes through a number of small villages and the pleasant town of Tromello. From shortly after the Abbazia Sant'Albino to Roventino the "Official Route" has recently changed. Unfortunately this new section of the route zig-zags through featureless rice fields making it very easy to get lost. We prefer and alternate more direct route via the village of Remondo. A further Alternate Route visits the Santuario Madonna della Bozzola.

Distance from Vercelli: 33km　　　Distance to St Peter's Square, Rome: 815km
Stage Ascent: 110m　　　　　　　Stage Descent: 123m

| Waypoint | Distance between waypoints | Total km | Directions | Verification Point | Compass | Altitude m |
|---|---|---|---|---|---|---|
| 63.001 | 0 | 0.0 | From the railway station in Mortara, go straight ahead on Corso Garibaldi | Railway station directly behind | E | 108 |
| 63.002 | 400 | 0.4 | Beside the town hall (municipio) bear right | Corso Cavour | SE | 111 |
| 63.003 | 270 | 0.7 | Continue straight ahead on Corso Cavour | Direction Sant'Albino | SE | 110 |
| 63.004 | 250 | 0.9 | At the roundabout go straight ahead on via Sant'Albinio Alcuino | Towards the water tower | E | 109 |
| 63.005 | 180 | 1.1 | Continue straight ahead to join the cycle track | Water tower immediately to the left | SE | 106 |
| 63.006 | 600 | 1.6 | Bear right on the cycle track | After crossing the waterway | S | 103 |
| 63.007 | 170 | 1.8 | Take subway under the main road (SS494) and then immediately turn left | Parallel to the main road | NE | 105 |
| 63.008 | 150 | 1.9 | Turn right on the gravel track | Abbazia Sant'Albino on the right | SE | 105 |
| 63.009 | 600 | 2.5 | At the junction bear right | Towards the railway track | S | 104 |
| 63.010 | 220 | 2.7 | Cross over the railway and turn left | Railway immediately on the left | SE | 104 |

| Waypoint | Distance between waypoints | Total km | Directions | Verification Point | Compass | Altitude m |
|---|---|---|---|---|---|---|
| 63.011 | 1200 | 3.9 | At the T-junction beside the irrigation channel turn left | Towards the gas plant | NE | 102 |
| 63.012 | 140 | 4.0 | Take the next turning to the right. Note:- a more more easily followed Alternate Route continues straight ahead | | SE | 104 |
| 63.013 | 500 | 4.6 | At the junction, turn left | Farm ahead | E | 104 |
| 63.014 | 600 | 5.2 | Continue straight ahead over the bridge | Cavour canal | NE | 103 |
| 63.015 | 600 | 5.8 | At the junction, keep right | | E | 103 |
| 63.016 | 150 | 5.9 | At the T-junction, turn right on the broad gravel road and continue straight ahead to the farm | | S | 105 |
| 63.017 | 1100 | 7.0 | Immediately before the farm turn left | Pass the farm building close on your right | E | 102 |
| 63.018 | 280 | 7.3 | Continue straight ahead and follow the track as it bears left and then right | Pass between the trees | NE | 102 |
| 63.019 | 400 | 7.7 | Turn right onto a grassy track | | SE | 101 |
| 63.020 | 1100 | 8.8 | At the junction, continue straight ahead | Trees on your left | S | 99 |
| 63.021 | 500 | 9.3 | Turn left on the grassy track | Between fields fringed with woods | SE | 98 |
| 63.022 | 500 | 9.8 | Cross the irrigation channel and turn left | Towards the woods | N | 101 |
| 63.023 | 300 | 10.2 | Cross another channel and turn right | Woods on the left at the junction | SE | 101 |
| 63.024 | 600 | 10.8 | Beside the gate turn left | Cross another channel | NE | 97 |
| 63.025 | 120 | 10.9 | Take the right fork | | E | 100 |

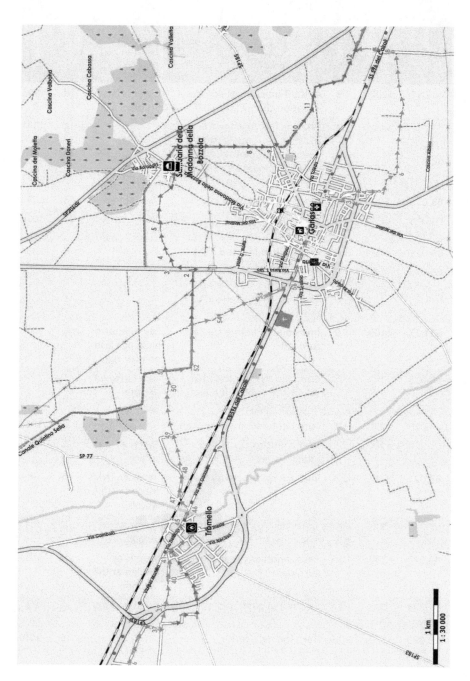

| Waypoint | Distance between waypoints | Total km | Directions | Verification Point | Compass | Altitude m |
|---|---|---|---|---|---|---|
| 63.026 | 250 | 11.1 | Close to cascina Donzellina, turn left | Follow the irrigation channel on your right | N | 100 |
| 63.027 | 600 | 11.8 | At the T-junction, after crossing another channel, turn right | | E | 97 |
| 63.028 | 400 | 12.1 | Cross a further channel and turn left at the T-junction | Follow the track as it bears right | NE | 98 |
| 63.029 | 250 | 12.4 | Pass through the gate and continue straight ahead | Channel on your left | SE | 98 |
| 63.030 | 500 | 12.8 | At the junction beside the farm, turn left on the broad track | Pass the buildings on your right | E | 96 |
| 63.031 | 800 | 13.6 | Turn left | Towards the hamlet of Roventino | N | 96 |
| 63.032 | 400 | 14.0 | Pass through the farm and then turn right and follow the track as it it turns right | Keep the buildings close on your right. Note:- the Alternate Route joins from the left | SE | 98 |
| 63.033 | 1100 | 15.1 | Pass through a clump of trees and at the T-junction turn left | | N | 101 |
| 63.034 | 250 | 15.4 | At the junction turn sharp right | Parallel to the main road | E | 98 |
| 63.035 | 300 | 15.7 | Continue straight ahead | Cross the Langosco canal | E | 99 |
| 63.036 | 300 | 16.0 | At the crossroads proceed straight ahead | Towards cascina San Vincenzo | SE | 97 |
| 63.037 | 800 | 16.8 | At the T-junction turn left | | E | 97 |

| Waypoint | Distance between waypoints | Total km | Directions | Verification Point | Compass | Altitude m |
|---|---|---|---|---|---|---|
| 63.038 | 70 | 16.8 | At the junction where the track becomes tarmac keep left. Note:- at the next Waypoint there is a crash barrier and dangerous road crossing to negotiate. Riders should turn right here and then left at the T-junction and follow the road into the centre of Tromello | Grass track, pass trees on the right | E | 97 |
| 63.039 | 220 | 17.0 | Carefully cross the main road (SS596) and continue straight ahead on the track | Towards the bell tower in the village | E | 94 |
| 63.040 | 400 | 17.5 | At the crossroads continue straight ahead on the tarmac road | Pass the garages on the left | E | 95 |
| 63.041 | 240 | 17.7 | At the junction with via Crispi continue straight ahead | Long brick wall to your left | E | 95 |
| 63.042 | 110 | 17.8 | At the T-junction, turn right on via Cavour | VF signs | SE | 96 |
| 63.043 | 400 | 18.2 | In piazza Campegi, in the centre of Tromello (XLII), turn left | Pass a café on your right | NE | 96 |
| 63.044 | 180 | 18.4 | At the crossroads, turn right | Direction Pavia | E | 95 |
| 63.045 | 70 | 18.5 | At the junction continue straight ahead | VF sign, bar on your right | SE | 96 |
| 63.046 | 190 | 18.6 | After crossing the bridge turn left | Towards Borgo S. Siro | NE | 95 |
| 63.047 | 180 | 18.8 | After crossing the railway, take the right fork | Via Cascinino, VF sign | E | 93 |
| 63.048 | 400 | 19.2 | Take the right fork on the track | Valve on the left at the junction | E | 92 |
| 63.049 | 500 | 19.7 | At the crossroads, continue straight ahead | Towards the power line | E | 94 |
| 63.050 | 700 | 20.4 | At the junction continue straight ahead | | E | 95 |

| Waypoint | Distance between waypoints | Total km | Directions | Verification Point | Compass | Altitude m |
|---|---|---|---|---|---|---|
| 63.051 | 230 | 20.6 | At the canal crossing, turn right | Keep canale Cavour on your left | S | 99 |
| 63.052 | 400 | 20.9 | At the junction, keep left | Remain beside the canal | E | 97 |
| 63.053 | 600 | 21.5 | At the next junction turn right. Note:- to visit the sanctuary of la Madonna della Bazzola turn left and follow the Alternate Route | Bridge on your left | S | 96 |
| 63.054 | 280 | 21.8 | At the junction, continue straight ahead | | SE | 94 |
| 63.055 | 800 | 22.5 | Continue straight ahead on the tarmac road | Cross the railway | SE | 94 |
| 63.056 | 300 | 22.9 | At the T-junction with the main road, turn left and continue straight ahead at the roundabout | Direction Centro | E | 94 |
| 63.057 | 700 | 23.6 | Arrive at Garlasco centre | Beside piazza Repubblica | | 95 |

| Alternate Route #63.A1 | | | | Length: 7.9km | | |
|---|---|---|---|---|---|---|
| Stage Summary: a more direct and more easily followed route to Roventino | | | | | | |
| Stage Ascent: 33m | | | | Stage Descent: 41m | | |
| 63A1.001 | 0 | 0.0 | Continue straight ahead | Towards gas plant | NE | 104 |
| 63A1.002 | 800 | 0.8 | Following the bend to the left, turn right, cross the bridge over Canal Cavour and bear right | Turning beside the gas plant | SE | 104 |
| 63A1.003 | 260 | 1.0 | Fork left | Over small bridge | E | 104 |
| 63A1.004 | 1100 | 2.1 | At the T-junction turn left | Cross over railway track | N | 102 |

| Waypoint | Distance between waypoints | Total km | Directions | Verification Point | Compass | Altitude m |
|---|---|---|---|---|---|---|
| 63A1.005 | 110 | 2.2 | Cross straight over the main road into the village of Casoni di Sant'Albino | Direction Guallina | N | 103 |
| 63A1.006 | 700 | 2.8 | Shortly after passing house n° 33, turn right onto an unmade road | Cross small bridge | E | 102 |
| 63A1.007 | 1300 | 4.1 | At the T-junction with the road, turn right | Cemetery ahead at the junction | S | 103 |
| 63A1.008 | 300 | 4.4 | At the crossroads, in the centre of Redondo, turn left | Direction Gambolò, bar on the left | E | 105 |
| 63A1.009 | 100 | 4.5 | At the crossroads, turn right on via Arturo Ferrarin | Church on the right, war memorial on the left | S | 103 |
| 63A1.010 | 150 | 4.6 | At junction continue straight ahead | Via Arturo Ferrarin | SE | 103 |
| 63A1.011 | 600 | 5.2 | Take the left fork | Pass apartments on your left | SE | 105 |
| 63A1.012 | 300 | 5.5 | Take the right fork | Water channel directly on the right | S | 101 |
| 63A1.013 | 400 | 5.9 | Continue straight ahead | Cross the railway | S | 101 |
| 63A1.014 | 70 | 5.9 | Recross the main road to continue on the track the other side | | S | 100 |
| 63A1.015 | 300 | 6.3 | Take the left fork | Towards the radio masts | SE | 99 |
| 63A1.016 | 280 | 6.5 | Continue straight ahead | Pass radio masts on the right | SE | 100 |
| 63A1.017 | 300 | 6.9 | Continue straight ahead | Towards the large tree on the right | SE | 99 |
| 63A1.018 | 1100 | 7.9 | Pass beside cascina Roventino and continue straight ahead. Note:- rejoin the "Official Route" | Archway on your right | | 96 |

| Alternate Route #63.A2 | | | Length: 6.0km | | | |
|---|---|---|---|---|---|---|
| Stage Summary: route visiting the Sanctuary of la Madonna della Bazzola | | | | | | |
| Stage Ascent: 33m | | | | Stage Descent: 38m | | |

| Waypoint | Distance between waypoints | Total km | Directions | Verification Point | Compass | Altitude m |
|---|---|---|---|---|---|---|
| 63A2.001 | 0 | 0.0 | Bear left and then right over the canal | Continue with the canal on your right | E | 96 |
| 63A2.002 | 700 | 0.7 | Cross over road and bear left on the track with the canal on the left | VF sign | N | 94 |
| 63A2.003 | 300 | 1.0 | Fork right away from the canal | VF sign, trees on your left | NE | 97 |
| 63A2.004 | 230 | 1.3 | Take the second turning on the right | VF sign, into trees | E | 96 |
| 63A2.005 | 400 | 1.7 | Turn left and then right | VF sign, trees on the left | E | 95 |
| 63A2.006 | 800 | 2.5 | At the junction in front of the sanctuary, turn left and immediately right | Pass the Sanctuary on your right | NE | 96 |
| 63A2.007 | 190 | 2.7 | Immediately after crossing over the bridge, turn right beside the canal | VF sign, canal on the right | S | 98 |
| 63A2.008 | 1300 | 3.9 | Continue straight ahead with a bridge on the right | VF sign, canal on the right | S | 92 |
| 63A2.009 | 280 | 4.2 | Cross the road and continue on the track beside the canal | Bridge on right | SE | 94 |
| 63A2.010 | 500 | 4.7 | Turn right, cross over bridge, then turn immediately left to skirt the large building on the right | Canal on the left | SE | 92 |

| Waypoint | Distance between waypoints | Total km | Directions | Verification Point | Compass | Altitude m |
|---|---|---|---|---|---|---|
| 63A2.011 | 400 | 5.1 | Beside bridge, continue straight ahead with water on left | VF sign | SE | 91 |
| 63A2.012 | 1000 | 6.0 | Cross over the sluice gate bridge, then cross the bridge to the left, bear right and at the T-junction, turn left to rejoin the "Official Route" | VF sign, continue with the canal on the right | | 91 |

### Accommodation & Facilities .... Mortara - Garlasco

Santuario Madonna della Bozzola,Piazzale Santuario, 1,27026 Garlasco(PV),Italy; Tel:+39 0382 822117; +39 0382 822428; Email:bozzola@madonnadellabozzola.org; Web-site:www.madonnadellabozzola.org; Price:D

Parrocchia San Martino,Via Branca, 1,27020 Tromello(PV),Italy; Tel:+39 0382 86020; +39 3356 609347; Price:D

Albergo Margherita,Via Don Minzoni, 5,27026 Garlasco(PV),Italy; Tel:+39 0382 822674; +39 3355 724907; Email:hotel.margherita@libero.it; Web-site:www.ristorantehotelmargherita.com; Price:A

Banca Popolare di Lodi,Via Biscaldi, 2,27020 Tromello(PV),Italy; Tel:+39 0382 809016

Croce - Studio Medico,Corso Cavour, 173,27026 Garlasco(PV),Italy; Tel:+39 0382 820191

Mozzato - Ambulatorio Veterinario,Piazza Garibaldi, 14,27026 Garlasco(PV),Italy; Tel:+39 0382 800553

Gallottibike di Gallotti Claudio,Via Alagna, 47,27026 Garlasco(PV),Italy; Tel:+39 0382 810483

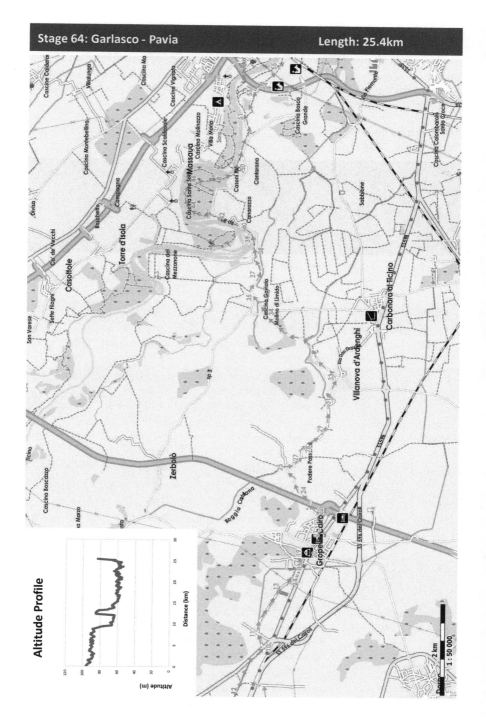

Altitude Profile

Stage Summary: the route will return to the canal-side paths after leaving Garlasco and pass through the small town of Gropello Cairoli before finally leaving the rice fields and entering Pavia beside the banks of the Ticino.

Distance from Vercelli: 57km
Stage Ascent: 153m

Distance to St Peter's Square, Rome: 792km
Stage Descent: 166m

| Waypoint | Distance between waypoints | Total km | Directions | Verification | Compass | Altitude m |
|---|---|---|---|---|---|---|
| 64.001 | 0 | 0.0 | From piazza Repubblica, continue on Corso Camillo Cavour | Church of San Rocco on your right | E | 96 |
| 64.002 | 600 | 0.5 | Immediately after passing the petrol station, turn right | Via Dorno | S | 93 |
| 64.003 | 400 | 1.0 | At the busy junction turn left beside the main road | Via Leonardo da Vinci | E | 91 |
| 64.004 | 210 | 1.2 | After crossing the small water course, turn right on the unmade road - via Albera | Between the industrial buildings and gardens | S | 91 |
| 64.005 | 300 | 1.5 | Bear left on the track | Between the fields | SE | 93 |
| 64.006 | 290 | 1.8 | Continue straight ahead on the main track | Track begins to bend to the left | E | 88 |
| 64.007 | 1700 | 3.5 | At the T-junction with a gravel track, turn left | Pass farm buildings on your right | N | 89 |
| 64.008 | 230 | 3.7 | At the crossroads, with great care cross the busy road and continue straight ahead on the unmade road | Cross the railway | N | 91 |
| 64.009 | 240 | 3.9 | Cross the canal bridge and then turn right. The Alternate Route joins from the left | Canal close on your right | SE | 91 |
| 64.010 | 1100 | 5.0 | At the crossroads with SP206 cross the road and continue on the track beside the canal | Canal on the left | E | 89 |

| Waypoint | Distance between waypoints | Total km | Directions | Verification | Compass | Altitude m |
|---|---|---|---|---|---|---|
| 64.011 | 400 | 5.3 | At the crossroads, continue straight ahead | Canal on the left | E | 87 |
| 64.012 | 150 | 5.5 | Fork right, away from the canale Cavour on the lower track direction Gropello Cairoli | VF sign | SE | 88 |
| 64.013 | 1000 | 6.5 | Continue straight ahead at the junction | After passing behind the cemetery | SE | 89 |
| 64.014 | 170 | 6.7 | Fork left on the track | Avoid the tarmac road ahead | E | 88 |
| 64.015 | 300 | 7.0 | Cross the canal and continue straight ahead | | E | 86 |
| 64.016 | 90 | 7.1 | Take the first road on the right | Between apartment buildings | S | 87 |
| 64.017 | 120 | 7.2 | At the end of the road, turn left | Via Verdi | E | 87 |
| 64.018 | 220 | 7.4 | At the end of the road, turn right and then immediately left | Via C. Battisti | SE | 90 |
| 64.019 | 140 | 7.6 | At the T-junction, turn right | Park entrance on your left | S | 90 |
| 64.020 | 90 | 7.7 | At the T-junction with the main road, turn left | Towards the centre of Gropello Caoroli | SE | 90 |
| 64.021 | 600 | 8.2 | Pass the church of San Rocco (in centre of main road) and immediately bear left on viale C.B. Zanotti | Sign for Centro Ippico Sant'Andrea | E | 86 |
| 64.022 | 600 | 8.8 | On leaving the town continue straight ahead on the bridge over the motorway | Pass telephone mast on the right | E | 88 |
| 64.023 | 270 | 9.0 | After crossing the bridge bear left on strada del Morgarolo | Factory on the right | NE | 83 |

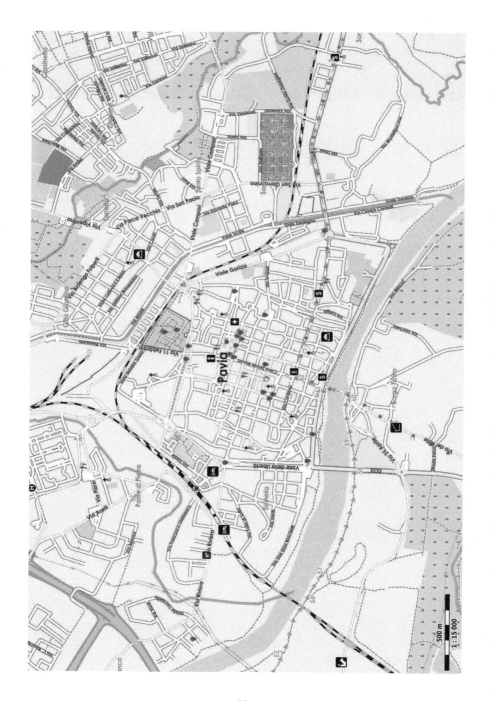

| Waypoint | Distance between waypoints | Total km | Directions | Verification | Compass | Altitude m |
|---|---|---|---|---|---|---|
| 64.024 | 400 | 9.4 | Continue straight ahead | Pass beside Centro Ippico Sant'Andrea | NE | 76 |
| 64.025 | 600 | 10.0 | At the junction before the canal bridge, turn right | Direction cascina Morgarolo | S | 66 |
| 64.026 | 190 | 10.2 | At the entrance to the farm turn left, cross over the canal and then immediately turn right between the buildings | Proceed with canal close on the right | SE | 67 |
| 64.027 | 250 | 10.4 | Take the left fork | Between broad and narrow channels | E | 65 |
| 64.028 | 190 | 10.6 | At the fork bear right | Channel close on the right | SE | 64 |
| 64.029 | 700 | 11.3 | After crossing a bridge bear left | Ditch close on the left | E | 64 |
| 64.030 | 600 | 11.9 | At the T-junction, turn right, away from the main irrigation channel | Bridge on the left at the junction | SE | 63 |
| 64.031 | 150 | 12.0 | At the fork, bear left into Villanova d'Ardenghi on the tarmac road | Uphill between trees | E | 64 |
| 64.032 | 400 | 12.4 | Continue straight ahead through the town | Via Pollini | E | 83 |
| 64.033 | 230 | 12.7 | At the crossroads turn left on via Roma | Direction Zerbolo | NE | 84 |
| 64.034 | 2200 | 14.9 | At the crossroads, continue straight ahead | VF sign | NE | 62 |
| 64.035 | 500 | 15.3 | At the junction, continue straight ahead on the raised road | Cascina Gaviola on the left | E | 59 |

| Waypoint | Distance between waypoints | Total km | Directions | Verification | Compass | Altitude m |
|---|---|---|---|---|---|---|
| 64.036 | 290 | 15.6 | Shortly after the bend to the right, descend from the embankment and take the grass track on the left. Note:- to avoid potentially wet ground, cyclists may wish to remain on the road for the 8.8km to the Ponte Coperto in Pavia | VF sign | SE | 59 |
| 64.037 | 300 | 15.9 | Turn right to follow the water-course | | E | 58 |
| 64.038 | 600 | 16.5 | Continue straight ahead on the path | River Ticino on the left | E | 59 |
| 64.039 | 270 | 16.8 | Continue straight ahead on the riverside path | | NE | 57 |
| 64.040 | 500 | 17.3 | Take the right fork, climb the embankment and continue straight ahead on the road | Village of Canarazzo on the right | NE | 61 |
| 64.041 | 220 | 17.5 | Bear left to leave the embankment and return to the riverside path | VF sign | NE | 59 |
| 64.042 | 300 | 17.8 | Cross a car park and at the T-junction turn left and then bear right | Path branches away from the road | N | 60 |
| 64.043 | 230 | 18.0 | Take the left fork | Right fork leads to farm buildings | NE | 60 |
| 64.044 | 500 | 18.6 | Continue straight ahead | Avoid the turning to the beach on the left | E | 56 |
| 64.045 | 500 | 19.0 | At the T-junction bear left | Towards the river | E | 61 |
| 64.046 | 170 | 19.2 | At the T-junction, turn right on the broad straight track | | SW | 58 |
| 64.047 | 270 | 19.5 | Bear left on the track | | S | 59 |

| Waypoint | Distance between waypoints | Total km | Directions | Verification | Compass | Altitude m |
|---|---|---|---|---|---|---|
| 64.048 | 300 | 19.8 | Continue straight ahead | Ignore the turning towards the river | S | 57 |
| 64.049 | 500 | 20.3 | Continue straight ahead on the riverside path | | E | 60 |
| 64.050 | 140 | 20.5 | Continue straight ahead | Pass beside a restaurant | E | 58 |
| 64.051 | 1200 | 21.7 | At the T-junction in the woods turn right | Pass a lake on the left | E | 60 |
| 64.052 | 500 | 22.2 | Take the right fork | | E | 58 |
| 64.053 | 110 | 22.3 | Continue straight ahead on the tarmac road | Towards the elevated highway | SE | 61 |
| 64.054 | 170 | 22.5 | Pass under the highway and continue straight ahead | The road ahead is closed to traffic | SE | 64 |
| 64.055 | 600 | 23.1 | Continue straight ahead on the unmade road | Parallel to the river | SE | 59 |
| 64.056 | 400 | 23.5 | Continue on the riverside track | Pass under the railway | SE | 54 |
| 64.057 | 250 | 23.8 | Continue straight ahead on the riverside path | Ignore the turning to the right | E | 56 |
| 64.058 | 700 | 24.4 | Continue straight ahead on the riverside path | Pass under the road bridge | E | 59 |
| 64.059 | 180 | 24.6 | Pedestrians continue on the riverside path. Cyclists and riders should turn right and take the road to the entrance to the Ponte Coperto | Borgo Ticino to the right and the Ponte Coperto directly ahead | E | 55 |
| 64.060 | 400 | 25.0 | Climb the steps and cross the covered bridge | No Entry Sign on the bridge | N | 64 |
| 64.061 | 220 | 25.2 | At the traffic lights cross the piazzale Ponte Ticino and take the road ahead | Corso Strada Nuova | NE | 67 |

| Waypoint | Distance between waypoints | Total km | Directions | Verification | Compass | Altitude m |
|---|---|---|---|---|---|---|
| 64.062 | 230 | 25.4 | Arrive at Pavia (XLI) centre. Note:- if you plan to use the Pò ferry from Corte Sant'Andrea, we recommend that you call well in advance, preferably between 20.00 and 22.00 in the evening and be flexible in the timing of your crossing. In case of difficulties with the ferry we suggest that you plan to stay in Orio Litta to avoid the risk of having to substantially extend your journey to the next stopping place if the ferry does not arrive | Crossroads with Corso Garibaldi | | 82 |

**Accommodation & Facilities .... Garlasco - Pavia**

Saint Maria In Betlem,Via Pasino Degli Eustachi, 7,27100 Pavia(PV),Italy; +39 3313 046459; Email:info@ostellosantamariainbetlem.com; Web-site:ostellosantamariainbetlem.com; Price:B; Note:Check in from 18.30,

Pro Loco,Via Roma, 18,27020 Carbonara-al-Ticino(PV),Italy; Tel:+39 0382 400425; Price:C

Parrocchia della Sacra Famiglia,Viale Ludovico il Moro,27100 1Pavia(PV),Italy; Tel:+39 0382 575381; +39 3383 555168; +39 3315 888313; Email:informazione@sacrafamigliapv.it; Web-site:www.sacrafamigliapv.it; Price:D

Casa della Carità,Via Giuseppe Pedotti, 14,27100 Pavia(PV),Italy; Tel:+39 0382 23138; +39 3334 477119; Price:D

Parrocchia San Giorgio,Via Libertà,27027 Gropello-Cairoli(PV),Italy; Tel:+39 0382 815049; +39 3386 178903; Price:D

Hotel Aurora,Viale Vittorio Emanuele II, 25,27100 Pavia(PV),Italy; Tel:+39 0382 23664; Email:info@hotel-aurora.eu; Web-site:www.hotel-aurora.eu; Price:A

Hotel Stazione,Via Bernardino de' Rossi, 8,27100 Pavia(PV),Italy; Tel:+39 0382 35477; Price:B

Albergo Italia Ristorante,Via Libertà, 144,27027 Gropello-Cairoli(PV),Italy; Tel:+39 0382 815082; Email:albitagropelloc@gmail.com; Web-site:albergoitaliagropello.it; Price:B

## Accommodation & Facilities .... Garlasco - Pavia

Hotel Motel Flower,Via Lecco, 14,27027 Gropello-Cairoli(PV),Italy; Tel:+39 0382 815154; Email: info@hotelmotelflower.it ; Web-site:www.hotelmotelflower.it; Price:B

Camping Ticino,Via Mascherpa, 16,27100 Pavia(PV),Italy; Tel:+39 0382 527094; +39 3391 166674; Email:camping.ticino@libero.it; Web-site:www.campingticino.it; Price:C; Note:Open April to September,

Il Centro Ippico di Pavia,Strada Per il Lido,27100 Pavia(PV),Italy; Tel:+39 3386 065179

Il Centro Ippico di Pavia,Strada Canarazzo,27100 Pavia(PV),Italy; Tel:+39 0382 308322; Web-site:www.lombardia-inform.com/

Tourist Office,Piazza Italia, 5,27100 Pavia(PV),Italy; Tel:+39 0382 597022

San Paolo,Corso Giuseppe Garibaldi, 52,27100 Pavia(PV),Italy; Tel:+39 0382 304401

Banca Popolare di Sondrio,Piazzale Ponte Ticino, 8,27100 Pavia(PV),Italy; Tel:+39 0382 301759; Web-site:www.popso.it/FixedPages/Common/ DoveSiamoFiliali.php/L/IT

Banca Regionale Europea,Piazzale del Policlinico, 5,27100 Pavia(PV),Italy; Tel:+39 0382 527482

San Paolo,Via Libertà, 108,27027 Gropello-Cairoli(PV),Italy; Tel:+39 0382 815701

Stazione Ferrovie,Piazzale della Stazione, 9,27100 Pavia(PV),Italy; Tel:+39 06 6847 5475; Web-site:www.renitalia.it

Azienda Ospedaliera,Via Carlo Forlanini, 1,27100 Pavia(PV),Italy; Tel:+39 0382 527549

Bolduri - Studio Medico,Via Defendente Sacchi, 25,27100 Pavia(PV),Italy; Tel:+39 0382 33622

Ambulatorio Veterinario Ticino,Via Riviera, 43,27100 Pavia(PV),Italy; Tel:+39 0382 526322

Rino Sport,Corso Garibaldi Giuseppe, 4,27100 Pavia(PV),Italy; Tel:+39 0382 26976

Bike Corner di Milazzo Luca,Viale Cremona, 186,27100 Pavia(PV),Italy; Tel:+39 0382 575040

Taxi Radio Pavese,Viale Montegrappa, 15,27100 Pavia(PV),Italy; Tel:+39 0382 577733

Stage Summary: after exiting the centre of Pavia, the route follows suburban roads before negotiating the crossing of the busy ring road. From there the "Official Route" follows a mix of quiet country roads and gravel tracks making for easy going for all groups. Belgioioso offers a broader range of facilities than Santa Cristina.

Distance from Vercelli: 82km          Distance to St Peter's Square, Rome: 766km
Stage Ascent: 183m                    Stage Descent: 195m

| Waypoint | Distance between waypoints | Total km | Directions | Verification Point | Compass | Altitude m |
|---|---|---|---|---|---|---|
| 65.001 | 0 | 0.0 | From the crossroads turn right | Corso Garibaldi | E | 82 |
| 65.002 | 1000 | 1.0 | At the traffic lights go straight ahead direction Piacenza | Cross the waterway on viale dei Partigiani | E | 69 |
| 65.003 | 1200 | 2.2 | At San Pietro in Verzolo continue straight ahead | Pass church on the right | E | 76 |
| 65.004 | 400 | 2.6 | Turn right on via Francana | VF sign, kiosk on the corner | SE | 66 |
| 65.005 | 700 | 3.2 | Continue straight ahead | Ignore the turning to the left on via Scarenzio | SE | 67 |
| 65.006 | 160 | 3.4 | At the end of the road continue straight ahead on the tarmac which quickly becomes an unmade track and winds from left to right and then turns back towards the main toad | | NE | 66 |
| 65.007 | 300 | 3.7 | At the crossroads at the end of the track take the tarmac road straight ahead | Uphill | NE | 66 |
| 65.008 | 90 | 3.8 | At the T-junction turn right on the broader road | Via Montebolone | SE | 71 |
| 65.009 | 160 | 3.9 | At the roundabout, continue straight ahead | Church on the right | E | 76 |

| Waypoint | Distance between waypoints | Total km | Directions | Verification Point | Compass | Altitude m |
|---|---|---|---|---|---|---|
| 65.010 | 130 | 4.1 | At the T-junction, turn right | Pedestrian and cycle path | SE | 75 |
| 65.011 | 600 | 4.7 | At the T-junction turn left on strada Scagliona | Factory buildings directly ahead at the junction | SE | 68 |
| 65.012 | 400 | 5.1 | Bear right | Direction Broni, VF sign | SE | 73 |
| 65.013 | 800 | 5.9 | At the roundabout, proceed with care to take the second exit | Direction San Leonardo | E | 60 |
| 65.014 | 4800 | 10.6 | At the sharp bend to the left, after passing through Ospedaletto, bear right on the tarmac and then turn right on the unmade road | Direction S. Giacomo | S | 70 |
| 65.015 | 500 | 11.0 | At the first crossroads turn left and follow the road through San Giacomo and Santa Margherita | VF sign | E | 71 |
| 65.016 | 4000 | 15.0 | Remain on the road into Belgioioso | Factory to the right | N | 62 |
| 65.017 | 1100 | 16.1 | In Belgioioso turn right on via P. Nenni | VF sign, direction carabinieri | E | 73 |
| 65.018 | 500 | 16.5 | At the T-junction, turn right on the SP9 towards Torre de' Negri | Exit Beligioioso | SE | 71 |
| 65.019 | 2100 | 18.6 | Pass through Torre de' Negri and on the crown of the right-hand bend continue on the road | Ignore the track to the left | S | 69 |
| 65.020 | 800 | 19.3 | On the crown of a further bend to the right, bear left on the gravel road | Direction Cascina Campobello, pass silos on the right | E | 69 |

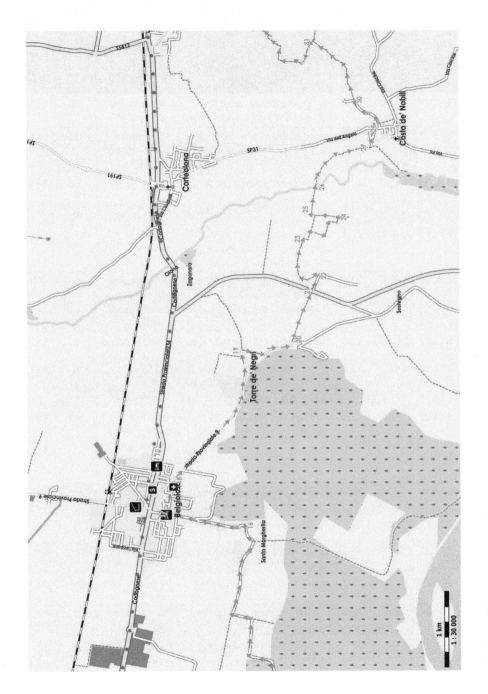

| Waypoint | Distance between waypoints | Total km | Directions | Verification Point | Compass | Altitude m |
|---|---|---|---|---|---|---|
| 65.021 | 700 | 20.0 | At the crossroads with the SP199 continue straight ahead | Towards the quarry | E | 66 |
| 65.022 | 230 | 20.3 | Besides the quarry buildings, turn left on the gravel track | Skirt the quarry on your right | E | 68 |
| 65.023 | 800 | 21.1 | Bear right following the fence | | SE | 68 |
| 65.024 | 700 | 21.8 | At the T-junction turn left | VF sign | N | 69 |
| 65.025 | 400 | 22.2 | At the next junction,at the end of the field, continue straight ahead | Slightly downhill | E | 69 |
| 65.026 | 300 | 22.5 | Cross the bridge and continue straight ahead on the broad track beside the canal | Woodland to the right and canal close on the left | SE | 56 |
| 65.027 | 1000 | 23.5 | Turn left over the next bridge | Via Aldo Moro | E | 56 |
| 65.028 | 260 | 23.8 | At the T-junction turn right on the main road into the village of Costa de' Nobili | Via Roma | S | 65 |
| 65.029 | 70 | 23.8 | Turn left towards Cascina Padulino | Shortly after turning the tarmac gives way to an unmade road | NE | 64 |
| 65.030 | 600 | 24.4 | By the farm entrance continue straight ahead | Farm on the left | NE | 55 |
| 65.031 | 1000 | 25.4 | At the T-junction turn left | | N | 53 |
| 65.032 | 2200 | 27.6 | Continue straight ahead into Santa Cristina | Conifers on the right | N | 63 |
| 65.033 | 120 | 27.7 | At the T-junction turn left | VF sign | NW | 70 |
| 65.034 | 60 | 27.7 | Take the next turning to the right | Via Gibelli, VF sign | N | 71 |
| 65.035 | 150 | 27.9 | Arrive at Santa-Cristina (XL) centre | Beside the church | | 70 |

Casa Pellegrino - Parrocchia San Michele,Via Giuseppe Garibaldi,27011 Belgioioso(PV),Italy; Tel:+39 0382 969093; Price:D

Parrocchia di Santa Cristina e Bissone,(Don Antonio Pedrazzini),Via Vittorio Veneto, 118,31055 Santa-Cristina(TV),Italy; Tel:+39 0382 70106; +39 3333 429685; Email:santacristina@parrocchie.diocesi.pavia.it; Web-site:www. parrocchiasantacristinaebissone.it; Price:D; Note:Credentials required,

S.Michele Arcangelo - Casa Canonica Parrocchia,Piazza Iv Novembre,27010 Miradolo-Terme-27010(PV),Italy; Tel:+39 0382 77116; Price:D

La Locanda della Pesa Ristorante Albergo,Via 20 Settembre, 111,27011 Belgioioso(PV),Italy; Tel:+39 0382 969073; Price:B

Hotel Gulliver,Via Cavallotti, 50,27011 Belgioioso(PV),Italy; Tel:+39 0382 969180; Price:B

La Castellana,Frazione San Giacomo,27011 Belgioioso(PV),Italy; Tel:+39 0382 970207

Banca Popolare di Lodi,27010 Miradolo-Terme(PV),Italy; Tel:+39 0382 721790; Web-site:www.poplodi.it

Istituto Bancario San Paolo di Torino,Piazza Vittorio Veneto, 15,27011 Belgioioso(PV),Italy; Tel:+39 0382 969015

Salvi - Studio Medico,Via Amendola, 6,27011 Belgioioso(PV),Italy; Tel:+39 0382 970567

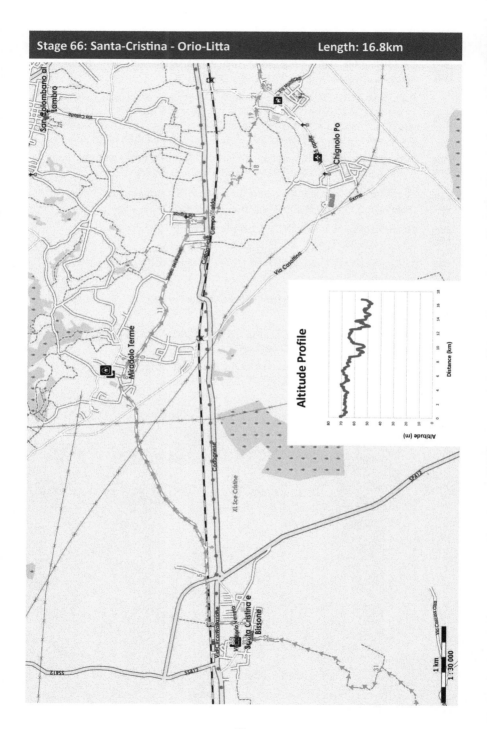

Stage Summary: we again use farm tracks and minor roads over generally level ground on this short section. Both Miradolo Terme and Cignolo Po offer a range of facilities.

Distance from Vercelli: 110km
Stage Ascent: 89m

Distance to St Peter's Square, Rome: 738km
Stage Descent: 105m

| Waypoint | Distance between waypoints | Total km | Directions | Verification | Compass | Altitude m |
|---|---|---|---|---|---|---|
| 66.001 | 0 | 0.0 | Facing the church in Santa Cristina turn right and proceed along the main street | Via Vittorio Veneto | E | 70 |
| 66.002 | 220 | 0.2 | Turn left on viale Rimembranze | Direction Stazione | N | 71 |
| 66.003 | 270 | 0.5 | Cross the main road (SS234) and continue straight ahead | Pedestrian traffic lights | N | 67 |
| 66.004 | 100 | 0.6 | Cross the railway line and immediately turn right on the path beside the railway | Open fields to the left and railway to the right | E | 67 |
| 66.005 | 700 | 1.2 | Turn right and then immediately left | Between the railway and the irrigation channel | E | 67 |
| 66.006 | 400 | 1.6 | Bear left over the irrigation channel | Continue between the open fields | NE | 66 |
| 66.007 | 2200 | 3.8 | Cross the main road and continue straight ahead on the road towards Miradolo Terme | Pass the cemetery on your left | NE | 66 |
| 66.008 | 500 | 4.2 | In piazza del Comune in Miradolo Terme, bear right towards Piacenza | Via Garibaldi | SE | 68 |
| 66.009 | 300 | 4.5 | Bear right | Via Garibaldi | S | 70 |
| 66.010 | 90 | 4.6 | Take the first turning to the left and follow the road into open country | Via San Marco, VF sign | SE | 70 |
| 66.011 | 800 | 5.4 | Take the left fork on the road | Pass between the trees | E | 66 |

| Waypoint | Distance between waypoints | Total km | Directions | Verification | Compass | Altitude m |
|---|---|---|---|---|---|---|
| 66.012 | 1300 | 6.7 | At the crossroads in the centre of Camporinaldo turn right | Via Cavour | S | 69 |
| 66.013 | 240 | 6.9 | At the T-junction with the main road turn left and then cross the road using the pedestrian crossing beside the traffic lights and continue beside the main road | SS234, via Cremona | E | 67 |
| 66.014 | 130 | 7.0 | Turn right on the first track between the fields | Towards the railway | S | 68 |
| 66.015 | 140 | 7.2 | Shortly after crossing the railway bear left | | SE | 66 |
| 66.016 | 500 | 7.7 | Turn right | Towards the canal | S | 66 |
| 66.017 | 130 | 7.8 | Turn right and then immediately left | Cross the small canal bridge | SE | 66 |
| 66.018 | 260 | 8.0 | At the T-junction turn left | Initially parallel to canal | E | 64 |
| 66.019 | 800 | 8.8 | At the road junction, continue straight ahead | Towards the Chignolo Po castle tower | E | 56 |
| 66.020 | 110 | 8.9 | Continue straight ahead | Towards the town centre | E | 55 |
| 66.021 | 160 | 9.1 | At the Stop sign, bear right | Castle to the left | SE | 56 |
| 66.022 | 130 | 9.2 | At the traffic lights bear left | Via Garibaldi, towards Lambrinia | E | 55 |
| 66.023 | 600 | 9.8 | At the crossroads with the SP193 continue straight ahead | Towards Lambrinia | E | 58 |
| 66.024 | 1400 | 11.2 | Continue straight ahead on the cycle track | Pass a cemetery on the right | E | 63 |
| 66.025 | 500 | 11.7 | At the fork bear left | Via Mameli | NE | 64 |

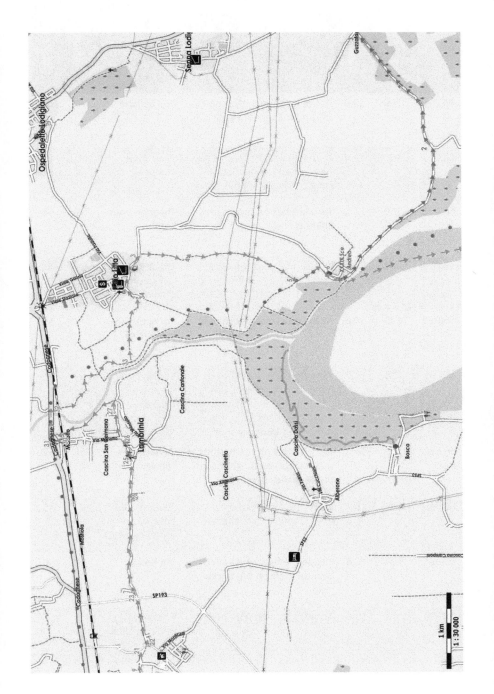

Ospedaletto Lodigiano

Senna Lodi...

Guzzafa...

S. Lco
(Andreo...

Viale Golita
Viale Vittoria

S

...Litta

Codognese

2

3

5

Lodigiana

Mulazzo
Cascina San Marinana
Via Marinana
Lambrinia

2

25
24
22

Mazzola

Cascina Cantonale

Cascina Dosi

Cascina Dosi

Bosco

SP53

Cascina Campagna
Cascinetta

Via Albarone
Alberone

Codognese

Mazzola

SP193

Via Monticelli

Cascina Camponi

1 km

1 : 30 000

48

| Waypoint | Distance between waypoints | Total km | Directions | Verification | Compass | Altitude m |
|---|---|---|---|---|---|---|
| 66.026 | 300 | 12.0 | At the junction in the centre of Lambrinia, bear right | Via Bellaria | E | 63 |
| 66.027 | 400 | 12.4 | At the end of the tarmac road, turn left and immediately right on the footpath | Near pink house | E | 62 |
| 66.028 | 150 | 12.6 | Turn left beside the irrigation channel | River on your right | NW | 55 |
| 66.029 | 900 | 13.5 | Turn left on the stony road | Cross the irrigation channel | SW | 54 |
| 66.030 | 120 | 13.6 | At the crossroads, turn right | Towards the main road | N | 59 |
| 66.031 | 100 | 13.7 | At the T-junction with the main road, turn right and continue beside the road using the guard rail for protection from the traffic | SS234, cross over river bridge | E | 58 |
| 66.032 | 500 | 14.2 | Immediately after crossing the river bridge, turn right onto the unmade road | Towards the railway | SE | 52 |
| 66.033 | 1500 | 15.7 | Leave the embankment on the second track to the left | Towards Orio Litta and between fields | E | 49 |
| 66.034 | 900 | 16.6 | Beside the first houses in Orio Litta turn left on the tarmac road | Via Roma | NE | 50 |
| 66.035 | 200 | 16.8 | Arrive at Orio-Litta centre | Piazza dei Benedettini to the left | | 55 |

Cascina San Pietro,Piazza dei Benedettini,20080 Orio-Litta(LO),Italy; Tel:+39 0377 944436; Price:D

Palestra Comunale,Piazza Aldo Moro, 2,26863 Orio-Litta(LO),Italy; +39 3356 468587; Price:D; Note:For large groups only,

Comune di Senna Lodigiana,Via Dante Alighieri, 1,26856 Senna-Lodigiana(LO),Italy; Tel:+39 0377 802155; +39 3391 268946; Email:comune.sennalodigiana@pec.regione.lombardia.it; Web-site:www.comune.sennalodigiana.lo.it; Price:C

B&B - la Conchiglia,Cascina Quaino, 4,27013 Chignolo-Po(PV),Italy; +39 3383 831889; +39 3201 457138; Email:info@beblaconchiglia.com; Web-site:www.beblaconchiglia.com; Price:B

Centro Ippico Visola,Strada dei Boschi, 29,26813 Graffignana(LO),Italy; Tel:+39 0371 209237

Banca Popolare di Lodi,Via Giuseppe Mazzini, 2,26863 Orio-Litta(LO),Italy; Tel:+39 0377 833472

Zucca - Studio Medico,Via 8 Marzo,27013 Chignolo-Po(PV),Italy; Tel:+39 0382 723095

Ambulatorio Veterinario,Via Garibaldi, 138,27013 Chignolo-Po(PV),Italy; Tel:+39 0382 766531

## Altitude Profile

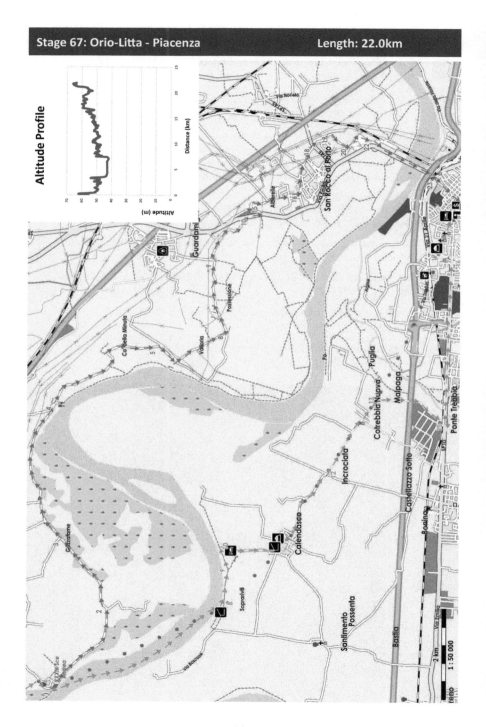

Stage Summary: the route leads from Orio Litta to the Guado di Sigerico (Pò ferry crossing) on farm tracks and the argine. From the ferry dock to the outskirts of Piacenza the route continues on pleasant country roads, but the long entry into Piacenza unfortunately uses the very busy via Emilia Pavese. An Alternate Route along the argine is available for those not able to take the ferry. The ferry crosses between 10.00 and 11.00 and 16:00 and 17:00, but only on request and should be booked at least 24 hours in advance: Danilo Parisi Tel:+39 0523 771607 Mobile:+39 3886 933850

Distance from Vercelli: 127km          Distance to St Peter's Square, Rome: 721km
Stage Ascent: 103m                     Stage Descent: 95m

| Waypoint | Distance between waypoints | Total km | Directions | Verification Point | Compass | Altitude m |
|---|---|---|---|---|---|---|
| 67.001 | 0 | 0.0 | From piazza dei Benedettini bear right | Via Roma | E | 55 |
| 67.002 | 280 | 0.3 | At the T-junction beside Villa Litta bear right | Via Montemalo | SE | 61 |
| 67.003 | 200 | 0.5 | At the bottom of the hill bear right on the unmade road | Beside the water course, Cascina Cantarana | S | 51 |
| 67.004 | 600 | 1.1 | Take the left fork beside the gas sub-station | Remain beside the water course | S | 49 |
| 67.005 | 1600 | 2.7 | At the T-junction turn left on the embankment, argine, above the river |  | SE | 51 |
| 67.006 | 400 | 3.0 | Turn right | Remain on the embankment | SW | 48 |
| 67.007 | 300 | 3.4 | Arrive beside the Pò river ferry (Guado di Sigerico). Note:- the ferry is only suitable for pedestrians or a small number of bikes. Horse riders and those not wishing to take the ferry will need to continue straight ahead on the Alternate Route | Corte Sant'Andrea (XXXIX) to the left | SE | 53 |

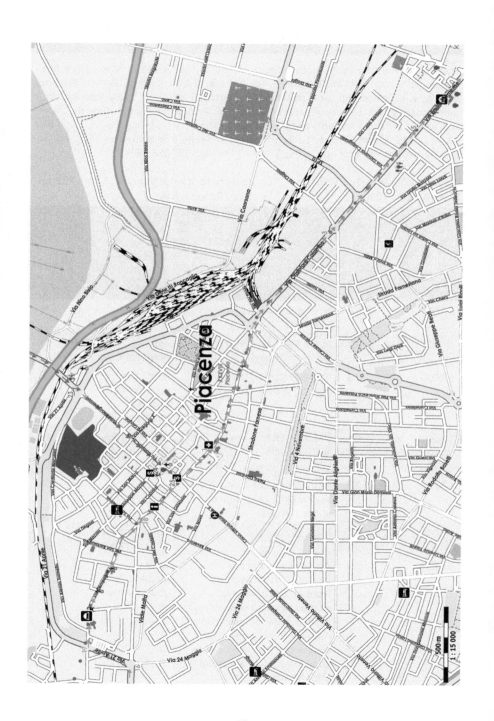

| Waypoint | Distance between waypoints | Total km | Directions | Verification Point | Compass | Altitude m |
|---|---|---|---|---|---|---|
| 67.008 | 4400 | 7.7 | After climbing from the ferry landing stage, proceed to the left on the gravel track | Pò on the left | E | 50 |
| 67.009 | 700 | 8.5 | At the fork in the track, continue straight ahead. Note:- 500m may be saved by taking the grass track to the right and then turning right at the T-junction | VF sign | E | 49 |
| 67.010 | 600 | 9.1 | At the crossroads on the embankment, turn right on the stony track | Towards the farm buildings, the track will become a tarmac road | S | 50 |
| 67.011 | 1300 | 10.3 | At the crossroads, turn left directly in front of a large building - Commune di Calendasco | Via Mazzini | SE | 52 |
| 67.012 | 2200 | 12.5 | On the crown of the bend to the right, in the hamlet of Incrociata, turn left | Direction Cotrebbia Nuova,VF sign | SE | 51 |
| 67.013 | 2000 | 14.5 | At the fork in Malpaga, bear right | Towards the Autostrada, VF sign | S | 51 |
| 67.014 | 1600 | 16.1 | After passing under the railway and the road bridges turn immediately right and climb the ramp | | W | 54 |
| 67.015 | 230 | 16.3 | At the junction with the main road, turn right to cross the bridge and continue on the long straight via Emilia Pavese. Note:- caution on the narrow pavement over the long bridge beside the very busy road | Direction Piacenza | E | 57 |
| 67.016 | 3700 | 20.0 | At the roundabout in piazzale Torino turn left on via XXI Aprile | Fountain in roundabout | NE | 55 |

| Waypoint | Distance between waypoints | Total km | Directions | Verification Point | Compass | Altitude m |
|---|---|---|---|---|---|---|
| 67.017 | 300 | 20.4 | At the next roundabout turn right on via Campagna | Pass park and citadel walls on the left | E | 53 |
| 67.018 | 900 | 21.3 | In piazza del Borgo go straight ahead | Via Garibaldi | SE | 63 |
| 67.019 | 400 | 21.7 | At the crossroads with corso Vittorio Emanuele II, go straight ahead. The Alternate Route joins from the left | Strada Sant'Antonino | SE | 64 |
| 67.020 | 270 | 22.0 | Arrive at Piacenza (XXXVIII) centre | Beside the church of Sant'Antonino | | 64 |

**Alternate Route #67.A1**                     **Length: 22.8km**

Stage Summary: route to Piacenza avoiding the Pò ferry. The route follows the argine and farms tracks before skirting San Rocco al Porto and approaching Piacenza on the pedestrian and cycle track over the new Pò river bridge

**Stage Ascent: 101m**                        **Stage Descent: 90m**

| Waypoint | Distance between waypoints | Total km | Directions | Verification Point | Compass | Altitude m |
|---|---|---|---|---|---|---|
| 67A1.001 | 0 | 0.0 | Continue straight ahead | Remain on the argine | SE | 52 |
| 67A1.002 | 2400 | 2.3 | Continue straight ahead on the embankment | Farm on the left | NE | 51 |
| 67A1.003 | 1800 | 4.2 | Continue straight ahead on the embankment | Village of Guzzafame on the left | E | 50 |
| 67A1.004 | 3500 | 7.6 | At the crossroads, continue straight ahead on the embankment | | SE | 48 |
| 67A1.005 | 3000 | 10.6 | Bear right on the embankment | Parallel to the road below | SW | 47 |
| 67A1.006 | 600 | 11.2 | Beside the village of Valloria, turn sharp left to leave the embankment | | NE | 46 |

| Waypoint | Distance between waypoints | Total km | Directions | Verification Point | Compass | Altitude m |
|---|---|---|---|---|---|---|
| 67A1.007 | 80 | 11.3 | Turn right and pass through the centre of Valloria | Via Dante Alighieri | SE | 46 |
| 67A1.008 | 1300 | 12.5 | At the junction with the embankment, turn left | Follow the embankment | E | 47 |
| 67A1.009 | 1700 | 14.2 | At the crossroads, continue straight ahead | Remain on the embankment | SE | 45 |
| 67A1.010 | 1400 | 15.7 | Shortly before the T-junction with the main road, turn right on the gravel track | Pass an industrial zone on your left | S | 45 |
| 67A1.011 | 230 | 15.9 | At the crossroads, turn left, carefully cross the main road and continue straight ahead into the industrial zone | Via Alberelle | E | 44 |
| 67A1.012 | 70 | 16.0 | Bear left on the road | Pass between industrial buildings | N | 45 |
| 67A1.013 | 210 | 16.2 | Bear right on the road | Remain close to the industrial building | E | 45 |
| 67A1.014 | 200 | 16.4 | Bear right on the road | Avoid the road on the left | S | 45 |
| 67A1.015 | 150 | 16.5 | Take the left fork | | S | 45 |
| 67A1.016 | 900 | 17.4 | At the crossroads in San Rocco al Porto, turn left on the small road | Via Giovanni Bosco | E | 45 |
| 67A1.017 | 130 | 17.6 | At the junction, cntinue straight ahead and skirt San Rocco al Porto on your right | Via Martiri della Libertà | E | 45 |
| 67A1.018 | 1000 | 18.5 | At the roundabout, continue straight ahead | Pass a lake on the right of the road | SE | 45 |

| Waypoint | Distance between waypoints | Total km | Directions | Verification Point | Compass | Altitude m |
|---|---|---|---|---|---|---|
| 67A1.019 | 500 | 19.1 | Bear right on the cycle track beside the road | Waterway on the left and industrial buildings on the right | SW | 42 |
| 67A1.020 | 500 | 19.6 | At the roundabout, turn left | Pass the rear of the hypermarket | SE | 44 |
| 67A1.021 | 300 | 19.9 | Bear right | Car park on the right | SW | 47 |
| 67A1.022 | 400 | 20.3 | At the roundabout, continue straight ahead and join the pedestrian path beside the main road | Cross the Pò bridge | SW | 47 |
| 67A1.023 | 1600 | 21.9 | At the roundabout, continue straight ahead | Memorial on roundabout | SW | 52 |
| 67A1.024 | 800 | 22.7 | Continue straight ahead on via Cavour | Pass Piazza Cavalli on the right | SW | 65 |
| 67A1.025 | 160 | 22.8 | At the crossroads, turn left and rejoin the "Official Route" | Via Sant'Antonio | | 63 |

**Accommodation & Facilities .... Orio-Litta - Piacenza**

Caupona Sigerico,Località Soprarivo, 21,29010 Calendasco(PC),Italy; Tel:+39 0523 771607; +39 3886 933850; Email:ser.pe@libero.it; Web-site:www.cauponasigerico-viafrancigena.it; Price:D

Ostello le Tre Corone,Via Mazzini Nuova, 59,29010 Calendasco(PC),Italy; Tel:+39 0523 772894; +39 3341 866556; Email:mszaniboni@yahoo.co.uk; Web-site:www.trecorone.it; Price:C

Oratorio Santa Maria Assunta,Via Verdi, 1,29010 Calendasco(PC),Italy; Tel:+39 0523 771497; Price:D

Santuario Santa Maria di Campagna,Piazzale delle Crociate, 5,29121 Piacenza(PC),Italy; Tel:+39 0523 490728; +39 3282 127017; Email:secondoballati@gmail.com; Price:D

Ostello San Pietro,(Don Pietro Bulla),Via Emilia Parmense, 71,29100 Piacenza(PC),Italy; Tel:+39 0523 614256; +39 3331 493595; Email:sanlazzaro@libero.it; Web-site:www.parrocchiasanlazzaropiacenza.com/ostello-sulla-via-francigena; Price:C

## Accommodation & Facilities .... Orio-Litta - Piacenza

San Giovanni Battista,Piazza 4 Novembre,26862 Guardamiglio(LO),Italy; Tel:+39 0377 51020; Price:D

Ostello Don Zermani,Via Luigi Zoni,29100 Piacenza(PC),Italy; Tel:+39 0523 712319; Email:info@ostellodipiacenza.it; Web-site:www.ostellodipiacenza.it; Price:B

Locanda - il Masero,Loc.Masero, 2,29010 Calendasco(PC),Italy; Tel:+39 0523 772787; +39 3461 306189; Email:info@locandailmasero.it; Web-site:www.locandailmasero.it; Price:A

B&B - Angela,Via Giuseppe Mazzini,29100 Piacenza(PC),Italy; Tel:+39 0523 499098; Email:angela.aime48@gmail.com; Web-site:www.bbangela.com; Price:B

B&B - Pilgrims,Via G.Morigi, 36,29121 Piacenza(PC),Italy; Tel:+39 0523 453527; +39 3286 751328; Email:contatti@bb-pilgrims.com; Web-site:bb-pilgrims.com; Price:A

Vip Hotel,Via Vittorio Cipelli, 41,29100 Piacenza(PC),Italy; Tel:+39 0523 712420; +39 0523 71208; Email:info@viphotel.it; Web-site:www.viphotel.it; Price:B

Provincia di Piacenza,Via Giuseppe Garibaldi, 50,29121 Piacenza(PC),Italy; Tel:+39 0523 7951

Banca di Piacenza,Via Giuseppe Mazzini, 20,29121 Piacenza(PC),Italy; Tel:+39 0523 347336

Unicredit,Largo Cesare Battisti, 26,29100 Piacenza(PC),Italy; Tel:+39 0523 308211

Stazione Ferrovie,Piazzale Marconi Snc, C/o C.C.Borgo Fax Hall,29100 Piacenza(PC),Italy; Tel:+39 06 6847 5475; Web-site:www.renitalia.it

Azienda Unita' Sanitaria Locale di Piacenza,Corso Vittorio Emanuele II, 169,29121 Piacenza(PC),Italy; Tel:+39 0523 301111; Web-site:www.ausl.pc.it

Zucchi Marco,Via Chiapponi, 46,29121 Piacenza(PC),Italy; Tel:+39 0523 336921

Ambulatorio Veterinario,Via Trebbia, 28,29121 Piacenza(PC),Italy; Tel:+39 0523 490272

Eightysix,Via Martiri della Resistenza, 36,29122 Piacenza(PC),Italy; Tel:+39 0523 751369

Vivo,Via Egidio Gorra, 5,29122 Piacenza(PC),Italy; Tel:+39 0523 716432

Tuttociclismo Tizzoni Tuttociclismo di Tizzoni & C.Sas,Via Pietro Cella, 39a,29121 Piacenza(PC),Italy; Tel:+39 0523 457578

Taxi,Piazzale Marconi Guglielmo,29121 Piacenza(PC),Italy; Tel:+39 0523 323853

Taxi Radio Taxi,1 Largo Anguissola Ercole,29100 Piacenza(PC),Italy; Tel:+39 0523 591919

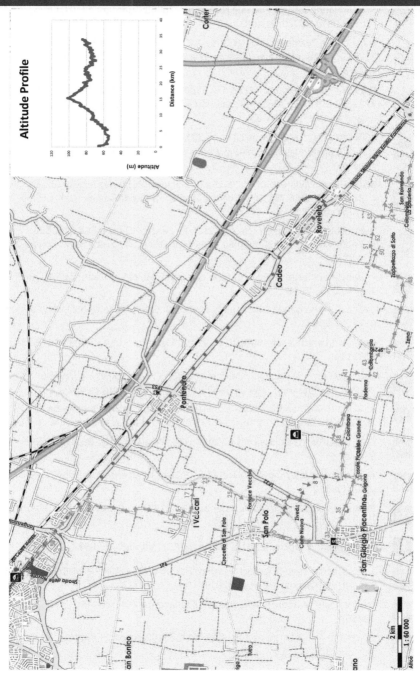

Stage Summary: a long section through farmland. The exit from Piacenza initially follows the dangerous via Emilia. Thereafter we enter the countryside where again there is the difficulty of navigation with few distinct landmarks but also with a number of river crossings to be negotiated or bypassed. After leaving the outskirts of Piacenza, there are limited opportunities for intermediate stops and so be sure that you have sufficient water and food for the day.

Distance from Vercelli: 149km
Stage Ascent: 200m

Distance to St Peter's Square, Rome: 699km
Stage Descent: 179m

| Waypoint | Distance between waypoints | Total km | Directions | Verification Point | Compass | Altitude m |
|---|---|---|---|---|---|---|
| 68.001 | 0 | 0.0 | From the church of Sant'Antonino continue straight ahead on via Sant'Antonino and via Scalabrini | Church to the right | E | 64 |
| 68.002 | 900 | 0.8 | In piazzale Roma continue straight ahead on the right side of the long, straight, broad road | Via Emilia Parmense | SE | 58 |
| 68.003 | 1000 | 1.8 | At the roundabout continue straight ahead on the via Emilia Parmense, SS9 | Hotel ahead and cycle track on the right | SE | 56 |
| 68.004 | 180 | 2.0 | At the next roundabout continue straight ahead | Direction Parma, spire ahead | SE | 55 |
| 68.005 | 700 | 2.6 | Continue straight ahead at the traffic lights | Pass the Parrocchia San Lazzaro on the right | SE | 54 |
| 68.006 | 500 | 3.1 | Continue straight ahead at the traffic lights | Via Emilia Parmense, SS9 | SE | 54 |
| 68.007 | 500 | 3.5 | Continue straight ahead on the pavement | Via Emilia Parmense, SS9 | SE | 54 |
| 68.008 | 600 | 4.1 | At the junction continue straight ahead on the cycle path | Large commercial centre to the right | SE | 58 |

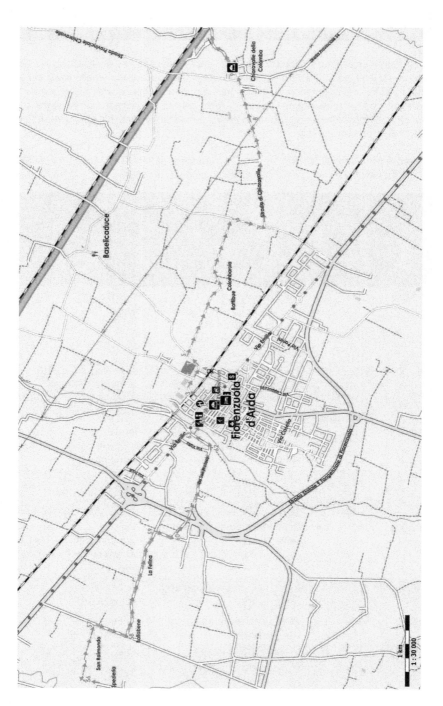

| Waypoint | Distance between waypoints | Total km | Directions | Verification Point | Compass | Altitude m |
|---|---|---|---|---|---|---|
| 68.009 | 250 | 4.3 | With great care cross the major highway intersection and continue straight ahead | Via Emilia Parmense, SS9 | SE | 58 |
| 68.010 | 1000 | 5.3 | Turn right to leave the via Emilia Parmese | Towards the office complex | S | 57 |
| 68.011 | 150 | 5.4 | At the roundabout, turn left | Follow the tarmac pathway | SE | 55 |
| 68.012 | 300 | 5.8 | Bear right on the cycle track | | SW | 60 |
| 68.013 | 300 | 6.1 | Bear left on the cycle track over the ditch and continue straight ahead on the country road | Pass telephone mast on your right! | S | 57 |
| 68.014 | 2600 | 8.7 | At the first crossroads in the hamlet of I Vaccari turn left on the road | Via L Rocci to the right at the junction | SE | 74 |
| 68.015 | 180 | 8.8 | At the T-junction turn right | Via G. Seti, VF sign | SW | 71 |
| 68.016 | 160 | 9.0 | At the T-junction, turn left on the tarmac road | Strada I Vaccari | E | 73 |
| 68.017 | 600 | 9.6 | Continue straight ahead on the gravel road | Farm buildings to the right | E | 72 |
| 68.018 | 220 | 9.8 | Continue straight ahead on the track | Metal gate | E | 71 |
| 68.019 | 100 | 9.9 | Turn right onto a partially obscured path into the trees | Path leads beside the river – torrente Nure | S | 71 |
| 68.020 | 50 | 9.9 | Fork left | VF sign | S | 72 |
| 68.021 | 220 | 10.2 | Fork left | | S | 72 |
| 68.022 | 100 | 10.3 | At the junction, keep left | VF sign | S | 72 |
| 68.023 | 130 | 10.4 | Take the right fork | River visible on the left | S | 72 |
| 68.024 | 120 | 10.5 | Keep left on the path | Remain beside the river | SW | 73 |

| Waypoint | Distance between waypoints | Total km | Directions | Verification Point | Compass | Altitude m |
|---|---|---|---|---|---|---|
| 68.025 | 700 | 11.2 | At the next intersection turn left | Remain beside the river, farm on your right | S | 76 |
| 68.026 | 600 | 11.8 | At the T-junction with the gravel road turn left | Remain beside the river, VF sign | S | 79 |
| 68.027 | 300 | 12.1 | Continue straight ahead | Between the fields and the river | S | 80 |
| 68.028 | 230 | 12.3 | Turn left and then right | Remain beside the river | SW | 81 |
| 68.029 | 500 | 12.8 | Turn right.  Note:- a stretch of the busy SP 6 can be avoided and the route reduced by approximately 2km by fording the river and following the Alternate Route.  This should only be attempted in high summer and when the river bed is clearly dry | Towards the farm | NW | 85 |
| 68.030 | 800 | 13.5 | At the T-junction with the main road | Turn left | S | 87 |
| 68.031 | 800 | 14.3 | Continue straight ahead over the bridge, SP6 | Direction San Giorgio | S | 94 |
| 68.032 | 1000 | 15.4 | Shortly after entering San Giorgio, turn left on via Garibaldi | Elaborately decorated house on the right at junction | E | 102 |
| 68.033 | 190 | 15.6 | Turn right | Via Manzoni | S | 98 |
| 68.034 | 100 | 15.7 | At the T-junction, turn left | Direction Montanaro | E | 99 |
| 68.035 | 700 | 16.4 | Continue straight ahead on the road | Pass the cemetery on the right | E | 94 |
| 68.036 | 1000 | 17.3 | Take the next turning on the left | Via Verona | N | 89 |

| Waypoint | Distance between waypoints | Total km | Directions | Verification Point | Compass | Altitude m |
|---|---|---|---|---|---|---|
| 68.037 | 400 | 17.7 | At the T-junction, turn right. The Alternate Route joins from the left | Towards the farm buildings | E | 86 |
| 68.038 | 1300 | 19.0 | At the junction, next to a farm, turn right on the white road | VF sign | E | 82 |
| 68.039 | 400 | 19.4 | At the T-junction beside the farm turn right, | VF sign | SE | 80 |
| 68.040 | 1100 | 20.4 | At the crossroads, continue straight ahead | Shortly after passing Castello di Paderna | E | 80 |
| 68.041 | 700 | 21.1 | After passing driveways on the right and left, turn right on the track | Towards trees | S | 74 |
| 68.042 | 500 | 21.6 | At the T-junction, turn left | Pass trees on your right | E | 77 |
| 68.043 | 400 | 22.0 | Bear right across the stream | Cross the field towards the trees | E | 76 |
| 68.044 | 100 | 22.1 | Turn right | Pass trees on your left, towards farm | S | 77 |
| 68.045 | 140 | 22.2 | At the T-junction, turn left | Farm on the right at the junction | SE | 78 |
| 68.046 | 400 | 22.6 | At the T-junction with the main road, turn right | Towards Zena | S | 75 |
| 68.047 | 300 | 22.9 | On the entry to the hamlet of Zena, turn left | Towards Chero | E | 81 |
| 68.048 | 2200 | 25.1 | At the T-junction turn left. Note:- beware of the traffic | Strada Zappellazzo | NE | 80 |
| 68.049 | 1000 | 26.1 | After passing the tower in Zappellazzo turn right on the tarmac road | | E | 73 |

| Waypoint | Distance between waypoints | Total km | Directions | Verification Point | Compass | Altitude m |
|---|---|---|---|---|---|---|
| 68.050 | 400 | 26.5 | At the end of the tarmac road ford the torrente Chero and turn left on the track | Keep trees to the left and cultivated field to the right | NE | 74 |
| 68.051 | 290 | 26.8 | Turn right passing a barrier | Track between fields | E | 75 |
| 68.052 | 250 | 27.0 | Continue straight ahead on the white road | Ignore the turning to the left | E | 72 |
| 68.053 | 600 | 27.7 | At the T-junction with the tarmac road, turn right | Keep trees to the left | S | 73 |
| 68.054 | 400 | 28.0 | Take the next turning to the left | Towards the trees and fording torrente Chiavenna | SE | 74 |
| 68.055 | 290 | 28.3 | Shortly after the ford turn left | Between fields, with trees on the left | N | 75 |
| 68.056 | 260 | 28.5 | Bear right | Pass between two farms | E | 70 |
| 68.057 | 800 | 29.4 | At the T-junction with the tarmac road, turn right | | S | 71 |
| 68.058 | 500 | 29.8 | Immediately after passing farm buildings, close on the left side of the road, turn left on the unmade road | Strada Vicinale della Felina | E | 75 |
| 68.059 | 1600 | 31.4 | Turn right on the tarmac road | VF sign | S | 77 |
| 68.060 | 260 | 31.7 | Bear left and then take the left fork | | SE | 78 |
| 68.061 | 500 | 32.2 | At the road junction after the underpass continue straight ahead | VF sign | E | 82 |
| 68.062 | 900 | 33.1 | Follow the main road to the left | Enter Fiorenzuola-d'Arda | NE | 80 |

| Waypoint | Distance between waypoints | Total km | Directions | Verification Point | Compass | Altitude m |
|---|---|---|---|---|---|---|
| 68.063 | 300 | 33.4 | Turn right on the cycle track | Cross the bridge over the river Arda | SE | 81 |
| 68.064 | 130 | 33.5 | Bear left towards the main road | | NE | 80 |
| 68.065 | 50 | 33.6 | Take the pedestrian crossing over the main road and turn right towards the centre of the town | SS9 | SE | 80 |
| 68.066 | 110 | 33.7 | Continue straight ahead on the main street | Corso Giuseppe Garibaldi | SE | 82 |
| 68.067 | 250 | 33.9 | Arrive at Fiorenzuola-d'Arda (XXXVII) centre | Crossroads with via della Liberazione | | 84 |

| Alternate Route #68.A1 | | | Length: 2.8km | | | |
|---|---|---|---|---|---|---|
| Stage Summary: shorter path avoiding the SP6 but fording the river - only attempt this in high summer and when the river bed is dry | | | | | | |
| Stage Ascent: 16m | | | Stage Descent: 15m | | | |
| 68A1.001 | 0 | 0.0 | Turn left and ford the river | | E | 85 |
| 68A1.002 | 220 | 0.2 | On the far side of the river, continue straight ahead | Towards the main road | SE | 84 |
| 68A1.003 | 240 | 0.5 | At the T-junction with the main road, turn right | | S | 85 |
| 68A1.004 | 400 | 0.9 | Turn left, towards the farm | Strada privata | E | 88 |
| 68A1.005 | 100 | 1.0 | Pass through the farm buildings, turn left and then immediately right on the track | | E | 87 |
| 68A1.006 | 500 | 1.4 | At the T-junction turn right | Remaining on the track | SE | 84 |

| Waypoint | Distance between waypoints | Total km | Directions | Verification Point | Compass | Altitude m |
|---|---|---|---|---|---|---|
| 68A1.007 | 300 | 1.7 | At the next T-junction turn right | Tarmac road | S | 83 |
| 68A1.008 | 300 | 2.1 | At the following T-junction turn left and then immediately right onto a white road | Località Montanaro | S | 86 |
| 68A1.009 | 700 | 2.7 | At the end of the track, turn left | Cascina del Lupo to the right | E | 89 |
| 68A1.010 | 140 | 2.8 | At the junction, continue straight ahead on the tarmac. Note:- the "Official Route" joins from the right | | | 86 |

**Accommodation & Facilities .... Piacenza - Fiorenzuola-d'Arda**

🛏 Bellotta Opera Diocesana Per la Preservazione della Fede,Frazione Valconasso,29010 Pontenure(PC),Italy; Tel:+39 0523 517110; Price:B

🛏 Parrocchia di San Fiorenzo,Piazza Molinari Fratelli, 15,29017 Fiorenzuola-d'Arda(PC),Italy; Tel:+39 0523 982247; Email:parrocchiasanfiorenzo@tin.it; Web-site:www.parrocchiasanfiorenzo.it; Price:C

🛏 Hotel Concordia,Via 20 Settembre, 54,29017 Fiorenzuola-d'Arda(PC),Italy; Tel:+39 0523 982827; Email:info@hotelconcordiapc.com; Web-site:www.hotelconcordiapc.com; Price:A

ℹ Comune di Fiorenzuola d'Arda,Corso Giuseppe Garibaldi, 53,29017 Fiorenzuola-d'Arda(PC),Italy; Tel:+39 0523 9891

💲 Banca di Piacenza,Via Patrioti, 9,29019 San-Giorgio-Piacentino(PC),Italy; Tel:+39 0523 377219

💲 Banca Farnese,Via Risorgimento,29017 Fiorenzuola-d'Arda(PC),Italy; Tel:+39 0523 985053

💲 Banca Nazionale del Lavoro,Via Scapuzzi, 2,29017 Fiorenzuola-d'Arda(PC),Italy; Tel:+39 0523 983626

🅗 Ospedale Civile,Via Roma, 35,29017 Fiorenzuola-d'Arda(PC),Italy; Tel:+39 0523 9890

## Accommodation & Facilities .... Piacenza - Fiorenzuola-d'Arda

➕ Bazzani - Medico Chirurgo,Piazza Molinari Fratelli, 5,29017 Fiorenzuola-d'Arda(PC),Italy; Tel:+39 0523 983411

➕ Anelli - Medico Chirurgo,Piazza Verdi,29017 Fiorenzuola-d'Arda(PC),Italy; Tel:+39 0523 981770

🐕 Carolfi - Veterinario,Via Mischi, 7,29017 Fiorenzuola-d'Arda(PC),Italy; Tel:+39 0523 984494

🚶 Ivan Sport,Via Brunani, 14,29017 Fiorenzuola-d'Arda(PC),Italy; Tel:+39 0523 982748

🚲 Cigala Cicli di Stori Sergio,Viale Giacomo Matteotti, 5,29017 Fiorenzuola-d'Arda(PC),Italy; Tel:+39 0523 941730

🚲 Bici Sprint di Graffi,Viale Giacomo Matteotti, 52,29017 Fiorenzuola-d'Arda(PC),Italy; Tel:+39 0523 943165

☎ Taxi ͰPiazza Caduti,29017 Fiorenzuola-d'Arda(PC),Italy; Tel:+39 0523 983396

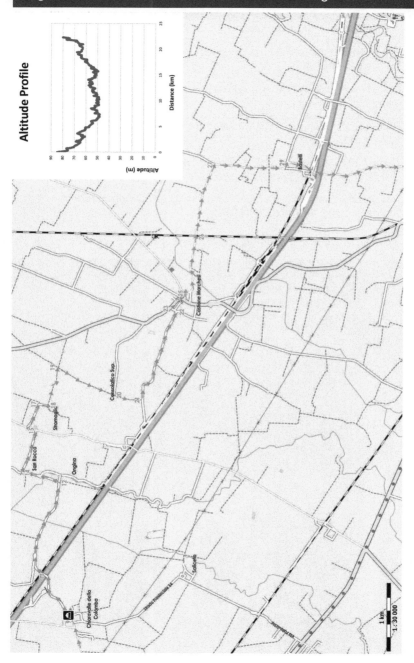

## Stage 69: Fiorenzuola-d'Arda - Fidenza                Length: 22.3km

Stage Summary: a gentle stage on level ground generally using country roads and passing beside the Abbey of Chiaravalle de Colomba.

Distance from Vercelli: 183km          Distance to St Peter's Square, Rome: 665km
Stage Ascent: 123m                     Stage Descent: 127m

| Waypoint | Distance between waypoints | Total km | Directions | Verification Point | Compass | Altitude m |
|---|---|---|---|---|---|---|
| 69.001 | 0 | 0.0 | From the centre of Fiorenzuola, near n° 55 Corso Garibaldi, turn left onto the narrow street | Via della Liberazione | NE | 84 |
| 69.002 | 90 | 0.1 | At the crossroads, continue straight ahead on the tree lined road | Direction Busseto, VF sign | NE | 81 |
| 69.003 | 210 | 0.3 | Pass under the railway and bear right on the road | Viale dei Tigli | E | 75 |
| 69.004 | 400 | 0.7 | Bear left on the pavement on the left side of the road | Pass beside the cemetery | NE | 76 |
| 69.005 | 250 | 1.0 | Just after the cemetery, cross the road and turn right | Towards agriturismo Battibue | E | 70 |
| 69.006 | 2200 | 3.1 | At the T-junction at the end of the road turn right | Towards the farm on the left of the road | S | 64 |
| 69.007 | 500 | 3.6 | Turn left on the road | Towards Chiaravalle, VF sign | E | 67 |
| 69.008 | 1500 | 5.1 | Continue straight ahead on the pathway on the left side of the road | Pass the cemetery on the left | E | 57 |
| 69.009 | 800 | 5.8 | Continue straight ahead | Towards the Abbey courtyard | E | 55 |
| 69.010 | 110 | 6.0 | In front of the Abbey of Chiaravalle de Colomba bear left to follow the road | Towards Busseto | NE | 55 |

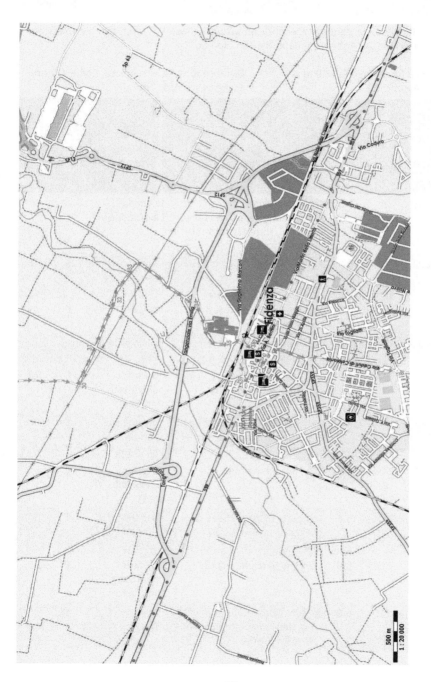

| Waypoint | Distance between waypoints | Total km | Directions | Verification Point | Compass | Altitude m |
|---|---|---|---|---|---|---|
| 69.011 | 700 | 6.7 | Continue straight ahead | Cross the Autostrada bridge | E | 49 |
| 69.012 | 1600 | 8.2 | Bear left on the road and ignore the junction to the right | Beside Cascina Ongina | N | 52 |
| 69.013 | 300 | 8.5 | Continue straight ahead on strada Borre | Beside the entrance to the village of San Rocco | N | 54 |
| 69.014 | 230 | 8.8 | Turn right | Before reaching church | E | 52 |
| 69.015 | 700 | 9.4 | At the T-junction at the end of the road turn left | Industrial area ahead at junction | N | 49 |
| 69.016 | 140 | 9.6 | Take the next turning to the right | Strada Orsi | SE | 51 |
| 69.017 | 400 | 10.0 | Bear right on the tarmac | Pass a barn on the right | S | 50 |
| 69.018 | 140 | 10.1 | Bear left on the unmade road | Entrance to farm on the right | E | 51 |
| 69.019 | 600 | 10.7 | At the crossroads, turn right | Bridge ahead | SW | 49 |
| 69.020 | 900 | 11.6 | Continue straight ahead on strada Fossa Superiore | Ignore the turning on the tarmac road to the left | S | 53 |
| 69.021 | 400 | 12.0 | At the T-junction with a tarmac road turn left | Strada Portone | E | 54 |
| 69.022 | 1500 | 13.4 | At the T-junction, turn left | Direction Fidenza | NE | 56 |
| 69.023 | 100 | 13.5 | At the traffic lights, turn right | Direction Fidenza | SE | 54 |
| 69.024 | 240 | 13.8 | After rounding the first bend turn left | Towards Bastelli | E | 56 |
| 69.025 | 130 | 13.9 | At the T-junction turn right | Towards Bastelli | E | 56 |

| Waypoint | Distance between waypoints | Total km | Directions | Verification Point | Compass | Altitude m |
|---|---|---|---|---|---|---|
| 69.026 | 900 | 14.8 | Continue straight ahead on the long straight road | Cross the railway | E | 52 |
| 69.027 | 1200 | 16.0 | At the T-junction turn right | Towards Bastelli | S | 51 |
| 69.028 | 1000 | 17.0 | In hamlet of Bastelli with silos on the right, turn left | Towards Soragna | SE | 57 |
| 69.029 | 110 | 17.1 | Turn right on the road and cross the railway and Autostrada | Towards Fidenza | S | 58 |
| 69.030 | 1900 | 19.0 | Shortly before reaching the power lines, turn left | Towards Fidenza | E | 67 |
| 69.031 | 400 | 19.4 | At the mini-roundabout, continue straight ahead | Direction Fidenza | E | 67 |
| 69.032 | 500 | 19.8 | Continue straight ahead | Cross Ponte Sigerico | SE | 64 |
| 69.033 | 500 | 20.3 | Keep right on the main road | | SW | 63 |
| 69.034 | 700 | 21.0 | Continue straight ahead | Pass under highway | SW | 64 |
| 69.035 | 700 | 21.6 | At the traffic lights turn right under the railway | Car park on the left at the junction | S | 68 |
| 69.036 | 130 | 21.8 | After emerging from under the railway, turn right direction Duomo | Pass Hotel Astoria on the left | W | 75 |
| 69.037 | 400 | 22.1 | Continue straight ahead at the roundabout and then quickly bear left towards the old city gate | Piazza Grandi, large VF sign on entry to piazza | SW | 75 |
| 69.038 | 110 | 22.3 | Arrive at Fidenza (XXXVI) centre | Piazza Cremoni, beside the Duomo | | 80 |

**Accommodation & Facilities .... Fiorenzuola-d'Arda - Fidenza**

Abbazia,Chiaravalle della Colomba,29010 Alseno(PC),Italy;
Tel:+39 0523 940132; Price:D

Parrocchia di S.Tommaso Becket,Via Cabriolo,43036 Fidenza(PR),Italy;
Tel:+39 0524 81912; +39 3294 130656; +39 3402 523983;
Email:parrocchiadicabriolo@libero.it; Web-site:cabriolo.altervista.org;
Price:D; Note:Open May to September,

Convento di San Francesco,Viale San Francesco, 7,43036 Fidenza(PR),Italy;
Tel:+39 0524 522035; +39 0524 520118; Price:D; Note:Credentials required,

Hotel Astoria,Via Gandolfi, 5,43036 Fidenza(PR),Italy; Tel:+39 0524 524314;
Email:Info@hotelastoriafidenza.it; Web-site:www.hotelastoriafidenza.it ;
Price:A

Albergo Ugolini,Via Cornini Malpeli, 90,43036 Fidenza(PR),Italy; Tel:+39 0524
83264; Web-site:www.albergougolinifidenza.it; Price:B

Affittacamere al Duomo,Via Arnaldo Da Brescia, 2,43036
Fidenza(PR),Italy; Tel:+39 0524 523930; +39 0347 5819; +39 3475 819065;
Email:affittacamerealduomo@hotmail.com;
Web-site:www.affittacamerealduomo.it; Price:B

Centro Ippico Montevalle – Castelnuovo Fogliani,Strada di Montevalle,29010
Alseno(PC),Italy; +39 3473 213281; Web-site:montevalle.it

Associazione Europea delle Vie Francigene,Piazza Duomo,43036
Fidenza(PR),Italy; Tel:+39 7513 517380; Email:segreteriagenerale@
associazioneviafrancigena.it; Web-site:www.viafrancigena.eu

Banca Popolare,Piazza Giuseppe Garibaldi, 24,43036 Fidenza(PR),Italy;
Tel:+39 0524 523928

Banca di Piacenza,Via Benedetto Bacchini, 2/4,43036 Fidenza(PR),Italy;
Tel:+39 0524 533436

Stazione Ferrovie,Via Giuseppe Mazzini,43036 Fidenza(PR),Italy;
Tel:+39 06 6847 5475; Web-site:www.renitalia.it

Fidenza San Secondo,Via Don Tincati, 5,43036 Fidenza(PR),Italy;
Tel:+39 0524 515111;
Web-site:www.ausl.pr.it/page.asp?IDCategoria=625&IDSezione=3930

Lannutti Ferdinando,43036 Fidenza(PR),Italy; Tel:+39 0524 523476

Medical Center Srl,Via Andrea Costa, 3,43036 Fidenza(PR),Italy;
Tel:+39 0524 528110

Cattivelli - Medico Veterinario,Frazione Fornio,43036 Fidenza(PR),Italy;
Tel:+39 0524 60171

Fitness,Via 24 Maggio,43036 Fidenza(PR),Italy; Tel:+39 0524 84328

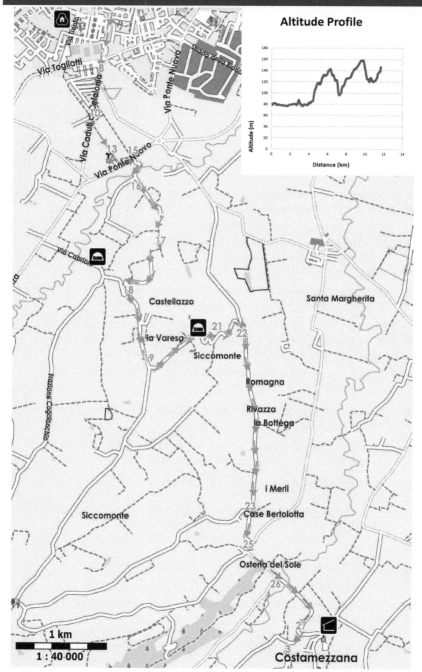

## Altitude Profile

Altitude (m)

Distance (km)

Via Tenia

Via Togliatti

Via Ponte Nuovo

Strada della Biada

Via Caduti di Cefalonia

Via Ponte Nuovo

Via Cabriolo

Castellazzo

Santa Margherita

la Varesa

Siccomonte

Frazione Coglonchio

Romagna

Rivazza

la Bottega

i Merli

Siccomonte

Case Bertolotta

Osteria del Sole

1 km

1 : 40.000

Costamezzana

## Stage 70: Fidenza - Costamezzana  Length: 11.6km

Stage Summary: after leaving Fidenza the well marked route begins to climb into the beautiful, rolling foothills of the Appenines. The section is largely conducted on small country roads and tracks, but can be challenging in hot weather and so be sure to carry enough water. For the next few days you will be travelling in the province of Parma that has provided some excellent support for the via Francigena. Costamezzana is a very small and isolated village but offers a warm welcome to pilgrims.

Distance from Vercelli: 205km  Distance to St Peter's Square, Rome: 643km
Stage Ascent: 192m  Stage Descent: 126m

| Waypoint | Distance between waypoints | Total km | Directions | Verification Point | Compass | Altitude m |
|---|---|---|---|---|---|---|
| 70.001 | 0 | 0.0 | From piazza Cremoni beside the Duomo pass in front of the church and turn left to skirt the church | Church on the left | SE | 80 |
| 70.002 | 120 | 0.1 | At the rear of the church turn right | Pedestrian zone, via Micheli. VF sign | E | 79 |
| 70.003 | 80 | 0.2 | Continue straight ahead across the small square and take via Antini | VF sign | E | 81 |
| 70.004 | 110 | 0.3 | Continue straight ahead in piazza del Palazzo, pass under the porch and turn right | Via Amendola | S | 81 |
| 70.005 | 90 | 0.4 | At the end of the road, bear left across the small park | Keep the playground on your left | SE | 81 |
| 70.006 | 90 | 0.5 | At the roundabout turn right into the tree lined street | Via Gramsci | S | 79 |
| 70.007 | 290 | 0.8 | At the roundabout, cross the main road – via 24 Maggio – and bear a little to the left towards the trees | Via Caduti di Cefalonia | S | 78 |
| 70.008 | 900 | 1.7 | At the roundabout continue straight ahead on the cycle track | Sports ground to the right before the roundabout | S | 76 |

| Waypoint | Distance between waypoints | Total km | Directions | Verification Point | Compass | Altitude m |
|---|---|---|---|---|---|---|
| 70.009 | 300 | 2.0 | Continue straight ahead on the pedestrian and cycle track on the right side of the road | Open field on your left | S | 79 |
| 70.010 | 180 | 2.2 | Continue straight ahead | Footpath sign and small wooden bridge on the left | S | 79 |
| 70.011 | 230 | 2.4 | Shortly after passing farm on the left, bear left on the tree lined track | VF sign | SE | 80 |
| 70.012 | 400 | 2.8 | Bear right into the trees | Towards the buildings | S | 83 |
| 70.013 | 80 | 2.9 | Turn left on the tarmac driveway Note:- to your right is Piave Cabriolo (dedicated to Thomas Becket) | Bell tower on your right at the junction | SE | 86 |
| 70.014 | 170 | 3.0 | At the T-junction with the main road, turn left | Pass cheese producer on left | NE | 80 |
| 70.015 | 170 | 3.2 | Take the first turning to the right | Towards the trees, VF sign | S | 77 |
| 70.016 | 280 | 3.5 | Continue straight ahead on the unmade road | Ignore the turning to the right | S | 79 |
| 70.017 | 1000 | 4.4 | Turn right towards the hilltop | Via Cabriolo | SW | 87 |
| 70.018 | 700 | 5.1 | At the junction with a tarmac road – on a sharp bend – turn left | Uphill, towards the top of the ridge | S | 115 |
| 70.019 | 1100 | 6.2 | At the junction, turn left | Towards Siccomonte | NE | 141 |
| 70.020 | 800 | 7.0 | In front of the Chiesa di Siccomonte turn right then left on the grassy path, downhill | Keep church to the left | E | 122 |
| 70.021 | 180 | 7.2 | Leave the grass and turn left on the road | VF sign | NE | 97 |

| Waypoint | Distance between waypoints | Total km | Directions | Verification Point | Compass | Altitude m |
|---|---|---|---|---|---|---|
| 70.022 | 400 | 7.6 | At the T-junction at the top of the hill, turn right on the tarmac road | Direction Tabiano, VF sign | S | 112 |
| 70.023 | 2200 | 9.8 | Take the left fork | Towards Pieve Cusignano, VF sign | S | 158 |
| 70.024 | 400 | 10.2 | At the T-junction, at the bottom of the hill, turn right, towards Costamezzana | Osteria on your left at the junction | SW | 126 |
| 70.025 | 130 | 10.3 | Turn left | Towards Costamezzana | SE | 124 |
| 70.026 | 400 | 10.7 | Keep left | Towards Costamezzana, VF sign | SE | 123 |
| 70.027 | 1000 | 11.6 | Arrive at Costamezzana | Village centre ahead | | 146 |

**Accommodation & Facilities  ....  Fidenza - Costamezzana**

 Ostello Comunale di Costamezzana,Via Costa Pavesi, 1,43015 Costamezzana(PR),Italy; Tel:+39 0521 629149; +39 0521 622137; Price:C; PR

 Casa di Preghiera S.Giovanni Battista,(Nicola),Frazione Siccomonte,43036 Fidenza(PR),Italy; +39 3492 825720; Email:siccomonte@hotmail.it; Web-site:www.siccomonte.altervista.org; Price:C

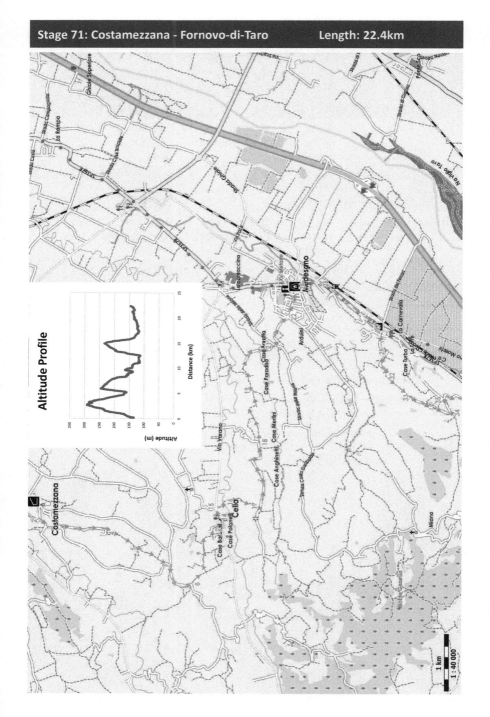

Altitude Profile

Stage Summary: the route continues to climb and fall on farm tracks and some small roads. Great care needs to be exercised on the final approach to Fornovo where the traffic can be heavy on the narrow river bridge.

Distance from Vercelli: 217km          Distance to St Peter's Square, Rome: 632km
Stage Ascent: 491m                     Stage Descent: 491m

| Waypoint | Distance between waypoints | Total km | Directions | Verification Point | Compass | Altitude m |
|---|---|---|---|---|---|---|
| 71.001 | 0 | 0.0 | From the junction at the entrance to Costamezzana, turn towards the Castello | Note:- at the time of writing there is a VF sign pointing the wrong way | SW | 146 |
| 71.002 | 200 | 0.2 | At the crossroads, just before reaching the farm, turn left | Via Costa Canali, VF sign | S | 135 |
| 71.003 | 170 | 0.4 | Take the narrow road to the left | Towards the Hostaria Castello, VF sign | S | 150 |
| 71.004 | 1000 | 1.4 | Beside the Castello di Costamezzana bear left and immediately right | Keep the trees close on your right, VF sign | SW | 219 |
| 71.005 | 700 | 2.1 | At the junction in the tracks, continue straight ahead between the vines | Farm on the left | SW | 249 |
| 71.006 | 500 | 2.6 | At the T-junction, turn left on the tarmac road | Towards the houses on the sky-line | S | 284 |
| 71.007 | 110 | 2.7 | At the T-junction with the road turn right | Leaving via Costa Canali | SW | 289 |
| 71.008 | 700 | 3.3 | On the crown of the bend to the right, take the track downhill to the left | VF sign, towards a small wood | SE | 280 |
| 71.009 | 700 | 4.0 | Beside the first farm, continue straight ahead | VF sign | E | 227 |
| 71.010 | 300 | 4.3 | Bear right towards the road below | | S | 205 |

| Waypoint | Distance between waypoints | Total km | Directions | Verification Point | Compass | Altitude m |
|---|---|---|---|---|---|---|
| 71.011 | 140 | 4.5 | At the T-junction turn left on the grass track | Farm buildings on the right | E | 193 |
| 71.012 | 140 | 4.6 | At the junction with the tarmac road, continue straight ahead, then bear right downhill | Pass house on your left | SE | 184 |
| 71.013 | 170 | 4.8 | At the T-junction with the main road, turn left and follow the pavement on the left | Car parks on the right and left at junction | E | 169 |
| 71.014 | 160 | 4.9 | In the centre of Cella, cross the road and continue straight ahead with care on the other side | Restaurant on the left | E | 168 |
| 71.015 | 190 | 5.1 | Just after a slight bend to the right in the road, turn right on the track | VF sign, house on the right | SE | 164 |
| 71.016 | 190 | 5.3 | Cross the river ford and continue straight ahead | Between fields and steeply uphill | S | 161 |
| 71.017 | 700 | 6.0 | At the T-junction, after a steep climb, turn left on a tarmac road | Large house on the hilltop to the right | E | 246 |
| 71.018 | 1400 | 7.3 | At a bend in the road to the left, continue straight ahead on an unmade road | Pass between farm buildings, VF sign | E | 220 |
| 71.019 | 1000 | 8.4 | At the T-junction, turn left on the track | Towards farm | NE | 160 |
| 71.020 | 50 | 8.4 | With the farm directly ahead, turn right | | SE | 161 |
| 71.021 | 1200 | 9.6 | At the crossroads, at the top of the hill, in the hamlet of Arduini, continue straight ahead | VF sign, via Giuseppe Verdi | SE | 163 |
| 71.022 | 600 | 10.2 | At the roundabout, at the entry to Medesano (XXXV), continue straight ahead | Towards the spire, VF sign | E | 141 |

| Waypoint | Distance between waypoints | Total km | Directions | Verification Point | Compass | Altitude m |
|---|---|---|---|---|---|---|
| 71.023 | 400 | 10.6 | At the crossroads with via Dante Alighieri, continue straight ahead | Footpath and cycleway on the right | E | 140 |
| 71.024 | 170 | 10.8 | Before reaching the main road turn right. Note:- riders should continue to the main road to avoid a flight of steps | Towards the church, VF sign | SE | 137 |
| 71.025 | 90 | 10.9 | Pass beside the church and turn right on the main road to leave the town | SP357R, pavement protected by crash barrier | S | 133 |
| 71.026 | 400 | 11.2 | Shortly after the end of the ramp cross with care to the left side of the main road and continue on the pedestrian and bike track | Pass under the gantry for the xit from Medesano | SW | 118 |
| 71.027 | 1400 | 12.6 | Shortly after entering Carnevala, turn right on via G. la Pira | VF sign | W | 114 |
| 71.028 | 140 | 12.7 | Just after crossing the small bridge, bear left and then immediately right on the road | Pass conifers on your left | W | 127 |
| 71.029 | 400 | 13.1 | Follow the road as it turns right | Metal gate ahead at the turning | NW | 162 |
| 71.030 | 280 | 13.4 | Turn left on the road | Uphill towards the houses | SW | 190 |
| 71.031 | 130 | 13.5 | Beside the farm bear right on the grassy track | | W | 195 |
| 71.032 | 100 | 13.6 | Bear left on the track | Straight track along the ridge | SW | 197 |
| 71.033 | 600 | 14.2 | Continue straight ahead on the gravel road | Driveway to a house on the right | S | 215 |
| 71.034 | 800 | 15.0 | At the T-junction, turn left on the tarmac road | Shrine on the left | NE | 234 |

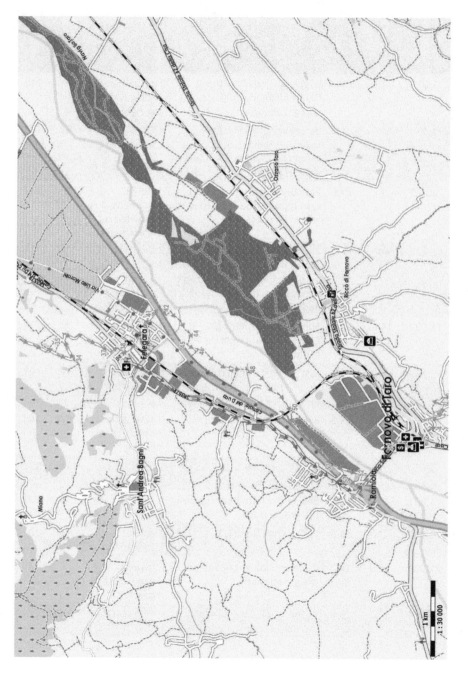

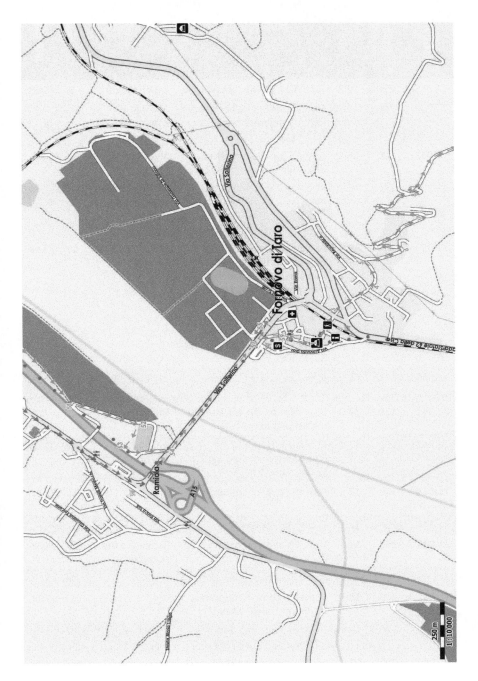

| Waypoint | Distance between waypoints | Total km | Directions | Verification Point | Compass | Altitude m |
|---|---|---|---|---|---|---|
| 71.035 | 270 | 15.3 | Turn right on the tarmac road | Steep descent | S | 223 |
| 71.036 | 700 | 15.9 | On the crown of a bend to the left, on the entry Felegara, turn right | Via Damiano Chiesa | SW | 147 |
| 71.037 | 150 | 16.1 | At the T-junction, turn left, downhill | Via Campioni | SE | 141 |
| 71.038 | 140 | 16.2 | At the T-junction with the main road, turn right | Via Repubblica towards the pharmacy, VF sign | SW | 133 |
| 71.039 | 160 | 16.4 | At the roundabout with a fountain, turn left. Note:- the riverside path ahead involves a number of water crossings. Cyclists may wish to continue straight ahead on the busy road to rejoin the "Official Route" on the bridge over the river Taro | Via G. Picelli, VF sign | SE | 133 |
| 71.040 | 500 | 16.9 | At the roundabout continue straight ahead | Via Pattigna | SE | 125 |
| 71.041 | 120 | 17.0 | Bear right on the track under the Autostrada | Chain barrier, VF sign | SE | 123 |
| 71.042 | 150 | 17.1 | At the exit from the underpass, turn right and immediately left | Initially with the river close on the left | SW | 119 |
| 71.043 | 400 | 17.5 | Ford the stream and bear right | | SW | 117 |
| 71.044 | 250 | 17.8 | Take the right fork | | W | 120 |
| 71.045 | 150 | 17.9 | Turn left on the footpath | Parallel to the Autostrada | SW | 123 |
| 71.046 | 140 | 18.1 | At the T-junction, turn left | | SW | 122 |
| 71.047 | 700 | 18.7 | At the junction in the tracks, continue straight ahead | | S | 124 |
| 71.048 | 120 | 18.8 | Cross a small ditch and continue straight ahead | Close beside the river | SW | 123 |
| 71.049 | 200 | 19.0 | Continue straight ahead | | SW | 124 |

| Waypoint | Distance between waypoints | Total km | Directions | Verification Point | Compass | Altitude m |
|---|---|---|---|---|---|---|
| 71.050 | 600 | 19.6 | Cross the stream, pass under the railway bridge and bear right | Keeping the quarry on the left | SW | 129 |
| 71.051 | 1000 | 20.6 | Take the left fork away from the motorway and close beside the quarry | Beside Fornace Grigolin and further barrier | S | 135 |
| 71.052 | 280 | 20.9 | On reaching the football field, turn right | Keep football field to the left | NW | 134 |
| 71.053 | 110 | 21.0 | Turn left in the parking area | Keep football field on the left | S | 138 |
| 71.054 | 200 | 21.2 | At the T-junction with the main road, turn left and cross the bridge over the river Taro. Note:- take great care as there is frequently heavy traffic on the bridge and only a narrow pavement | Bar ahead at the junction | SE | 140 |
| 71.055 | 700 | 21.9 | At the end of the bridge turn sharp left | VF sign | NW | 138 |
| 71.056 | 110 | 22.0 | At the bottom of the hill turn left, piazza Mercato | Pass under the bridge | SW | 137 |
| 71.057 | 40 | 22.1 | Immediately after passing under the bridge turn left | Via Pietro Zuffardi | SE | 138 |
| 71.058 | 100 | 22.2 | At the end of the road turn right and immediately left in the small piazza | | S | 140 |
| 71.059 | 60 | 22.3 | Bear right across piazza Giacomo Matteotti | Direction Duomo, via 20 Settembre | S | 143 |
| 71.060 | 110 | 22.4 | Arrive at Fornovo-di-Taro (XXXIV) centre | Piazza IV Novembre in front of the Duomo | | 146 |

Villa Santa Maria,Località Magnana,43045 Fornovo-di-Taro(PR),Italy; Tel:+39 0525 3595; +39 3493 757441; Email:novellabaldini@alice.it; Price:C

Ostello Parrochia Santa Maria Assunta,Piazza 4 Novembre,43045 Fornovo-di-Taro(PR),Italy; Tel:+39 0525 2218; +39 3391 260100; Price:D

Oratorio Don Bosco,Via Conciliazione, 2,43014 Medesano(PR),Italy; Tel:+39 0525 420447; Email:dontorri@libero.it; Web-site:www.parrocchiadimedesano.it; Price:D

Comune di Medesano,Piazza Guglielmo Marconi, 6,43014 Medesano(PR),Italy; Tel:+39 0525 422711

Associazione Turistica Pro Loco,Via dei Collegati, 19,43045 Fornovo-di-Taro(PR),Italy; Tel:+39 0525 2599

Banca Reggiana,Via Giuseppe Verdi, 4a,43014 Medesano(PR),Italy; Tel:+39 0525 422011; Web-site:www.bancareggiana.it

Banca Monte dei Paschi di Siena,Piazza del Mercato, 10,43045 Fornovo-di-Taro(PR),Italy; Tel:+39 0525 30290

Stazione Ferrovie,Via Antonio Gramsci, 22,43045 Fornovo-di-Taro(PR),Italy; Tel:+39 06 6847 5475; Web-site:www.renitalia.it

Simsmieh - Medico Chirurgo,Via Grazia Deledda, 12,43040 Medesano(PR),Italy; Tel:+39 0525 430716

Barbarese - Ambulatorio,Via Nazario Sauro, 5,43045 Fornovo-di-Taro(PR),Italy; Tel:+39 0525 39917

Associazione Veterinaria il Castello,V.Carnevala, 18,43014 Medesano(PR),Italy; Tel:+39 0525 420280

Clinica Veterinaria,Strada della Cisa, 23,43045 Fornovo-di-Taro(PR),Italy; Tel:+39 0525 400393

City Sport,Via 24 Maggio, 16,43045 Fornovo-di-Taro(PR),Italy; Tel:+39 0525 401053

Taxi,Via Antonio Gramsci, 25,43045 Fornovo-di-Taro(PR),Italy; Tel:+39 0525 3281

## Stage 72: Fornovo-di-Taro - Cassio Length: 21.0km

Strada Statale 62 della Cisa
Caselle
La salita
Respiccio
Le Capanne
Piantonia
Roncolongo
Sivizzano
Altitude Profile
Altitude (m)
Distance (km)
1 km
1 : 30 000

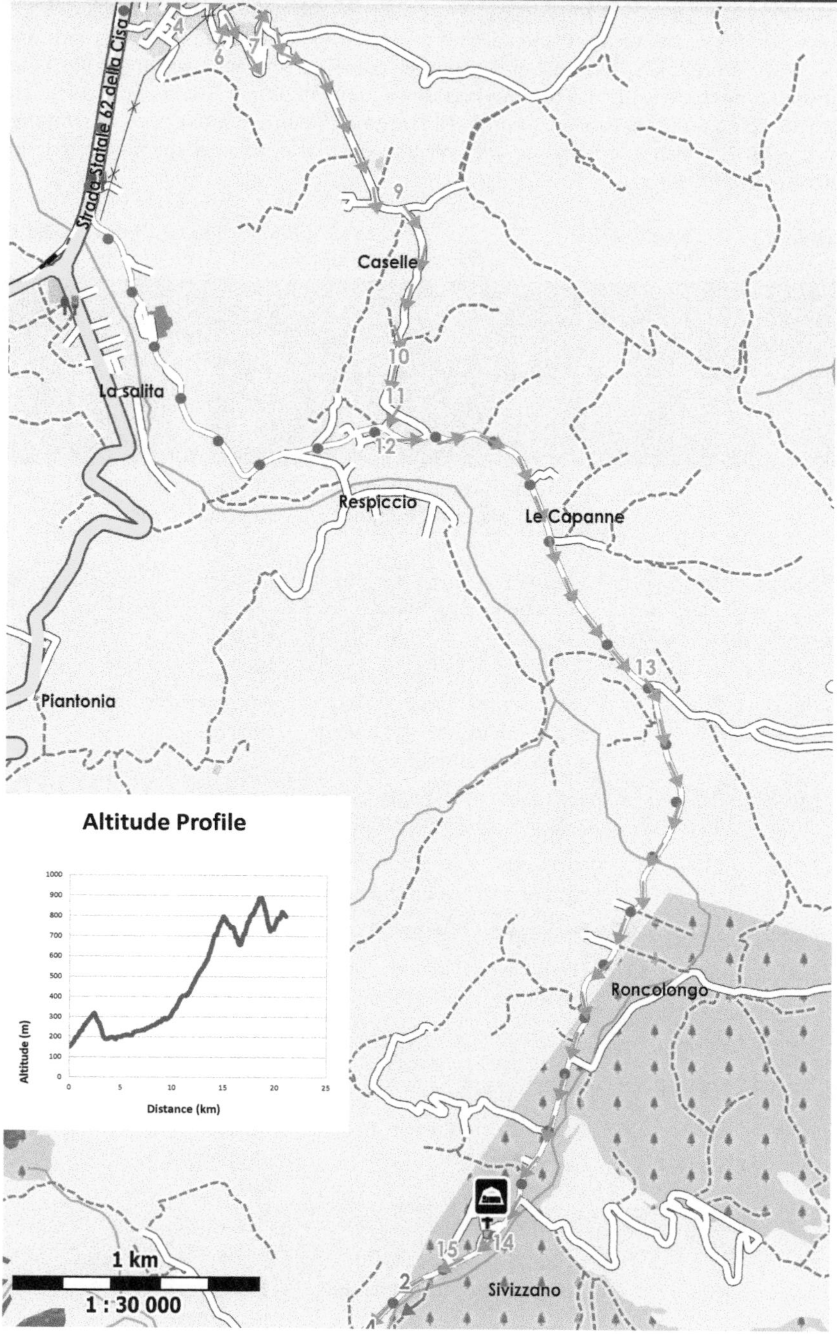

Stage Summary: the climb to the summit of the Cisa Pass begins on minor roads and the SP39 before taking to forest and mountain tracks. If you are travelling in spring or autumn then there is the risk of snow near the summit (1200m). Some of the tracks are narrow, steep and over broken ground. The route includes a number of short stretches on the SS62, which is a favourite with high-speed motorcycle groups particularly on Sundays and holidays.

Distance from Vercelli: 239km          Distance to St Peter's Square, Rome: 609km
Stage Ascent: 1224m                    Stage Descent: 575m

| Waypoint | Distance between waypoints | Total km | Directions | Verification Point | Compass | Altitude m |
|---|---|---|---|---|---|---|
| 72.001 | 0 | 0.0 | From the Duomo in Fornovo di Taro, take via XXIV Maggio | VF sign, pass the Duomo on the left | SE | 149 |
| 72.002 | 130 | 0.1 | Cross piazza Tarasconi and continue straight ahead | Kiosk on the right, pedestrian zone | SE | 156 |
| 72.003 | 50 | 0.2 | Cross the main road (SS62) and continue straight ahead on via Guglielmo Marconi | Pass bank on the right | SE | 158 |
| 72.004 | 170 | 0.3 | At the end of the pavement bear left on the road uphill | Via Guglielmo Marconi | E | 170 |
| 72.005 | 130 | 0.5 | Follow the road as it turns right and winds up the hill | Via Guglielmo Marconi | SE | 181 |
| 72.006 | 180 | 0.6 | Bear left on the road | | SE | 197 |
| 72.007 | 400 | 1.0 | Continue to follow the road to the left as it climbs the hill | Avoid road to right | NE | 222 |
| 72.008 | 400 | 1.4 | Continue straight ahead | Direction Caselle, VF sign | SE | 251 |
| 72.009 | 1000 | 2.4 | At the fork in Caselle, bear right, downhill | Narrow road, shrine on the left | S | 318 |
| 72.010 | 600 | 3.0 | Bear right and downhill on the tarmac road | House on the hill to your left | S | 248 |
| 72.011 | 400 | 3.4 | Take the right fork downhill | Towards the main road | SW | 196 |

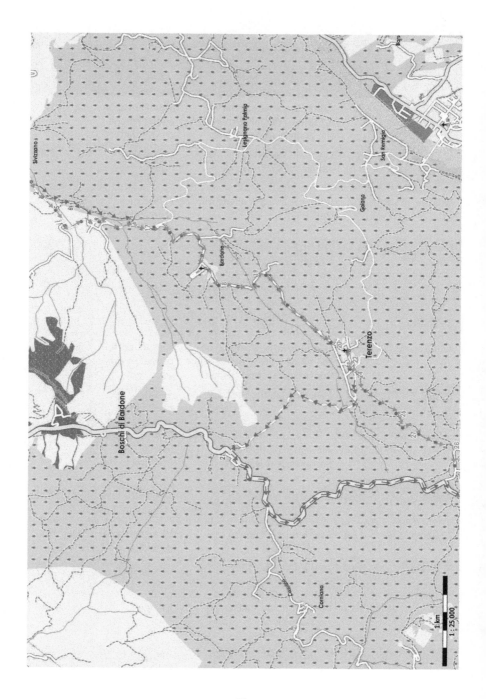

| Waypoint | Distance between waypoints | Total km | Directions | Verification Point | Compass | Altitude m |
|---|---|---|---|---|---|---|
| 72.012 | 80 | 3.5 | At the T-junction at the bottom of the hill turn left on the main road, SP39 | Metal fence on embankment on your left | SE | 189 |
| 72.013 | 1700 | 5.2 | Continue straight ahead on strada Val Sporzona | Ignore the turning to San Vitale | S | 206 |
| 72.014 | 2500 | 7.7 | Continue straight ahead on the SP39 | Village of Sivizzano to the right | SW | 247 |
| 72.015 | 300 | 8.0 | The "Official Route" continues straight ahead on the road. Note:- if you need some relief from the tarmac the Alternate Route follows a marked path through the woods on the left | | SW | 255 |
| 72.016 | 1500 | 9.5 | Continue straight ahead on the road. Note:- the Alternate Route rejoins from the left | Pass modern bungalow on your right | S | 287 |
| 72.017 | 280 | 9.7 | Fork right on the road | VF sign, direction Bardone | SW | 300 |
| 72.018 | 1300 | 11.0 | After passing through Bardone bear left | Strada Ca'di Bardone to the right | S | 407 |
| 72.019 | 600 | 11.6 | Bear right up the hill | Ca'di Fucinello to the left | SW | 422 |
| 72.020 | 1200 | 12.8 | Fork left into Terenzo | VF sign, strada della Posta | SW | 535 |
| 72.021 | 170 | 13.0 | At the T-junction, in front of the Piave di Terenzo turn right | Strada della Posta | W | 545 |
| 72.022 | 90 | 13.1 | Fork left up a small paved passageway | VF sign | W | 553 |
| 72.023 | 140 | 13.2 | At the T-junction, turn left uphill | VF sign, via Capoluogo | SW | 566 |

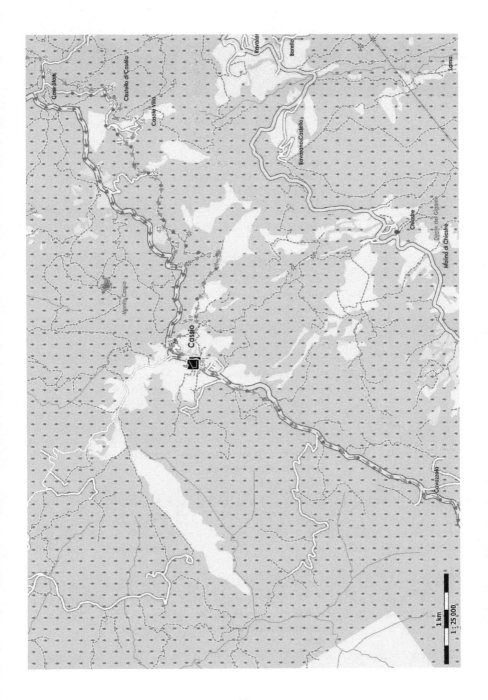

| Waypoint | Distance between waypoints | Total km | Directions | Verification Point | Compass | Altitude m |
|---|---|---|---|---|---|---|
| 72.024 | 160 | 13.3 | Turn left at the top of the hill. Note:- the route ahead is off-road and strenuous with steep climbs over broken ground. Cyclists are advised to turn right on the Alternate Route joining the SS62 | VF sign | E | 583 |
| 72.025 | 60 | 13.4 | Turn right onto unmade road | VF sign | SW | 582 |
| 72.026 | 700 | 14.1 | Continue straight ahead on the track | Fence on your right | SW | 706 |
| 72.027 | 400 | 14.6 | Continue straight ahead towards the top of the hill | | S | 749 |
| 72.028 | 400 | 15.0 | Bear right on the widening track | Large VF sign on left | SW | 796 |
| 72.029 | 60 | 15.0 | At the T-junction, turn right onto a minor road | VF sign, towards the large pylon | W | 792 |
| 72.030 | 120 | 15.1 | Just after passing the house on the left, turn left on the grassy path | VF sign, towards the church tower | S | 787 |
| 72.031 | 600 | 15.7 | Continue straight ahead on the track | Citi di Bardone route | S | 741 |
| 72.032 | 200 | 15.9 | In Castello di Casola cross the tarmac road and continue straight ahead | Downhill | SW | 743 |
| 72.033 | 240 | 16.1 | Cross the track and continue straight ahead on the faint path | Between the trees | W | 711 |
| 72.034 | 300 | 16.4 | Fork right | Towards the houses | S | 665 |
| 72.035 | 120 | 16.6 | Turn right between the houses in Villa di Casola | Strada Vici Villa | SW | 657 |
| 72.036 | 40 | 16.6 | Continue straight ahead on the tarmac and then bear right | Wooden fence on the left | SW | 659 |
| 72.037 | 50 | 16.6 | Take the left fork | VF sign, strada Cà Chioldi | NW | 659 |

| Waypoint | Distance between waypoints | Total km | Directions | Verification Point | Compass | Altitude m |
|---|---|---|---|---|---|---|
| 72.038 | 110 | 16.7 | Continue straight ahead at the crossroads | Strada della Fontana, VF sign | NW | 674 |
| 72.039 | 80 | 16.8 | Proceed straight ahead onto a small track | Garden on the right | N | 690 |
| 72.040 | 90 | 16.9 | At the T-junction turn left | VF sign | W | 707 |
| 72.041 | 30 | 16.9 | Turn left onto the grassy track | VF sign | SW | 713 |
| 72.042 | 600 | 17.5 | Cross the unmade road and continue straight ahead on the footpath | VF sign | W | 784 |
| 72.043 | 800 | 18.2 | At the junction following a bend in the track, continue straight ahead | Signpost to Cassio | W | 859 |
| 72.044 | 190 | 18.4 | Take the left fork. Note:- cyclists and walkers in wet conditions may find the route ahead difficult. If in doubt, continue straight ahead to the road junction and turn left for the final kilometre to Cassio | | SW | 888 |
| 72.045 | 400 | 18.8 | At the junction in the tracks, turn left. Note:- the track to the right again leads to the road | | SE | 865 |
| 72.046 | 260 | 19.1 | At the junction keep right on the broad track | | S | 818 |
| 72.047 | 170 | 19.3 | Turn right on the footpath | | W | 768 |
| 72.048 | 900 | 20.1 | Join a track and continue straight ahead | Uphill | W | 783 |
| 72.049 | 40 | 20.2 | Continue straight ahead | Ignore turnings on both sides | W | 787 |
| 72.050 | 70 | 20.3 | Join a broadening track and turn to the right | | NW | 788 |
| 72.051 | 300 | 20.6 | Take the right fork | Enter Cassio | NW | 814 |
| 72.052 | 100 | 20.7 | Turn left along the main street through Cassio | Pieve di Cassio ahead | SW | 821 |

| Waypoint | Distance between waypoints | Total km | Directions | Verification Point | Compass | Altitude m |
|---|---|---|---|---|---|---|
| 72.053 | 270 | 21.0 | At the end of the street turn right and then left on the main road – SS62 | Towards the old hostel | SW | 800 |
| 72.054 | 80 | 21.0 | Arrive at Cassio | Beside Ostello di Cassio | | 798 |

**Alternate Route #72.A1**          Length: 1.4km

Stage Summary: route parallel to the SP39 via woodland paths. The track includes a number of river crossings which may be difficult for cyclists.

Stage Ascent: 40m          Stage Descent: 8m

| Waypoint | Distance between waypoints | Total km | Directions | Verification Point | Compass | Altitude m |
|---|---|---|---|---|---|---|
| 72A1.001 | 0 | 0.0 | Bear left on the track | VF sign, direction Campo Sportivo | SW | 255 |
| 72A1.002 | 130 | 0.1 | After crossing the river and passing a group of buildings on your left, turn right on the faint track on the edge of the field | Trees close on your right | SW | 255 |
| 72A1.003 | 210 | 0.3 | At the T-junction with broader track, turn right | Towards the river | SW | 262 |
| 72A1.004 | 50 | 0.4 | Cross the river and continue straight ahead | | SW | 262 |
| 72A1.005 | 50 | 0.4 | At the T-junction, turn left | | S | 263 |
| 72A1.006 | 160 | 0.6 | Bear right | River close on the left | SW | 271 |
| 72A1.007 | 140 | 0.7 | Take the right fork, then bear left | House on the hill to the right | S | 270 |
| 72A1.008 | 90 | 0.8 | Take the left fork, cross the river and continue straight ahead | Uphill | S | 274 |
| 72A1.009 | 140 | 1.0 | Bear right on the faint track | Field on your left, trees on right | S | 278 |

| Waypoint | Distance between waypoints | Total km | Directions | Verification Point | Compass | Altitude m |
|---|---|---|---|---|---|---|
| 72A1.010 | 400 | 1.3 | Turn right. Note:- riders ford the river | Over footbridge | NW | 288 |
| 72A1.011 | 80 | 1.4 | At the T-junction with the road, turn left and rejoin the "Official Route" | Bungalows ahead at the junction | | 286 |

| Alternate Route #72.A2 | | Length: 9.6km | |
|---|---|---|---|

Stage Summary: route for cyclists and those not wishing to deal with the steepest climbs over broken ground in the woods. The route links with the main road to Cassio.

| Stage Ascent: 463m | | | | Stage Descent: 249m | | |
|---|---|---|---|---|---|---|
| 72A2.001 | 0 | 0.0 | Turn right on the road | Strada Terenzo-Calestano | NW | 587 |
| 72A2.002 | 2100 | 2.1 | At T-junction turn left on the main road | SS62 direction Cassio and Berceto | SW | 657 |
| 72A2.003 | 4800 | 6.9 | Continue straight ahead on the main road | | SW | 875 |
| 72A2.004 | 2800 | 9.6 | Arrive in Cassio and rejoin the "Official Route" | | | 800 |

### Accommodation & Facilities  ....   Fornovo-di-Taro - Cassio

Ostello di Cassio,Loc.Cassio via Nazionale,43040 Terenzo(PR),Italy; Tel:+39 0525 629072; Email:forestalepassocisa@libero.it; Web-site:www. ostellipassocisa.it; Price:C

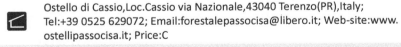
Parrocchia di Santa Margherita,(Pietro Adorni),Località Sivizzano Centro, 18,43045 Fornovo-di-Taro(PR),Italy; Tel:+39 0525 56258; +39 3497 839051; Price:C

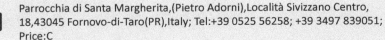
Affittacamere Da Veronica,Via Nazionale 51 Loc.Cassio,43040 Terenzo(PR),Italy; Tel:+39 0525 526002; +39 3204 480116; Email:albergo-bonora@hotmail.it; Price:B

## Altitude Profile

Cassio

Cavazzola

La Costa

Casaselvati

Castellonchio

Fugazzolo di Sotto

Frassano

Case di Monte Marino

Fugazzolo di Sopra

1 km

1 : 40 000

97

Stage Summary: the "Official Route" initially follows the SS62 before making diversions onto forest and farm tracks and descending into the centre of the town of Berceto. Bike riders will should plan to remain on the SS62 to avoid the steepest climbs.

Distance from Vercelli: 260km     Distance to St Peter's Square, Rome: 588km
Stage Ascent: 809m     Stage Descent: 626m

| Waypoint | Distance between waypoints | Total km | Directions | Verification Point | Compass | Altitude m |
|---|---|---|---|---|---|---|
| 73.001 | 0 | 0.0 | Continue straight ahead on the SS62 | Ostello on your right | SW | 797 |
| 73.002 | 500 | 0.5 | On a bend in the road to the left take the footpath to the right | Second track on right after strada Perdella | SW | 768 |
| 73.003 | 500 | 1.0 | Rejoin the main road and continue straight ahead on the right side of the road | Km 75, SS62 | SW | 742 |
| 73.004 | 2400 | 3.3 | On the crown of the bend to the right take the small tarmac road to the left. Note:- heavily packed bike riders may prefer avoid the steep tracks ahead and remain on the road | Sign Cavazzola di Sopra 700m | S | 748 |
| 73.005 | 400 | 3.7 | After a stretch on a level track, turn right | Steep forest track uphill | SW | 766 |
| 73.006 | 500 | 4.2 | Bear left on the track | | SW | 866 |
| 73.007 | 170 | 4.4 | At the fork in the tracks, keep right | Downhill | SW | 879 |
| 73.008 | 160 | 4.6 | Take the left fork | | S | 893 |
| 73.009 | 180 | 4.7 | Join a track and bear left | Under the electricity lines | SW | 914 |
| 73.010 | 120 | 4.9 | Turn right into the main street | Castellonchio | W | 912 |
| 73.011 | 70 | 4.9 | Bear left, downhill | Church to the right | S | 909 |
| 73.012 | 500 | 5.4 | Take the last turning to the left before reaching the main road | VF sign | S | 901 |

| Waypoint | Distance between waypoints | Total km | Directions | Verification Point | Compass | Altitude m |
|---|---|---|---|---|---|---|
| 73.013 | 270 | 5.6 | Continue straight ahead on the unmade road | Wooden fence on your left | S | 913 |
| 73.014 | 120 | 5.8 | Take the right fork | On the footpath | SW | 923 |
| 73.015 | 100 | 5.9 | At the junction with the main road turn right, cross over and continue on the left side of the road | SS62 | SW | 930 |
| 73.016 | 170 | 6.0 | On the crown of the next bend, turn left on the track | Into the woods | W | 935 |
| 73.017 | 160 | 6.2 | In the woods take the left fork | | S | 939 |
| 73.018 | 180 | 6.4 | Bear right | Ignore the turning to the left | SW | 956 |
| 73.019 | 160 | 6.5 | Shortly before reaching the main road turn right on the track | Towards the edge of the woods | W | 951 |
| 73.020 | 80 | 6.6 | Continue straight ahead | Keep close to the woods on your right | W | 957 |
| 73.021 | 180 | 6.8 | Bear left | Avoid the turning to the right | S | 975 |
| 73.022 | 130 | 6.9 | Bear right | Trees on your right, field on your left | W | 964 |
| 73.023 | 90 | 7.0 | At the T-junction with the road, turn left | | S | 955 |
| 73.024 | 700 | 7.7 | Beside the road junction, bear right on the track into the woods. Take the track closest to the main road. To avoid obstacles in the path, cyclists and riders should remain on the road | Pilgrim milestone at the entry to the woods | SW | 940 |
| 73.025 | 170 | 7.8 | Continue straight ahead over the stile on the path through the woods | Main road close on the left | S | 943 |

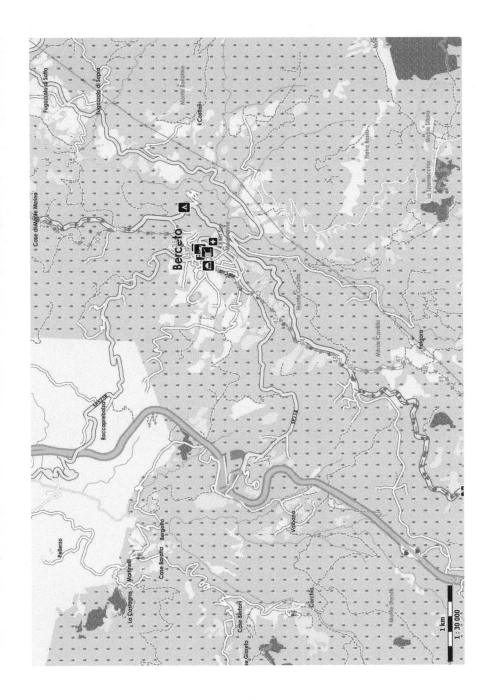

| Waypoint | Distance between waypoints | Total km | Directions | Verification Point | Compass | Altitude m |
|---|---|---|---|---|---|---|
| 73.026 | 130 | 8.0 | Continue straight ahead | Path joins a track | SW | 939 |
| 73.027 | 80 | 8.0 | Continue straight ahead | Track broadens into a road | SW | 942 |
| 73.028 | 260 | 8.3 | Bear left towards the radio mast | Across stile | S | 951 |
| 73.029 | 260 | 8.5 | After a short paved section turn right on the footpath | | S | 957 |
| 73.030 | 220 | 8.8 | Bear right on the track | | SE | 944 |
| 73.031 | 240 | 9.0 | Pass through the cattle gate and continue on the path | Towards the main road | S | 907 |
| 73.032 | 80 | 9.1 | Bear right on the main road remaining on the right side | SS62 (IV) marker on the left | S | 896 |
| 73.033 | 300 | 9.4 | As the road bears left, bear right on the footpath | Towards Berceto below | S | 883 |
| 73.034 | 500 | 9.9 | Take the right fork | Downhill, towards Berceto | SW | 866 |
| 73.035 | 180 | 10.1 | Continue straight ahead on the tarmac | Via Ripasanta | SW | 838 |
| 73.036 | 160 | 10.2 | Continue straight ahead | Castle to the left | S | 818 |
| 73.037 | 60 | 10.3 | In Largo Castello continue towards the centre of the town on the paved road | Via Rossi | SW | 812 |
| 73.038 | 130 | 10.4 | At the crossroads of via Martiri Libertà and via P.M. Rossi in the centre of Berceto (XXXIII), take via Romea | Pass in front of the Duomo | S | 807 |
| 73.039 | 30 | 10.4 | Continue on via Romea | Information Office to the left | SW | 806 |
| 73.040 | 90 | 10.5 | At the end of the small cobbled street in piazzale le Baruti, turn right and then immediately left | Via al Seminario, VF sign | SW | 806 |

| Waypoint | Distance between waypoints | Total km | Directions | Verification Point | Compass | Altitude m |
|---|---|---|---|---|---|---|
| 73.041 | 120 | 10.6 | Proceed straight ahead onto via E. Colli | VF sign | SW | 809 |
| 73.042 | 700 | 11.3 | At T-junction with main road turn right and almost immediately left onto a gravel track | VF sign | SW | 785 |
| 73.043 | 600 | 11.9 | At the fork, bear right | VF sign | SW | 819 |
| 73.044 | 400 | 12.2 | Fork right at the top of the rise | VF sign | S | 850 |
| 73.045 | 700 | 12.9 | In the parking area follow the tarmac to the junction with the main road | VF sign | SW | 872 |
| 73.046 | 140 | 13.0 | Cross the main road and continue straight ahead towards Monte Valoria. Note:- to avoid climbing on further forest tracks which include stiles follow the SS62 to the right to the end of the section beside the Ostello-della-Cisa | VF sign | S | 871 |
| 73.047 | 900 | 13.9 | Take the right fork | Farm Felgara to the left | SW | 938 |
| 73.048 | 260 | 14.2 | On the crown of a bend to the left bear right on the track | Uphill | S | 957 |
| 73.049 | 400 | 14.6 | Continue straight ahead | Altitude 1000m | SW | 1014 |
| 73.050 | 500 | 15.1 | Take the right fork | | SW | 1064 |
| 73.051 | 700 | 15.7 | Turn right. Note:- if you wish to bypass the hostel continue straight ahead and follow the instructions for the next section | Follow sign for the VF hostel | W | 1118 |
| 73.052 | 500 | 16.2 | Keep left | | W | 1098 |
| 73.053 | 500 | 16.7 | Turn sharp right | | N | 1030 |
| 73.054 | 100 | 16.8 | Bear left | | N | 1020 |

| Waypoint | Distance between waypoints | Total km | Directions | Verification Point | Compass | Altitude m |
|---|---|---|---|---|---|---|
| 73.055 | 210 | 17.0 | At the T-junction with the main road, turn right | Follow road downhill and across the river | N | 993 |
| 73.056 | 200 | 17.2 | Arrive at Ostello-della-Cisa | Hostel on the left | | 980 |

### Accommodation & Facilities ....   Cassio - Ostello-della-Cisa

Casa della Gioventù,Via Martino Iasoni,43042 Berceto(PR),Italy; Tel:+39 0525 60087; Price:D

Ostello via Francigena,Frazione Passo Cisa,43042 Berceto(PR),Italy; Tel:+39 0525 629072; Email:forestalepassocisa@libero.it ; Web-site:www. ostellipassocisa.it; Price:C

Ostello Seminario,Via Seminario,43042 Berceto(PR),Italy; Tel:+39 0521 234225; +39 3479 776652; Email:berceto@seminariovescovile.parma.it; Price:C

Albergo Ristorante Vittoria Da Rino,Via Guglielmo Marconi, 5,43042 Berceto(PR),Italy; Tel:+39 0525 64306; Email:info@darino.it; Web-site:www. darino.it; Price:A

Camping I Pianelli,Località I Pianelli, 146,43042 Berceto(PR),Italy; Tel:+39 0525 64521; Email:info@campingipianelli.it; Web-site:www.campingipianelli.it; Price:C

Ufficio Turistico,Via Romea, 5,43042 Berceto(PR),Italy; Tel:+39 0525 629027

Banca Monte Parma,Vicolo Marina,43042 Berceto(PR),Italy; Tel:+39 0525 629011

Croce Rossa Italiana - Delegazione,Salita P.Silva,43042 Berceto(PR),Italy; Tel:+39 0525 60040

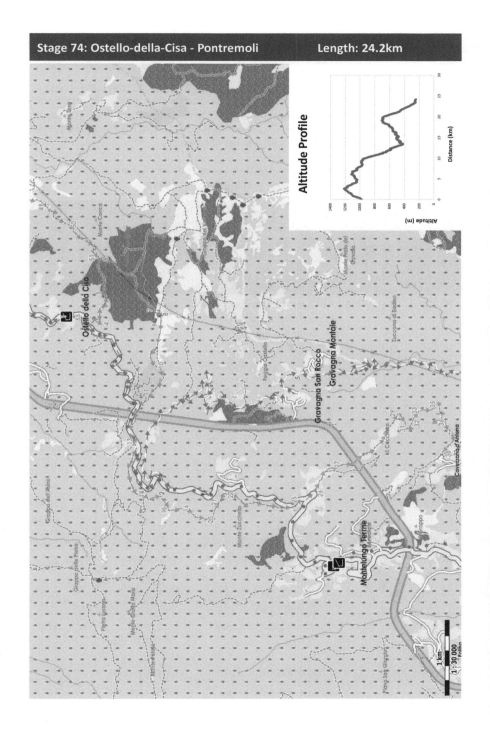

Stage Summary: this is a long and strenuous section with few intermediate facilities. The "Official Route" remains largely off-road, but after a pleasant descent from the summit of the Cisa Pass the route again climbs the 700m Crocetta Pass. A less strenuous Alternate Route descends gently on minor roads to the outskirts of Pontrmoli and avoids the Crocetta Pass. Pontremoli offers a full range of facilities.

Distance from Vercelli: 278km          Distance to St Peter's Square, Rome: 571km
Stage Ascent: 1016m                    Stage Descent: 1749m

| Waypoint | Distance between waypoints | Total km | Directions | Verification Point | Compass | Altitude m |
|---|---|---|---|---|---|---|
| 74.001 | 0 | 0.0 | With the Ostello-della-Cisa directly behind you, turn right on the road | Uphill | S | 979 |
| 74.002 | 210 | 0.2 | After crossing the river, turn left on the path. Note:- if the traffic conditions permit, the route can be reduced by 2km by remaining on the road to the summit of the pass. Cyclists and horse-riders are advised to follow this route to avoid further obstacles. | Uphill into the woods | S | 991 |
| 74.003 | 200 | 0.4 | Bear right | | S | 1015 |
| 74.004 | 120 | 0.5 | Turn sharp left | | E | 1030 |
| 74.005 | 500 | 1.0 | Bear right | | E | 1098 |
| 74.006 | 500 | 1.5 | At the T-junction, turn right | Uphill | SW | 1124 |
| 74.007 | 1200 | 2.6 | Near the summit of Valoria take the right fork | Towards the summit | SW | 1213 |
| 74.008 | 80 | 2.7 | At the summit take the path to the right | Along the ridge | W | 1207 |
| 74.009 | 160 | 2.9 | Continue straight ahead | Ignore the turning to the right | W | 1176 |
| 74.010 | 600 | 3.5 | Continue straight ahead | Cross the stile | W | 1130 |
| 74.011 | 500 | 4.0 | After a steep descent, continue straight ahead | Cross a second stile | NW | 1078 |

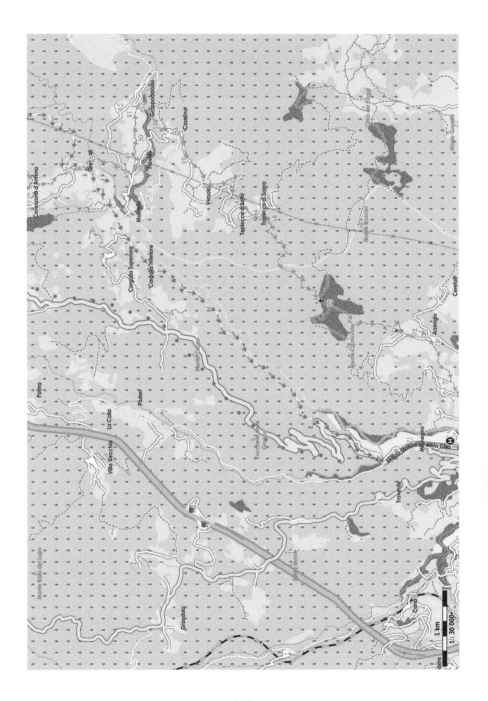

| Waypoint | Distance between waypoints | Total km | Directions | Verification Point | Compass | Altitude m |
|---|---|---|---|---|---|---|
| 74.012 | 50 | 4.0 | Join a track and bear right | | W | 1069 |
| 74.013 | 800 | 4.8 | At the summit of the Cisa Pass, cross the main road and bear right on the footpath.  Note:- the Alternate Route offers a pleasant descent to Pontremoli on generally quiet roads and may be preferred by cyclists and horse riders.  The "Official Route" includes sometimes difficult water crossings as well as steep descents and steps and a further climb over the Crocetta  There are many intersecting CAI routes also using red and white signs and so be sure to check for the pilgrim on the signs | Parallel to the steps to the church | W | 1039 |
| 74.014 | 800 | 5.5 | At an intersection between 3 tracks, take the left track | Downhill, red and white sign | SW | 1077 |
| 74.015 | 600 | 6.1 | Continue straight ahead across the stream | Cairn ahead | S | 1117 |
| 74.016 | 140 | 6.3 | Take the left fork | Downhill | SW | 1103 |
| 74.017 | 200 | 6.5 | Bear right and cross the stream | Continue on the small track | SW | 1095 |
| 74.018 | 50 | 6.5 | Bear left, cross the stream and a small grassy area and bear right | Re-enter woods | S | 1097 |
| 74.019 | 110 | 6.6 | Turn right on the forest road | Red and white sign | SW | 1096 |
| 74.020 | 30 | 6.7 | Turn left on another forest road | Cross another stream | SE | 1101 |
| 74.021 | 400 | 7.0 | At a T-junction of forest-tracks, turn right | | SE | 1061 |
| 74.022 | 100 | 7.2 | Ignore a turning to the right and continue straight ahead | Downhill | E | 1045 |

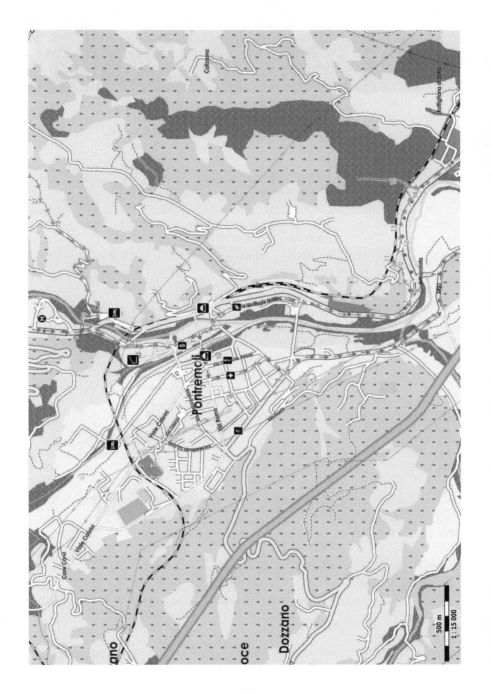

| Waypoint | Distance between waypoints | Total km | Directions | Verification Point | Compass | Altitude m |
|---|---|---|---|---|---|---|
| 74.023 | 30 | 7.2 | Turn right on the path | Gentle descent, parallel to the main road below | S | 1034 |
| 74.024 | 900 | 8.1 | The path enters a track, bear right down the hill | Parallel and closer to the main road | SE | 983 |
| 74.025 | 190 | 8.3 | At the junction with the main road bear right on the road | SS62 - Km53 | SE | 972 |
| 74.026 | 200 | 8.5 | On the apex of the next bend, bear left on the unmade road. Note:- to visit Montelungo (XXXII) follow the main road with care. The main road continues to Pontremoli | Via Francigena sign | SE | 967 |
| 74.027 | 600 | 9.1 | Pass a radio mast and continue straight ahead | Descend in an open space between woods | SE | 982 |
| 74.028 | 1000 | 10.1 | Continue straight ahead | Ignore the turning to the right | SE | 916 |
| 74.029 | 70 | 10.2 | At the T-junction with a broader track, turn right | Downhill | SW | 904 |
| 74.030 | 140 | 10.3 | At the fork in the tracks, bear right | Follow the larger track | SW | 884 |
| 74.031 | 120 | 10.4 | At a T-junction in the tracks, bear left | Downhill | SE | 863 |
| 74.032 | 80 | 10.5 | Continue straight ahead | Ignore turning to the right | SE | 846 |
| 74.033 | 220 | 10.7 | Continue straight ahead | Ignore the turning to the left and to the right | S | 799 |
| 74.034 | 170 | 10.9 | Continue straight ahead downhill | Ignore turning to right | SE | 760 |

| Waypoint | Distance between waypoints | Total km | Directions | Verification Point | Compass | Altitude m |
|---|---|---|---|---|---|---|
| 74.035 | 120 | 11.0 | At a turn in the track continue straight ahead on the path | Into the woods | W | 738 |
| 74.036 | 400 | 11.4 | Continue straight ahead | Ignore the turning to the right | SW | 695 |
| 74.037 | 300 | 11.7 | At a fork in the tracks, take the right fork | | W | 646 |
| 74.038 | 400 | 12.0 | At a T-junction with a grassy track, turn left | Church ahead, ignore VF sign to the right | SE | 591 |
| 74.039 | 400 | 12.4 | At the fork in the tracks, take the right fork | Downhill | S | 590 |
| 74.040 | 500 | 12.9 | Continue straight ahead on the tarmac road | Enter Groppoli | SE | 510 |
| 74.041 | 60 | 12.9 | At the intersection with the tarmac road continue straight ahead on the cobbled road | Pass between houses | S | 499 |
| 74.042 | 120 | 13.0 | Continue straight ahead | Narrow cobbled path | S | 486 |
| 74.043 | 100 | 13.1 | At the exit from Gropolli take the left fork | | E | 467 |
| 74.044 | 40 | 13.2 | At the junction with the main road turn right and immediately left on the track.  Note:- to reduce total distance by 2.5km and avoid further off-road tracks and the climb over the Crocetta pass continue to the right on the road and join the Alternate Route | Vines and wooden fence on the right | SE | 461 |
| 74.045 | 300 | 13.5 | Continue straight ahead and take the difficult ford across the Civasola torrente | Uphill | SW | 418 |

| Waypoint | Distance between waypoints | Total km | Directions | Verification Point | Compass | Altitude m |
|---|---|---|---|---|---|---|
| 74.046 | 400 | 13.9 | At the intersection with the tarmac road, turn right and immediately left onto a footpath | Steep descent into Previdè | SW | 463 |
| 74.047 | 120 | 14.0 | On reaching Previdè turn left onto the tarmac and then immediately left again | Towards the village centre | E | 454 |
| 74.048 | 110 | 14.1 | At the exit from the village take the left fork, uphill on the grass track | Shrine on the left | E | 448 |
| 74.049 | 190 | 14.3 | Take care to locate an indistinct junction and bear right over a dry wall | Between the olive trees | E | 474 |
| 74.050 | 270 | 14.6 | After an uphill section take a footpath to the right | Across the hillside | E | 496 |
| 74.051 | 400 | 14.9 | Continue straight ahead | Enter Groppodalosio | E | 506 |
| 74.052 | 100 | 15.0 | In the centre of the village turn right | Down a flight of steps | SW | 506 |
| 74.053 | 140 | 15.2 | Continue straight ahead | Over the old river Magra bridge | SW | 476 |
| 74.054 | 290 | 15.5 | Join a tarmac road and turn right | Towards the village of Casalina | SW | 502 |
| 74.055 | 70 | 15.5 | Bear left away from the road on a footpath | | SW | 501 |
| 74.056 | 150 | 15.7 | At the first junction in Casalina continue straight ahead | On the paved road | S | 509 |
| 74.057 | 150 | 15.8 | Continue straight ahead | Pass an old mill | W | 527 |
| 74.058 | 260 | 16.1 | Continue straight ahead on the road | Between the stone walls | SW | 508 |
| 74.059 | 160 | 16.2 | Bear left on the well signed path | Into the woods | SW | 512 |
| 74.060 | 400 | 16.6 | Join the track and bear left | | SW | 556 |

| Waypoint | Distance between waypoints | Total km | Directions | Verification Point | Compass | Altitude m |
|---|---|---|---|---|---|---|
| 74.061 | 80 | 16.7 | At a bend to the left in the track, continue straight ahead on the path | | S | 556 |
| 74.062 | 400 | 17.1 | Cross a stream and turn sharply to the right | | W | 559 |
| 74.063 | 500 | 17.5 | After a steep climb turn right on the track | Towards the village | W | 579 |
| 74.064 | 100 | 17.6 | At the junction with the tarmac road turn left on the road | Uphill | SW | 587 |
| 74.065 | 50 | 17.7 | Bear left on a footpath | Skirt the village of Toplecca di Sopra | SW | 594 |
| 74.066 | 50 | 17.7 | At the T-junction turn left | | SW | 599 |
| 74.067 | 120 | 17.8 | Cross the tarmac road and continue straight ahead | Shrine on your left | S | 606 |
| 74.068 | 180 | 18.0 | Continue straight ahead | Over the bridge | SW | 607 |
| 74.069 | 1800 | 19.8 | At the summit of the Crocetta pass, after a long climb, continue straight ahead on the track | Pass beside the chapel | SW | 696 |
| 74.070 | 40 | 19.8 | Take the grass track to the left and downhill | Towards the village of Arzengio | S | 692 |
| 74.071 | 1300 | 21.1 | At the first houses in Arzengio, take the tarmac road to the left | | SW | 487 |
| 74.072 | 220 | 21.3 | Take the first turning to the left | Village centre on the hilltop to the right | SE | 460 |
| 74.073 | 130 | 21.5 | On the far side of the village take the small path to the left | Between the olive trees | S | 457 |
| 74.074 | 70 | 21.5 | At the next junction turn right on the path | Across the hillside | W | 444 |

| Waypoint | Distance between waypoints | Total km | Directions | Verification Point | Compass | Altitude m |
|---|---|---|---|---|---|---|
| 74.075 | 60 | 21.6 | Cross the tarmac road and take right fork on the small road beside the house | Initially parallel to the tarmac road on the left | SW | 446 |
| 74.076 | 130 | 21.7 | Continue straight ahead | The road becomes a track | SW | 437 |
| 74.077 | 600 | 22.3 | Continue straight ahead | Ignore the turning to the right | SW | 366 |
| 74.078 | 180 | 22.5 | Continue straight ahead | Tarmac road | W | 342 |
| 74.079 | 900 | 23.4 | At the T-junction with the road, turn right | Conifers in the garden on your right | NW | 253 |
| 74.080 | 50 | 23.5 | Continue straight ahead over the old bridge over the Magra | Towards the hospital | W | 250 |
| 74.081 | 80 | 23.6 | Pass through the archway and at the junction with the main road turn left | SS62, VF sign | S | 256 |
| 74.082 | 60 | 23.6 | At the fork in the road, bear right. Note:- to avoid a pedestrian subway bear left on the main road and then turn right to the centre of Pontremoli | Via di Porta Parma | SW | 254 |
| 74.083 | 170 | 23.8 | Bear right and continue straight ahead through the underpass | Beneath railway | S | 256 |
| 74.084 | 80 | 23.9 | Turn right after coming up from the underpass and go around the mini roundabout | VF sign, shrine directly in front | W | 256 |
| 74.085 | 0 | 23.9 | Go under the archway – Porta Parma – and into the narrow street ahead | Via Garibaldi | S | 256 |
| 74.086 | 300 | 24.2 | Arrive at Pontremoli centre (XXXI) | Piazza della Repubblica | | 245 |

| Alternate Route #74.A1 | | | | Length: 19.8km | | |
| --- | --- | --- | --- | --- | --- | --- |

Stage Summary: a less challenging descent to Pontremoli. After a short stretch on the main road, the route follows quiet country roads for much of its length before rejoining the SS62 for the final 2km to Pontremoli. The route is recommended for cyclists.

Stage Ascent: 723m          Stage Descent: 1498m

| Waypoint | Distance between waypoints | Total km | Directions | Verification Point | Compass | Altitude m |
| --- | --- | --- | --- | --- | --- | --- |
| 74A1.001 | 0 | 0.0 | Continue straight ahead on the main road | Church on the right | SW | 1032 |
| 74A1.002 | 1100 | 1.1 | Turn left away from the SS62. Note:- to visit Montelungo (XXXII) follow the main road with care. The main road continues to Pontremoli | Direction Gravagna | SE | 1026 |
| 74A1.003 | 5400 | 6.5 | At the bottom of the hill continue straight ahead into the village of Gravagna San Rocco | VF sign | E | 707 |
| 74A1.004 | 230 | 6.8 | At the bottom of the hill continue straight ahead | VF sign | SE | 696 |
| 74A1.005 | 400 | 7.2 | Fork right before entering Gravagna Montale | Large house directly in front | S | 693 |
| 74A1.006 | 4900 | 12.1 | Continue straight ahead on the road | The "Official Route" crosses from the right | SW | 452 |
| 74A1.007 | 1200 | 13.3 | A the T-junction turn right | Towards Pontremoli | SW | 396 |
| 74A1.008 | 4100 | 17.4 | At the T-junction, turn left and proceed with caution on the potentially busy road | SS62, downhill, towards Pontremoli | S | 363 |
| 74A1.009 | 2400 | 19.8 | Rejoin the "Official Route" and continue straight ahead on the road | Towards the centre of Pontremoli | | 257 |

**Accommodation & Facilities** .... **Ostello-della-Cisa - Pontremoli**

Casa Alpina San Benedetto,(Signora Rita),54020 Montelungo(MS),Italy;
Tel:+39 3391 741919; Price:C

Castello del Piagnaro,Via dei Voltoni,54027 Pontremoli(MS),Italy; Tel:+39 0187
831439; +39 0187 831400; Email:istruzione@comune.pontremoli.ms.it; Web-
site:www.comune.pontremoli.ms.it; Price:C

Convento Cappuccini,Via dei Cappuccini, 2,54027 Pontremoli(MS),Italy;
Tel:+39 0187 830395; Web-site:www.cappuccinipontremoli.it; Price:C;
Note:Credentials required, ; PR

Ex Seminario de Pontremoli,Piazza San Francesco,54027 Pontremoli(MS),Italy;
+39 3386 876886; +39 3345 446198; Price:D

Prioria Sant'Andrea Apostolo,Località Scorcetoli,54023 Filattiera(MS),Italy;
Tel:+39 0187 457191; Email:luciofilippi@treemmei.com

B&B Ca' Battista,Località Montelungo Superiore, 63,54027
Pontremoli(MS),Italy; Tel:+39 0187 64338; +39 3278 387687; +39 3409
800929; Email:info@cabattista.eu; Web-site:www.cabattista.eu; Price:B

Ai Chiosi Bed & Breakfast,Via Chiosi, 15,54027 Pontremoli(MS),Italy; +39 3402
357383; +39 3405 065620; Email:aichiosi@libero.it  ;
Web-site:www.aichiosi.it; Price:A

Agriturismo il Paradiso,Via Costa San Nicolò, 2,54027 Pontremoli(MS),Italy;
+39 3409 231129; Email:info@agriparadiso.it; Web-site:www.agriparadiso.it;
Price:A

Comune di Pontremol,Via Generale Reisoli, 11,54027 Pontremoli(MS),Italy;
Tel:+39 0187 830056

Banca Monte dei Paschi di Siena,Via Pietro Bologna, 10,54027
Pontremoli(MS),Italy; Tel:+39 0187 461542

Stazione Ferrovie,Piazzale Bruno Raschi,54027 Pontremoli(MS),Italy;
Tel:+39 06 6847 5475; Web-site:www.renitalia.it

Ospedale Civile Sant'Antonio Abate,Via Nazionale,54027 Pontremoli(MS),Italy;
Tel:+39 0187 46211

Arrighi - Medico Chirurgo,Via Pirandello, 46,54027 Pontremoli(MS),Italy;
Tel:+39 0187 831252

Ballestracci Natale,Via Mazzini, 56,54027 Pontremoli(MS),Italy;
Tel:+39 0187 833204

El Nino Cicli di Ambrosini Fabrizio,Via Europa, 74,54027 Pontremoli(MS),Italy;
Tel:+39 0187 830457

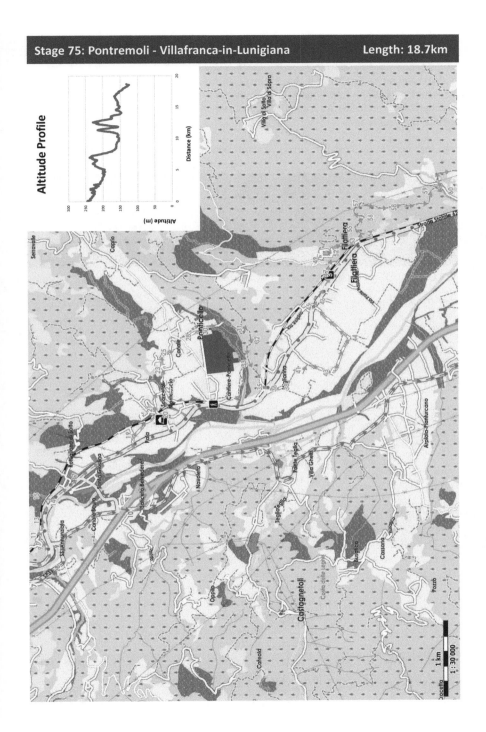

# Stage 75: Pontremoli - Villafranca-in-Lunigiana

## Length: 18.7km

Altitude Profile

## Stage 75: Pontremoli - Villafranca-in-Lunigiana — Length: 18.7km

Stage Summary: the "Official Route" involves mixed conditions varying from short stretches on busy and potentially dangerous roads near Pontremoli to isolated tracks through hilly woodland. A cycle route is available on more level ground on the western side of the river Magra.

Distance from Vercelli: 302km
Stage Ascent: 317m

Distance to St Peter's Square, Rome: 547km
Stage Descent: 431m

| Waypoint | Distance between waypoints | Total km | Directions | Verification Point | Compass | Altitude m |
|---|---|---|---|---|---|---|
| 75.001 | 0 | 0.0 | Cross piazza della Repubblica into the narrow street ahead | Via Armani | SE | 245 |
| 75.002 | 150 | 0.2 | At the crossroads continue straight ahead. Note:- to use the Cycle Route turn right and continue over the bridge on the Alternate Route | Via Cavour | S | 243 |
| 75.003 | 100 | 0.3 | Turn left and cross the river bridge | Ponte Cesare Battisti | E | 235 |
| 75.004 | 80 | 0.3 | Pass through the archway and turn right | Via Mazzini | S | 237 |
| 75.005 | 600 | 0.9 | At the crossroads continue straight ahead to join the main road, remain on the right-hand side | VF sign, direction Aulla | S | 228 |
| 75.006 | 700 | 1.6 | Continue straight ahead | Pass beside the church of San Lazzaro | SE | 224 |
| 75.007 | 130 | 1.7 | Cross the road and bear left on the narrow paved street. Note:- where possible the route will try and avoid this busy road. However, in light traffic conditions cyclists may prefer to stay on the road | Via Santissima Annunziata | E | 225 |
| 75.008 | 70 | 1.8 | With house n° 32 immediately on your right, turn left and then right at the end of the short street | | NE | 226 |

117

| Waypoint | Distance between waypoints | Total km | Directions | Verification Point | Compass | Altitude m |
|---|---|---|---|---|---|---|
| 75.009 | 70 | 1.9 | Join the track between the trees and the church and continue uphill | Pass the stone walled terraces on your left | NE | 234 |
| 75.010 | 170 | 2.0 | Bear right around the brick building | Towards the small road | E | 236 |
| 75.011 | 50 | 2.1 | At the T-junction with the road, turn right, downhill | Vines on your right | SE | 230 |
| 75.012 | 120 | 2.2 | Continue straight ahead on the elevated road | Main road on your right | E | 219 |
| 75.013 | 100 | 2.3 | At the hairpin, continue straight ahead | No Through Road | E | 222 |
| 75.014 | 250 | 2.5 | Bear left on the track | Towards the railway | NE | 214 |
| 75.015 | 120 | 2.7 | Cross the stream and turn right onto the small road | Return under the railway bridge | S | 225 |
| 75.016 | 160 | 2.8 | At the T-junction with the main road, turn left and follow the road with great care | | SE | 208 |
| 75.017 | 500 | 3.3 | At the junction beside the petrol station, continue straight ahead | Direction Villafranca, VF sign | SE | 204 |
| 75.018 | 800 | 4.1 | Turn left and leave the main road | VF sign, pass shop on your right | E | 197 |
| 75.019 | 140 | 4.3 | Take the right fork onto the gravel track | VF sign, large drainage ditch to your right | SE | 196 |
| 75.020 | 500 | 4.7 | At the junction with a minor road turn sharp left on the road | VF sign, towards railway | NE | 194 |
| 75.021 | 120 | 4.8 | Take the right fork | Direction Ponticello | E | 200 |
| 75.022 | 300 | 5.1 | At the junction, continue straight ahead | Up the hill | E | 199 |

| Waypoint | Distance between waypoints | Total km | Directions | Verification Point | Compass | Altitude m |
|---|---|---|---|---|---|---|
| 75.023 | 280 | 5.4 | Fork left on the road | Direction Canale, VF sign | E | 214 |
| 75.024 | 200 | 5.6 | At the end of the parking area, continue to the right on the road | VF sign | SE | 222 |
| 75.025 | 120 | 5.7 | At the crossroads, continue straight ahead on the gravel track | VF sign | SE | 222 |
| 75.026 | 130 | 5.9 | At the T-junction with a minor road, turn left | VF sign | E | 224 |
| 75.027 | 110 | 6.0 | At the road junction, cross over and pass the church on your right | Borgo de Ponticello, red and white sign | SE | 228 |
| 75.028 | 50 | 6.0 | Pass under an archway and turn right | Volta a Crociera | S | 229 |
| 75.029 | 70 | 6.1 | Bear left | Pass under a second arch | S | 227 |
| 75.030 | 180 | 6.3 | At the crossroads take the second turning on the left | The track crosses a river and climbs the ridge | S | 223 |
| 75.031 | 800 | 7.0 | Turn sharp right | VF sign | SW | 237 |
| 75.032 | 180 | 7.2 | Take the right fork onto the grassy track | VF sign | W | 233 |
| 75.033 | 400 | 7.6 | Take the left fork | Line of trees and fence on the left, VF sign | SW | 204 |
| 75.034 | 400 | 7.9 | At the T-junction, turn right | Pass under the railway | SW | 179 |
| 75.035 | 40 | 7.9 | Bear left and then turn right in a narrow passageway | Red and white signs | SW | 175 |
| 75.036 | 40 | 8.0 | Cross straight over the main road and continue straight ahead | VF sign | SW | 173 |

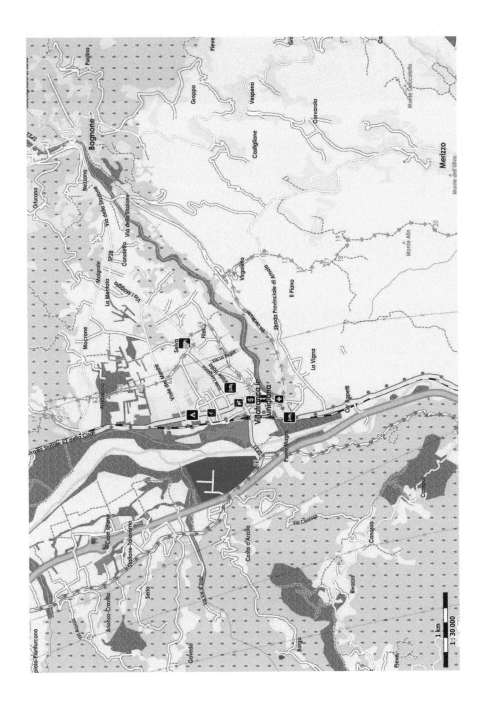

| Waypoint | Distance between waypoints | Total km | Directions | Verification Point | Compass | Altitude m |
|---|---|---|---|---|---|---|
| 75.037 | 50 | 8.0 | Turn left between houses | Red and white signs | S | 173 |
| 75.038 | 170 | 8.2 | At the fork in the track, bear left | Yellow VF sign, vines on your left | SE | 167 |
| 75.039 | 210 | 8.4 | At the end of the vines on your left, continue straight ahead on the faint track | Line of trees on your right | SE | 163 |
| 75.040 | 140 | 8.6 | At the T-junction, turn right | Towards farm buildings | SW | 161 |
| 75.041 | 90 | 8.7 | Turn left | Keep the farm buildings to the right | SE | 162 |
| 75.042 | 100 | 8.8 | At the T-junction with the tarmac road turn right | Yellow VF sign, field on the right | SW | 161 |
| 75.043 | 400 | 9.1 | At the junction, turn left between the fences | Yellow VF sign | SE | 161 |
| 75.044 | 600 | 9.7 | At the T-junction, turn left between the trees | Farm on your left, VF sign | NE | 154 |
| 75.045 | 600 | 10.3 | At the T-junction with the main road, turn right | Towards the church – Pieve di Sorano | E | 158 |
| 75.046 | 80 | 10.4 | Take the left fork and leave the SS62 | Direction Biglio | SE | 158 |
| 75.047 | 500 | 10.8 | Turn left under the railway bridge and turn right at the T-junction | Brown VF sign | E | 158 |
| 75.048 | 280 | 11.1 | Turn right up a flight of steps.  Note:- riders should remain on the road and then bear right into the centre of the village | Filattiera Alta | N | 180 |
| 75.049 | 130 | 11.2 | Continue straight ahead | Pass through the car park | N | 202 |

| Waypoint | Distance between waypoints | Total km | Directions | Verification Point | Compass | Altitude m |
|---|---|---|---|---|---|---|
| 75.050 | 20 | 11.2 | At the road junction turn sharp right | Towards the square in the centre of Filattiera | SE | 204 |
| 75.051 | 110 | 11.3 | Turn right to leave the square | Pass a café on your left | S | 214 |
| 75.052 | 100 | 11.4 | At the end of the road take the left fork | Pass through the archway, VF sign | SE | 208 |
| 75.053 | 500 | 11.9 | At the T-junction, turn left and then right over a bridge and climb the hill on a stony track | Railway bridge on the right at the junction | SE | 157 |
| 75.054 | 170 | 12.1 | Bear left towards the chapel on the brow of the hill | Yellow VF sign | NE | 185 |
| 75.055 | 150 | 12.2 | Take the right fork | VF signs | SE | 205 |
| 75.056 | 210 | 12.4 | Take the left fork | Into the trees | E | 213 |
| 75.057 | 300 | 12.8 | Turn right towards the pylon | Yellow VF sign | S | 213 |
| 75.058 | 400 | 13.1 | Continue straight ahead | | S | 177 |
| 75.059 | 800 | 13.9 | Turn right beside the river | Red and white signs | S | 151 |
| 75.060 | 200 | 14.1 | At the road junction, turn left | Brown VF sign | NE | 146 |
| 75.061 | 180 | 14.3 | Turn right on the broad gravel track | Brown VF sign | S | 149 |
| 75.062 | 800 | 15.0 | At the junction with the road turn left and then immediately right on the stony track | Brown VF sign, electricity station on the left | S | 152 |
| 75.063 | 600 | 15.5 | Continue straight ahead on the narrow track | Trees on the right, field on the left | S | 156 |
| 75.064 | 140 | 15.7 | Continue straight ahead | Between the trees | S | 157 |
| 75.065 | 110 | 15.8 | Bear left onto the road | Golf course on the right | S | 156 |

| Waypoint | Distance between waypoints | Total km | Directions | Verification Point | Compass | Altitude m |
|---|---|---|---|---|---|---|
| 75.066 | 270 | 16.1 | At the crossroads with the SP29, continue straight ahead into Filetto | Via San Genesio | SE | 158 |
| 75.067 | 600 | 16.7 | At the end of the road, turn left | Into Filetto old town | NE | 164 |
| 75.068 | 120 | 16.8 | Immediately after leaving the old town, turn right | Via del Canale | SE | 166 |
| 75.069 | 400 | 17.1 | At the T-junction, turn right | Parallel to the river and wooded ridge | SW | 159 |
| 75.070 | 900 | 18.1 | At the T-junction, turn left | Via Chiusura | SW | 138 |
| 75.071 | 270 | 18.3 | Bear left across piazza della Resistenza | Towards the main road | SW | 129 |
| 75.072 | 90 | 18.4 | Cross the main road and bear left across the piazza Aeronautica to take the old bridge over the river | Into the old town of Villafranca | SW | 127 |
| 75.073 | 260 | 18.7 | Arrive at Villafranca-in-Lunigiana old town centre | Beside the church | | 131 |

**Alternate Route #75.A1**                     **Length: 21.6km**

Stage Summary: cycle route to Terrarossa on the outskirts of Aulla. This tarmac route remains in the valley on the western side of the river Magra. The section to Ponte Magra (near Villafranca) is generally flat, before a stiff climb to Lusuolo

**Stage Ascent: 422m**                     **Stage Descent: 591m**

| Waypoint | Distance between waypoints | Total km | Directions | Verification Point | Compass | Altitude m |
|---|---|---|---|---|---|---|
| 75A1.001 | 0 | 0.0 | At the crossroads turn right and cross the river bridge | Via Pietro Bologna | W | 242 |
| 75A1.002 | 140 | 0.1 | At the next crossroads, continue straight ahead | Via Roma | W | 241 |
| 75A1.003 | 170 | 0.3 | At the crossroads, turn left | Via Pirandello | SE | 246 |
| 75A1.004 | 400 | 0.7 | At the T-junction turn right | Strada di Maggio Galante | SW | 238 |
| 75A1.005 | 170 | 0.9 | At the crossroads, turn left onto via Europa and via Groppomontone | Factory building straight ahead | SE | 239 |

| Waypoint | Distance between waypoints | Total km | Directions | Verification Point | Compass | Altitude m |
|---|---|---|---|---|---|---|
| 75A1.006 | 100 | 1.0 | Bear right on via Groppomontone | Keep river and bridge to the left | S | 235 |
| 75A1.007 | 700 | 1.7 | Continue straight ahead, cross the bridge over the Magra tributary | Via Antonino Siligato | SE | 232 |
| 75A1.008 | 400 | 2.1 | Take the left fork – remain beside the river | Direction La Spezia | E | 220 |
| 75A1.009 | 280 | 2.3 | Bear right on SP31 | Between the hill and the river plane | SE | 227 |
| 75A1.010 | 1100 | 3.4 | Continue straight ahead, direction Villafranca | Motorway entrance on the left | SE | 232 |
| 75A1.011 | 9000 | 12.4 | In Ponte Magra, turn right onto via Pontemagra. Note:- to rejoin the "Official Route", turn left and cross the bridge into the centre of Villafranca | Direction Lusuolo | S | 122 |
| 75A1.012 | 2000 | 14.4 | Continue straight ahead on the road | Avoid the turning to the right | S | 189 |
| 75A1.013 | 1800 | 16.2 | At the junction beside the hairpin bend, bear left | Enter Lusuolo | S | 181 |
| 75A1.014 | 2300 | 18.4 | At the junction, bear left remaining on the road | VF cycle route sign | SE | 100 |
| 75A1.015 | 900 | 19.3 | Bear right into Barbarasco | Via Chiesa | SW | 108 |
| 75A1.016 | 100 | 19.4 | At the T-junction in Barbarasco, turn left | SP23, via Roma | SE | 112 |
| 75A1.017 | 1500 | 20.9 | After crossing the river, continue straight ahead | Via Barbarasco | SE | 74 |
| 75A1.018 | 260 | 21.2 | At the T-junction, turn right. Note:- riders route joins from the left | Via Nazionale, direction Aulla | SE | 74 |
| 75A1.019 | 500 | 21.6 | At the Stop sign rejoin the "Official Route" and continue straight ahead across the main road | Pass the castle on your right | | 74 |

## Accommodation & Facilities .... Pontremoli - Villafranca-in-Lunigiana

Appartamenti Gredo,Piazza Immacolata, 30,54028 Villafranca-In-Lunigiana(MS),Italy; +39 3498 487416; Email:info@appartamentigredo.com; Web-site:www.appartamentigredo.com; Price:A

Villa Magnolia,Viale Italia, 33,54028 Villafranca-In-Lunigiana(MS),Italy; Tel:+39 0187 495563; Price:B

Albergo Manganelli,Piazza San Nicolò, 5,54028 Villafranca-In-Lunigiana(MS),Italy; Tel:+39 0187 493062; Price:B

Camping il Castagneto,Via Nazionale,54028 Villafranca-In-Lunigiana(MS),Italy; Tel:+39 0187 493492; Email:info@campingilcastagneto.it; Web-site:www.campingilcastagneto.it; Price:C; Note:Bungalows also available,

Comune di Villafranca In Lunigiana,Via Monsignor Razzoli, 2,54028 Villafranca-In-Lunigiana(MS),Italy; Tel:+39 0187 493013

Banca Monte dei Paschi di Siena,Via Ponte Provinciale, 41,54023 Filattiera(MS),Italy; Tel:+39 0187 458540

Banca Toscana,Via Chiusura, 22,54028 Villafranca-In-Lunigiana(MS),Italy; Tel:+39 0187 493018

Natali - Medico Chirurgo,Via Baracchini, 53,54028 Villafranca-In-Lunigiana(MS),Italy; Tel:+39 0187 494193

Ambulatorio Medico Veterinario,Via Aldo Moro, 2,54028 Villafranca-In-Lunigiana(MS),Italy; Tel:+39 0187 495193

Bortolasi,Via Provinciale, 2,54023 Filattiera (MS),Italy; Tel:+39 0187 458017

Dueruote di Pagani Emanuele Sas,Via Aldo Moro, 94,54028 Villafranca-In-Lunigiana(MS),Italy; Tel:+39 0187 495811

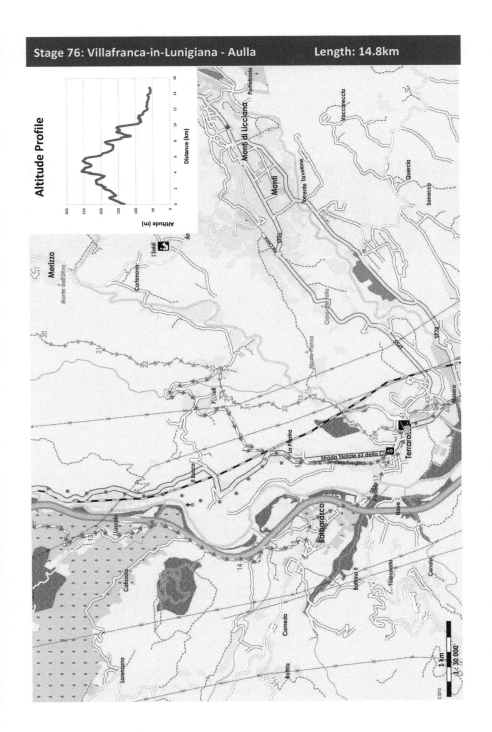

Stage Summary: the route leaves Villafranca on a minor road before returning to the woodland tracks some of which are both steep and narrow. The route briefly rejoins the busy SS62 between Terrarosa and the large town of Aulla.

Distance from Vercelli: 320km          Distance to St Peter's Square, Rome: 528km
Stage Ascent: 315m                     Stage Descent: 388m

| Waypoint | Distance between waypoints | Total km | Directions | Verification Point | Compass | Altitude m |
|---|---|---|---|---|---|---|
| 76.001 | 0 | 0.0 | Cross the piazza, turn left and leave the old town | Church on your left | S | 131 |
| 76.002 | 70 | 0.1 | Cross the main road and bear left onto via della Libertà | Direction Virgoletta, SP26, VF sign | E | 134 |
| 76.003 | 700 | 0.7 | Fork left | Direction Virgoletta | NE | 170 |
| 76.004 | 1100 | 1.8 | Turn right | Direction Virgoletta Centre | SE | 175 |
| 76.005 | 40 | 1.8 | After the turn to the left bear right on the path in the direction of the church | Shrine on left | NE | 178 |
| 76.006 | 80 | 1.9 | At the crossroads continue straight ahead. Note:- to avoid a flight of steps, riders should turn right and then right again | Pass under the arches | NE | 185 |
| 76.007 | 180 | 2.1 | Turn right through the arch and then turn right at the foot of the steps | VF sign at the foot of the steps | S | 193 |
| 76.008 | 60 | 2.1 | Turn left on the road | Pass the water source on the left | S | 189 |
| 76.009 | 180 | 2.3 | Bear left continuing up the hill | Via delle Fontane | SE | 194 |
| 76.010 | 600 | 2.9 | At the crossroads, continue straight ahead towards the cemetery | Red and white painted sign | S | 213 |

| Waypoint | Distance between waypoints | Total km | Directions | Verification Point | Compass | Altitude m |
|---|---|---|---|---|---|---|
| 76.011 | 140 | 3.0 | As the road becomes a track, continue straight ahead with the football pitch on the left | Red and white painted sign | S | 214 |
| 76.012 | 210 | 3.2 | Fork left downhill onto a narrow grassy track | Garden on the right | SW | 206 |
| 76.013 | 70 | 3.3 | Continue straight ahead | Ignore turning to the right | SW | 201 |
| 76.014 | 260 | 3.5 | Fork left across the stream and continue on the narrow track | Red and white painted sign | SE | 190 |
| 76.015 | 20 | 3.6 | After crossing the stream take the right fork | | SE | 189 |
| 76.016 | 180 | 3.7 | Take the right fork up the hill | Red and white painted sign | S | 203 |
| 76.017 | 400 | 4.1 | At the T-junction with the small road, at the top of the hill, turn left | Wooden balustrade on left | SE | 252 |
| 76.018 | 30 | 4.2 | Fork left | Avoid stony track on the right | SE | 256 |
| 76.019 | 400 | 4.5 | Turn sharp right | Between the embankments | S | 247 |
| 76.020 | 1200 | 5.8 | At the fork bear right | Red and white painted sign | S | 243 |
| 76.021 | 1000 | 6.7 | Continue straight ahead | Roman road | SW | 173 |
| 76.022 | 500 | 7.2 | Bear left | Following the red and white signs | S | 164 |
| 76.023 | 1100 | 8.3 | At the T-junction with minor road, bear left direction La Valle del Sole. Note:- horse riders should take the Alternate Route to the right to avoid a treacherous pathway and steps | VF sign | S | 140 |
| 76.024 | 40 | 8.4 | Skirt the house and turn right on a gravel track | Red and white painted sign | SW | 140 |

| Waypoint | Distance between waypoints | Total km | Directions | Verification Point | Compass | Altitude m |
|---|---|---|---|---|---|---|
| 76.025 | 50 | 8.4 | Turn right to go between two buildings, then immediately turn left | Red and white painted sign | W | 140 |
| 76.026 | 400 | 8.8 | After a steep ascent and a rough flight of steps, bear left with an old building immediately on the left and a wall on right | Red and white painted sign | W | 129 |
| 76.027 | 60 | 8.9 | Turn left onto the road | Up the hill | SW | 134 |
| 76.028 | 10 | 8.9 | Turn left up the steep narrow track | VF sign | S | 135 |
| 76.029 | 180 | 9.0 | Bear right on track | Red and white painted sign | SW | 144 |
| 76.030 | 220 | 9.3 | Turn left at the T-junction | Private property on the right | S | 150 |
| 76.031 | 150 | 9.4 | Take the right fork | | S | 145 |
| 76.032 | 400 | 9.8 | Take the left fork | | S | 151 |
| 76.033 | 400 | 10.2 | Bear right | In the clearing | SE | 95 |
| 76.034 | 40 | 10.2 | Bear right on the broader track | White house directly on left | SW | 90 |
| 76.035 | 800 | 11.0 | Take the right fork | Red and white painted sign | SW | 86 |
| 76.036 | 250 | 11.2 | Track emerges onto a minor tarmac road – via dei Pini, immediately turn left on the track | Cemetery on right at the junction | SE | 86 |
| 76.037 | 200 | 11.4 | Bear right on the tarmac road | Pass apartment buildings on the left | S | 77 |
| 76.038 | 250 | 11.7 | At the T-junction with the SS62, bear left and briefly follow the main road | Childrens playground on the right at the junction | SE | 75 |
| 76.039 | 80 | 11.8 | At the crossroads turn left on the narrow road | Pass the castle on your right | E | 74 |

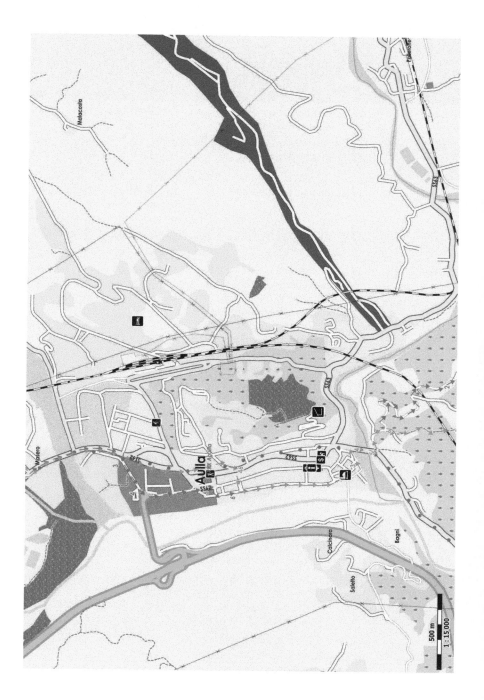

Malacosta

Mozzero

Aulla

Calcinara

Bagni

Saletto

500 m

1 : 15 000

| Waypoint | Distance between waypoints | Total km | Directions | Verification Point | Compass | Altitude m |
|---|---|---|---|---|---|---|
| 76.040 | 70 | 11.8 | Just before the archway, turn right and then left | Pass over the river bridge | SE | 70 |
| 76.041 | 110 | 11.9 | After crossing the bridge turn right on the road | Continue under the power lines | S | 66 |
| 76.042 | 230 | 12.2 | Bear left on the road | Pass building materials store on your left | SE | 64 |
| 76.043 | 180 | 12.3 | At the T-junction, turn right | Shopping street | SW | 67 |
| 76.044 | 170 | 12.5 | At the time of writing it has been proposed to provide an entry to the disused railway directly ahead at the T-junction. Unfortunately we have not been able to verify if this work has been completed. If access is clear then turn left on the old railway. If not then carefully follow the Alternate Route along the main road to the left | Pass through the gap in the trees | S | 66 |
| 76.045 | 1300 | 13.8 | At the road junction, turn right | Towards the church | SW | 64 |
| 76.046 | 90 | 13.9 | At the T-junction, continue straight ahead, climb the short flight of steps and descend into the piazza. Then continue ahead to join the road beside the river | Piazza Giuseppe Mazzini | W | 62 |
| 76.047 | 170 | 14.1 | At the T-junction, turn left. Note:- the Alternate Route via the main road and the industrial zone joins from the right | Keep the river close on your right | S | 56 |
| 76.048 | 700 | 14.8 | Arrive at Aulla (XXX) centre beside Abbazia di San Caprasio | Bridge over the river Magra to your right | | 58 |

Stage Summary: riders route avoiding a flight of steps and a steep descent but at the cost of some additional distance on the main road

Stage Ascent: 68m                          Stage Descent: 133m

| Waypoint | Distance between waypoints | Total km | Directions | Verification Point | Compass | |
|---|---|---|---|---|---|---|
| 76A1.001 | 0 | 0.0 | Take the road to the right | Direction Finoli | NW | 140 |
| 76A1.002 | 1400 | 1.4 | At the T-junction in Fornoli, turn right | Via dell'Ardito | W | 156 |
| 76A1.003 | 90 | 1.5 | At the fork bear left | Via dell'Ara | SW | 158 |
| 76A1.004 | 1600 | 3.1 | At the T-junction with the main road turn left | SS62, via Cisa | S | 87 |
| 76A1.005 | 500 | 3.5 | Turn right | Via Camposagna | S | 87 |
| 76A1.006 | 1200 | 4.7 | Join the Cycle Route from Pontremoli and continue straight ahead to rejoin the "Official Route" beside the castle in the centre of Terrarossa | Direction Aulla, via Nazionale | | 74 |

Stage Summary: Alternate Route to Aulla initially following the SS62

Stage Ascent: 2m                          Stage Descent: 12m

| Waypoint | Distance between waypoints | Total km | Directions | Verification Point | Compass | |
|---|---|---|---|---|---|---|
| 76A2.001 | 0 | 0.0 | At the T-junction, turn left and follow the main road with great care | Direction Massa | S | 66 |
| 76A2.002 | 600 | 0.6 | Shortly after passing a Tabacchi on your left, turn right into a pedestrian tunnel under the railway | VF sign | W | 63 |
| 76A2.003 | 30 | 0.7 | After emerging from the tunnel, turn left onto viale Lunigiana | VF sign | SW | 63 |
| 76A2.004 | 220 | 0.9 | Bear left away from the motorway entrance | Viale Lunigiana | S | 62 |

| Waypoint | Distance between waypoints | Total km | Directions | Verification Point | Compass | |
|---|---|---|---|---|---|---|
| 76A2.005 | 500 | 1.4 | At the major crossroads, turn right and bear left still on viale Lunigiana | VF sign, proceed beside the river | S | 58 |
| 76A2.006 | 220 | 1.6 | At the pedestrian crossing, continue beside the riverside road. Note:- the revised "Official Route" joins from the left | | | 56 |

### Accommodation & Facilities .... Villafranca-in-Lunigiana - Aulla

Castello Malaspina,Via Nazionale Cisa,54019 Terrarossa(MS),Italy; Tel:+39 0187 474942; +39 3289 438652; +39 3398 296074; Price:C

Fortezza "la Brunella",Parco della Brunella,54011 Aulla(MS),Italy; Tel:+39 0187 409077; Email:coopnatur@libero.it; Price:C

Abbazia di San Caprasio,(Don Giovanni Perini),Piazza Abbazia,54011 Aulla(MS),Italy; Tel:+39 0187 420148; +39 3396 380331; Email:cultura@comune.aulla.ms.it; Web-site:www.sancaprasio.it; Price:D

B&B Casa Barani,Via Sprini,54011 Aulla(MS),Italy; Tel:+39 3474 657930; Price:B

Agricamping Ulivetta,Via Molesana,54016 Licciana-Nardi(MS),Italy; Tel:+39 3472 343196

Pro Loco,Piazza Gramsci, 24,54011 Aulla(MS),Italy; Tel:+39 0187 421439

Cassa di Risparmio,Strada Statale della Cisa, 55,54016 Licciana-Nardi(MS),Italy; Tel:+39 0187 421371

Stazione Ferrovie,Piazza Roma, 18,54011 Aulla(MS),Italy; Tel:+39 06 6847 5475; Web-site:www.renitalia.it

Peselli - Studio Medico,Piazza della Vittoria, 7,54011 Aulla(MS),Italy; Tel:+39 0187 495002

Crespo - Studio Veterinario,Via Nazionale, 26,54011 Aulla(MS),Italy; Tel:+39 0187 421967

Bortolasi,Via Nazionale, 196B,54011 Aulla(MS),Italy; Tel:+39 0187 422544

Bi.Ciclo di Petacchi Elisabetta e C.Snc - Ingrosso e Dettaglio Biciclette,Via Cerri,54011 Aulla(MS),Italy; Tel:+39 0187 408020

Taxi Servizio,Piazza Giuseppe Mazzini, 29,54033 Carrara(MS),Italy; Tel:+39 3474 810994

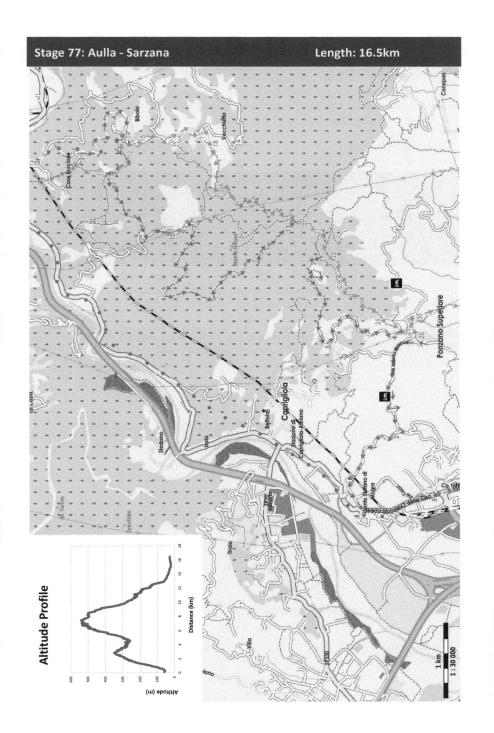

Stage Summary: this is another rugged section over the final ridge before the coastal plain. The Alternate Routes offer options for all groups to bypass the most difficult forest tracks and also to visit Santo Stefano di Magra (XXIX). Sarzana offers a full range of facilities with a frequent train service to La Spezia and the Cinque Terre.

Distance from Vercelli: 335km          Distance to St Peter's Square, Rome: 513km
Stage Ascent: 892m                     Stage Descent: 923m

| Waypoint | Distance between waypoints | Total km | Directions | Verification Point | Compass | Altitude m |
|---|---|---|---|---|---|---|
| 77.001 | 0 | 0.0 | With the bridge over the river Magra behind you and Abbazia di San Caprasio to your left, bear right | Piazza Abazzia, direction La Spezia | SE | 58 |
| 77.002 | 80 | 0.1 | At the T-junction, turn right, pass under the arch and then turn left | Towards the riverside | SE | 59 |
| 77.003 | 50 | 0.1 | At the riverside, turn left, direction Massa and La Spezia | Piazza L. Corbani | NE | 57 |
| 77.004 | 130 | 0.3 | At the T-junction, turn right and cross the river bridge | SS62, direction La Spezia | S | 57 |
| 77.005 | 180 | 0.4 | At the end of the bridge, turn left across a disused railway line and then bear left | Direction Bibola, VF sign | E | 59 |
| 77.006 | 200 | 0.6 | Bear right, uphill and away from the larger road. Note:– the Alternate Route to the left offers a longer but easier option for all groups and is recommended for cyclists and horse-riders | Via Prascara | S | 83 |
| 77.007 | 60 | 0.7 | Bear left on the footpath | Beside the wall | S | 90 |
| 77.008 | 400 | 1.1 | Cross the track and continue ahead up the hill | Beside the vineyard | S | 153 |
| 77.009 | 90 | 1.2 | At the junction with the road turn right and immediately left on the steep footpath | Into the woods | SE | 172 |

| Waypoint | Distance between waypoints | Total km | Directions | Verification Point | Compass | Altitude m |
|---|---|---|---|---|---|---|
| 77.010 | 600 | 1.8 | At the T-junction with the gravel road, turn right | The road makes a sharp left turn | S | 265 |
| 77.011 | 500 | 2.3 | At the crossroads in the clearing, keep left on the gravel road- the Alternate Route crosses the "Official Route" and continues to the right | Uphill towards Bibola | SE | 296 |
| 77.012 | 500 | 2.8 | Approaching the top of the hill take the footpath to the right | | E | 347 |
| 77.013 | 200 | 3.0 | Rejoin the broad track and turn right downhill | Bibola is on the hilltop to the left | E | 335 |
| 77.014 | 90 | 3.1 | Take the next turning to the right and then immediately right again on the gravel road | Pass the bus stop on your left | S | 331 |
| 77.015 | 500 | 3.6 | At the junction, bear right on the tarmac | Towards Vecchietto | S | 298 |
| 77.016 | 900 | 4.5 | Take the right fork into the village of Vecchietto | VF sign, towards bell tower | S | 269 |
| 77.017 | 180 | 4.6 | Turn right under the archway | Red and white stripe sign, via Fontana | W | 260 |
| 77.018 | 140 | 4.8 | On the edge of the village, bear right on the track, beside the olive grove | Climbing into the forest | W | 270 |
| 77.019 | 1000 | 5.7 | Take the steep footpath to the right | In the clearing | SW | 387 |
| 77.020 | 1600 | 7.3 | At the crossroads continue straight ahead on the forest track – the Alternate Route joins from the right | At the top of the hill | S | 537 |

| Waypoint | Distance between waypoints | Total km | Directions | Verification Point | Compass | Altitude m |
|---|---|---|---|---|---|---|
| 77.021 | 400 | 7.7 | Continue straight ahead. Note:- the turning to the left leads to a viewpoint overlooking La Spezia and the coast | | W | 519 |
| 77.022 | 400 | 8.1 | Continue straight ahead on the narrow track - the descent on the "Official Route" is over broken ground and is unsuitable for bikes and difficult for horses. The Alternate Route leaves to the right and descends on a broader easier track | | SW | 495 |
| 77.023 | 500 | 8.6 | Continue straight ahead down a narrow track | VF sign direction Sarzana | W | 489 |
| 77.024 | 130 | 8.7 | Fork left | | SW | 463 |
| 77.025 | 700 | 9.4 | At the junction, continue straight ahead | Between olive groves towards the village | S | 358 |
| 77.026 | 220 | 9.7 | Turn right onto a small tarmac road | Downhill | SW | 318 |
| 77.027 | 90 | 9.7 | Turn left | Enter Ponzano Superiore | S | 306 |
| 77.028 | 190 | 9.9 | Turn left in piazza Aia di Croce direction Sarzana - the pathway ahead has narrow sections over rough ground with steep descents and bypasses Santo Stefano di Magra (XXIX). Cyclists and those wishing to visit Santo Stefano should bear right on the Alternate Route | Via Cesare Orsini | NE | 284 |
| 77.029 | 50 | 10.0 | The road becomes a grassy track following the line of the ridge | Red and white stripe sign | E | 283 |

| Waypoint | Distance between waypoints | Total km | Directions | Verification Point | Compass | Altitude m |
|---|---|---|---|---|---|---|
| 77.030 | 240 | 10.2 | Turn right onto a minor road and proceed downhill on via Cattarello | Red and white stripe sign | S | 266 |
| 77.031 | 1300 | 11.5 | Fork right | Up the hill | S | 196 |
| 77.032 | 290 | 11.8 | Bear right at the top of the hill | Archaeological dig site | S | 188 |
| 77.033 | 80 | 11.9 | After passing the archaeological site, bear right | Down the hill | S | 185 |
| 77.034 | 800 | 12.7 | Take the lower track to the left | Red and white stripe sign | S | 107 |
| 77.035 | 200 | 12.8 | Turn left onto the small tarmac road | | S | 68 |
| 77.036 | 50 | 12.9 | Turn left at the T-junction | Via Lago | E | 62 |
| 77.037 | 130 | 13.0 | In the valley turn right at the T-junction, direction Sarzana | Red and white stripe sign, via Falcinello | S | 57 |
| 77.038 | 1500 | 14.5 | After crossing a small bridge, turn left at the crossroads - the Alternate Route rejoins from the right | Bar and shop on the left, VF sign | SE | 28 |
| 77.039 | 170 | 14.7 | Turn right on via Turi | Apartments on your right | SW | 27 |
| 77.040 | 600 | 15.3 | At the crossroads, turn left | Via Cisa, VF sign | SE | 20 |
| 77.041 | 700 | 16.0 | Go straight ahead to enter Sarzana old town | Pass through Porta Parma | SE | 24 |
| 77.042 | 500 | 16.5 | Arrive at Sarzana centre | Beside the church of Santa Maria | | 27 |

Stage Summary: an easier route suitable for cyclists and horse-riders taking a quiet road to Bibola and then broad gravel tracks over the ridge.

Stage Ascent: 960m      Stage Descent: 511m

| Waypoint | Distance between waypoints | Total km | Directions | Verification Point | Compass | |
|---|---|---|---|---|---|---|
| 77A1.001 | 0 | 0.0 | Bear left on the road over a small bridge | Direction Bibola | SE | 88 |
| 77A1.002 | 1100 | 1.0 | Fork right up the hill | Woodland to the right | S | 172 |
| 77A1.003 | 800 | 1.8 | Remain on the road to Bibola | Pass VF sign | SE | 236 |
| 77A1.004 | 1200 | 3.0 | Fork right on the road | Direction Bibola | W | 290 |
| 77A1.005 | 400 | 3.4 | Turn right at the top of the hill in the direction of Bibola centre | VF sign | N | 329 |
| 77A1.006 | 40 | 3.4 | At T-junction turn left | Away from the hill-top centre of Bibola | W | 332 |
| 77A1.007 | 90 | 3.5 | Bear right onto the gravel track | VF sign | NW | 335 |
| 77A1.008 | 900 | 4.3 | At the junction take the first track on the left | | SW | 299 |
| 77A1.009 | 1100 | 5.4 | Turn left onto a minor road and proceed uphill | Towards the quarry | S | 343 |
| 77A1.010 | 700 | 6.1 | Bear right on the gravel track | Quarry entrance on your left | SE | 416 |
| 77A1.011 | 230 | 6.3 | At fork bear right | Away from quarry | W | 453 |
| 77A1.012 | 60 | 6.4 | At T-junction turn right | | S | 451 |
| 77A1.013 | 3900 | 10.3 | At the crossroads in the tracks, rejoin the "Official Route" and turn right | | | 536 |

## Alternate Route #77.A2 — Length: 3.5km

Stage Summary: the route allows cyclists and riders to avoid a difficult descent in the forest.

Stage Ascent: 115m          Stage Descent: 297m

| Waypoint | Distance between waypoints | Total km | Directions | Verification Point | Compass | |
|---|---|---|---|---|---|---|
| 77A2.001 | 0 | 0.0 | Turn right | | N | 490 |
| 77A2.002 | 90 | 0.1 | At the junction, bear right | | W | 465 |
| 77A2.003 | 2000 | 2.1 | Take the left fork | Pass la Volpara restaurant - provides excellent regional food | S | 325 |
| 77A2.004 | 1400 | 3.5 | At the junction, rejoin the "Official Route" and turn right | Into the village of Ponzano Superiore | | 309 |

## Alternate Route #77.A3 — Length: 9.6km

Stage Summary: route for cyclists and those wishing to visit Santo Stefano di Magra (XXIX). The route includes approximately 3km on the busy SP62

Stage Ascent: 75m          Stage Descent: 332m

| Waypoint | Distance between waypoints | Total km | Directions | Verification Point | Compass | |
|---|---|---|---|---|---|---|
| 77A3.001 | 0 | 0.0 | In piazza Aia di Croce bear right on the road | Proceed down the hill on via Antonio Gramsci | W | 285 |
| 77A3.002 | 2000 | 2.0 | 400 metres after third right-hand hairpin turn sharp right leaving the road. | Via Brigate Alpine | NW | 146 |
| 77A3.003 | 1400 | 3.5 | At the T-junction at the entry to Santo Stefano di Magra (XXIX), turn left | Via Roma | SW | 56 |
| 77A3.004 | 290 | 3.7 | At the T-junction, turn left | SP62, via Cisa Sud | S | 53 |
| 77A3.005 | 1100 | 4.8 | At the roundabout, continue straight ahead | SP62, via Cisa Sud | S | 26 |

| Waypoint | Distance between waypoints | Total km | Directions | Verification Point | Compass | |
|---|---|---|---|---|---|---|
| 77A3.006 | 1200 | 6.0 | At broad junction in Ponzano Magra bear right on the smaller road | Via Cisa Vecchio | S | 25 |
| 77A3.007 | 300 | 6.4 | After passing under the railway, join via Seconda Piano Vezzano and proceed straight ahead | Keep railway to the left | SE | 22 |
| 77A3.008 | 1600 | 8.0 | At the mini-roundabout, turn left, cross the railway and immediately turn right at the roundabout | Rejoin SS62 | SE | 18 |
| 77A3.009 | 140 | 8.1 | With a bridge over the road ahead, bear left to leave the main road | Uphill | S | 21 |
| 77A3.010 | 400 | 8.5 | At the T-junction with the SS62, turn left | Enter Sarzana | S | 20 |
| 77A3.011 | 270 | 8.8 | At the fork, bear left on the small road | Via San Gottardo | E | 16 |
| 77A3.012 | 800 | 9.6 | At the crossroads, continue straight ahead and rejoin the "Official Route" | Bar ahead on the left | | 28 |

## Accommodation & Facilities .... Aulla - Sarzana

Convento San Francesco D'assisi,(Don Renzo Cortese),Via Agostino Paci, 9,19038 Sarzana(SP),Italy; Tel:+39 0187 620356; Price:D

Hotel la Trigola,Via Antonio Gramsci, 63,19037 Santo-Stefano-di-Magra(SP),Italy; Tel:+39 0187 630292; Price:B

B&B - la Costa Bed,Via Mario Baria, 11,19037 Santo-Stefano-di-Magra(SP),Italy; Tel:+39 0187 630037; +39 3339 999870; Email:miria.giannoni@libero.it; Web-site:www.bblacosta.it; Price:B

Albergo la Villetta,Via Sobborgo Emiliano, 24a,19038 Sarzana(SP),Italy; Tel:+39 0187 620195; Email:info@albergolavilletta.it; Web-site:www.albergolavilletta.it; Price:A

B&B - il viale,Viale Giuseppe Mazzini, 75,19038 Sarzana(SP),Italy; Tel:+39 0187 610866; +39 3337 705145; Email:info@ilvialedivaleria.it; Web-site:www.ilvialedivaleria.it; Price:B

River Ranch Sarzana,Via Navonella,19038 Sarzana(SP),Italy; +39 3382 979071

Comune di Sarzana,Via Antonio Bertoloni, 1,19038 Sarzana(SP),Italy; Tel:+39 0187 614300

Unicredit Banca,Via Sobborgo Emiliano, 32,19038 Sarzana(SP),Italy; Tel:+39 0187 029411; Web-site:www.unicreditbanca.it/?ucid=LEC-GMAP_163

Stazione Ferrovie,Piazza Guido Jurgens, 20,19038 Sarzana(SP),Italy; Tel:+39 06 6847 5475; Web-site:www.renitalia.it

Presidio Ospedaliero San Bartolomeo,Via Cisa,19038 Sarzana(SP),Italy; Tel:+39 0187 6041

Battistini - Studio Medico,Via Domenico Fiasella, 30,19038 Sarzana(SP),Italy; Tel:+39 0187 622138

Studio Medico Veterinario,Via Paganino Da Sarzana,19038 Sarzana(SP),Italy; Tel:+39 0187 621726

Alberti,Via Circonvallazione, 10,19038 Sarzana(SP),Italy; Tel:+39 0187 627387

Bike Station Srl,Via Cisa, 142,19038 Sarzana(SP),Italy; Tel:+39 0187 916668

Taxi,Piazza Cesare Battisti,19038 Sarzana(SP),Italy; Tel:+39 0187 967303

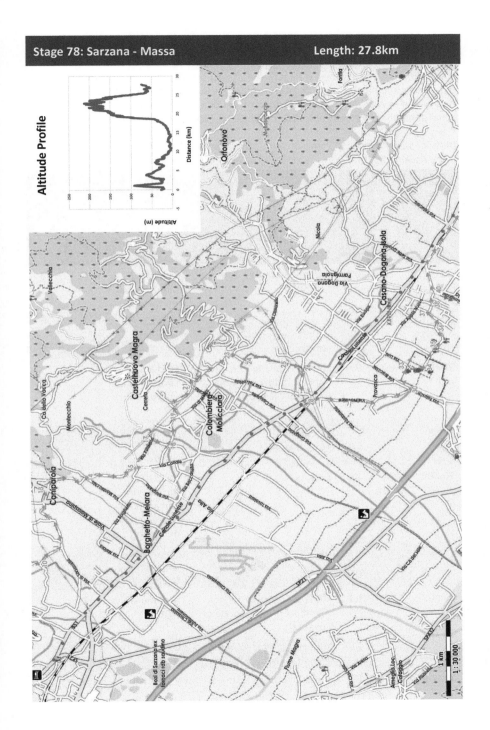

Stage 78: Sarzana - Massa

Length: 27.8km

Altitude Profile

144

Stage Summary: this section is largely undertaken on suburban roads before climbing onto tracks and narrow roads through the vineyards. The Alternate Route from Luni to Pietrasanta provides an opportunity to stroll beside the Mediterranean beaches, avoids some dangerous stretches of road and reduces the total distance to Pietrasanta.

Distance from Vercelli: 352km      Distance to St Peter's Square, Rome: 497km
Stage Ascent: 807m            Stage Descent: 760m

| Waypoint | Distance between waypoints | Total km | Directions | Verification Point | Compass | Altitude m |
|---|---|---|---|---|---|---|
| 78.001 | 0 | 0.0 | Continue along via Giuseppe Mazzini | Church of Santa Maria on the left | SE | 27 |
| 78.002 | 250 | 0.2 | At the roundabout, turn left on the narrow via San Francesco | Pass bar on your right | N | 20 |
| 78.003 | 400 | 0.6 | Shortly after the road bends to the left, turn right on the small road towards the hillside | Pass a small shrine in the wall on your left | E | 23 |
| 78.004 | 50 | 0.7 | Bear right on the track | Towards the fortress on the hilltop | NE | 25 |
| 78.005 | 400 | 1.0 | Bear right | Keep the fortress of Sarzanello immediately on the left | E | 83 |
| 78.006 | 90 | 1.1 | Turn left on the cobbled road | Continue to skirt the fortress | NE | 92 |
| 78.007 | 130 | 1.2 | At the junction, turn right downhill on via Montata di Sarzanello | Red and white sign | E | 78 |
| 78.008 | 600 | 1.8 | At the Stop sign, continue straight ahead | Over the bridge | SE | 25 |
| 78.009 | 120 | 1.9 | At the T-junction bear left | Via Canalburo | SE | 24 |

| Waypoint | Distance between waypoints | Total km | Directions | Verification Point | Compass | Altitude m |
|---|---|---|---|---|---|---|
| 78.010 | 800 | 2.7 | Bear left and remain on via Canalburo | Ignore turning to the right with bridge over the road | SE | 20 |
| 78.011 | 400 | 3.1 | At the T-junction, turn left | Red and white sign and bus stop (Fermata) on the left | E | 43 |
| 78.012 | 800 | 3.9 | At the complex junction continue straight ahead on via Caniparola | Pass small parking area on your left | E | 63 |
| 78.013 | 160 | 4.0 | On the apex of a bend to the left continue straight ahead on the small road | Pass an archway on your right | S | 61 |
| 78.014 | 700 | 4.7 | At the T-junction, turn right and then immediately left on via Montecchio and enter Colombiera | Olive grove on the left at the junction | S | 46 |
| 78.015 | 800 | 5.4 | At the crossroads turn left on via Provinciale | Direction Castellnuovo Magra - Centro Historico | E | 30 |
| 78.016 | 100 | 5.5 | Turn right on via Paradiso | Red and white sign, electricity sub-station on the right | SE | 29 |
| 78.017 | 400 | 5.9 | Turn right on via Bologna | Red and white sign | SW | 28 |
| 78.018 | 230 | 6.1 | At the crossroads, turn left | Towards parking area and dyke | E | 22 |
| 78.019 | 500 | 6.6 | At the next crossroads, turn left | Beside school, red and white sign | NE | 25 |
| 78.020 | 220 | 6.8 | At the crossroads turn right | Via Pedemontana, red and white sign | SE | 37 |

| Waypoint | Distance between waypoints | Total km | Directions | Verification Point | Compass | Altitude m |
|---|---|---|---|---|---|---|
| 78.021 | 400 | 7.2 | At the Stop sign, continue straight ahead on via Molino del Piano | Pharmacy on your right | E | 40 |
| 78.022 | 90 | 7.3 | At the crossroads, turn right on via Olmarello | Road bears left after the turn | SE | 39 |
| 78.023 | 700 | 8.0 | Turn right on the narrow via Corta | Red and white sign | SW | 28 |
| 78.024 | 160 | 8.1 | Immediately after crossing the water channel, turn left on the grass track | Keep the waterway on your left | S | 20 |
| 78.025 | 700 | 8.8 | At the road junction, continue straight ahead on the grass track | Bridge on the left | S | 20 |
| 78.026 | 170 | 9.0 | At the next road junction, turn right | Enter Palvotrisia | W | 19 |
| 78.027 | 400 | 9.4 | At the Stop sign, continue straight ahead | No through road | W | 10 |
| 78.028 | 110 | 9.5 | At the T-junction with the very busy via Aurelia, cross the pedestrian crossing and turn left.  Continue with care on the right hand side of the road | Towards traffic lights | SE | 9 |
| 78.029 | 110 | 9.6 | Beside the traffic lights, turn right and pass under the railway | Red and white sign, via Provasco | S | 9 |
| 78.030 | 1300 | 10.9 | At the crossroads with the main road continue straight ahead | Towards the archaeological site of Luni (XXVIII) | SE | 1 |
| 78.031 | 80 | 11.0 | At the entrance to the site, turn left and follow the path around the site | Keep the site on the right | NE | 2 |
| 78.032 | 190 | 11.2 | At the end of the fence turn right | Keep the site on the right | SE | 5 |
| 78.033 | 230 | 11.4 | Cross via Luni and take the footpath ahead and slightly to the right | Footpath quickly turns right | S | 7 |

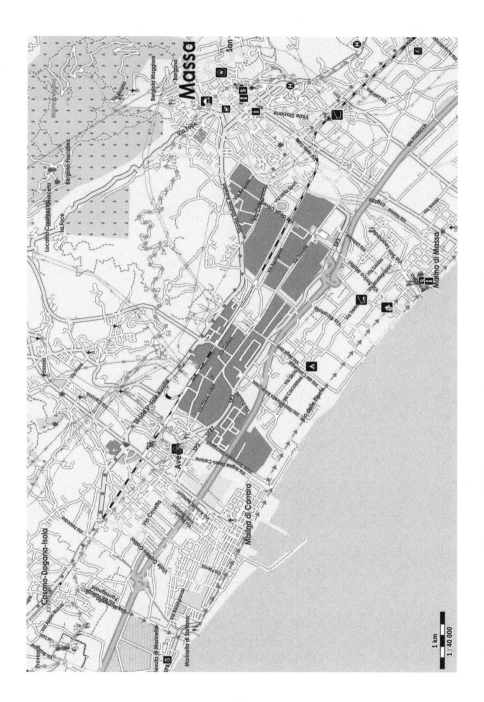

| Waypoint | Distance between waypoints | Total km | Directions | Verification Point | Compass | Altitude m |
|---|---|---|---|---|---|---|
| 78.034 | 260 | 11.6 | Turn left on the road | Via Appia | SE | 4 |
| 78.035 | 400 | 12.0 | Continue straight ahead | Luni amphitheatre on the left | E | 3 |
| 78.036 | 270 | 12.3 | Take the right fork | Via Appia | NE | 5 |
| 78.037 | 260 | 12.6 | Turn right on via Marina | Red and white sign | E | 9 |
| 78.038 | 140 | 12.7 | At the crossroads, continue straight ahead | No Entry sign | E | 10 |
| 78.039 | 150 | 12.8 | At the T-junction, cross the road and take the footbridge. Note: - to join the Alternate Route beside the sea, turn right | Red and white sign | E | 8 |
| 78.040 | 50 | 12.9 | Bear left on the road on via del Parmignola | Beside the waterway and then the railway track | E | 9 |
| 78.041 | 1400 | 14.2 | At the crossroads continue straight ahead | Railway bridge on the left | SE | 5 |
| 78.042 | 1300 | 15.6 | At the roundabout, continue straight ahead | Via Giovan-Pietro, pass bar on the right | SE | 10 |
| 78.043 | 600 | 16.1 | After passing the fortress on your left, immediately turn left | Pass through the arch | NE | 10 |
| 78.044 | 60 | 16.2 | At the T-junction, turn left | | NW | 11 |
| 78.045 | 70 | 16.2 | At the end of the road, turn right on Via Colombera | No Entry sign | NE | 12 |
| 78.046 | 500 | 16.7 | At the T-junction, turn left | Over the level crossing | NE | 14 |
| 78.047 | 160 | 16.9 | At the crossroads, turn right | Marble yard on the right | NE | 16 |
| 78.048 | 400 | 17.3 | At the traffic lights, continue straight ahead | Tyre store on the left | NE | 21 |

| Waypoint | Distance between waypoints | Total km | Directions | Verification Point | Compass | Altitude m |
|---|---|---|---|---|---|---|
| 78.049 | 600 | 17.8 | At the roundabout, cross the via Provinciale Nazzano and continue straight ahead | Direction Bonascola | NE | 28 |
| 78.050 | 150 | 18.0 | Turn right uphill | Via Forma Bassa | SE | 32 |
| 78.051 | 700 | 18.7 | Continue straight ahead on the track | | SE | 51 |
| 78.052 | 240 | 18.9 | Turn right | Into the woods | W | 97 |
| 78.053 | 130 | 19.0 | Turn left | Towards the farm | SW | 94 |
| 78.054 | 40 | 19.1 | Turn left beside the farm and then left again uphill | Towards the electricity pylon and between the vines | NE | 99 |
| 78.055 | 400 | 19.5 | At the top of the ridge turn right on the road, via Forma Alta | Vines on the right | SE | 122 |
| 78.056 | 270 | 19.7 | At the road junction, continue straight ahead | Metal fence and vines to the right | SE | 144 |
| 78.057 | 50 | 19.8 | At top of the hill, turn left on the narrow road | Along the ridge | E | 147 |
| 78.058 | 700 | 20.5 | Bear left | Quarry on the right | NE | 150 |
| 78.059 | 500 | 20.9 | Bear right on the white road, via dell'Uva | Between the vines | E | 175 |
| 78.060 | 1200 | 22.1 | Beside the restaurant, turn sharp left, uphill | Via dell'Uva | E | 170 |
| 78.061 | 3300 | 25.4 | At the end of the road, turn sharp right | | SE | 69 |
| 78.062 | 110 | 25.5 | Cross the main road and take the smaller road opposite | Via Ponte del Vescovo, No Entry | E | 65 |
| 78.063 | 150 | 25.7 | At the T-junction, turn left into piazza della Libertà and then immediately right | Via San Vitale | SE | 65 |

| Waypoint | Distance between waypoints | Total km | Directions | Verification Point | Compass | Altitude m |
|---|---|---|---|---|---|---|
| 78.064 | 600 | 26.3 | At the T-junction with the main road, turn right | Via Foce, Mirteto sign on the left | SE | 63 |
| 78.065 | 140 | 26.4 | Turn left, opposite the pharmacy | Direction Lavacchio, via Frangola | NE | 63 |
| 78.066 | 70 | 26.5 | Take the first turning to the right | Via Ortola | SE | 67 |
| 78.067 | 190 | 26.7 | Turn left and then right | Take the bridge over the stream | SE | 61 |
| 78.068 | 180 | 26.9 | At the T-junction turn left | Keep the river on the right | NE | 52 |
| 78.069 | 80 | 27.0 | Turn right over the bridge | Continue on via Ponte Vecchio | S | 57 |
| 78.070 | 220 | 27.2 | Bear right and immediately take the left fork | Via Palestro towards the centre of Massa | SE | 60 |
| 78.071 | 500 | 27.7 | At the mini roundabout continue straight ahead on via Cavour | No Entry sign, Seminary on the left | SW | 71 |
| 78.072 | 50 | 27.7 | Turn left | Towards the Duomo | S | 72 |
| 78.073 | 60 | 27.8 | Arrive at Massa centre | Beside the Duomo | | 73 |

Stage Summary: the shorter route, by 6.5km, to Pietrasanta, provides relief from further climbs and descents by following the broad promenade beside the Mediterranean before turning inland on the cycle track to find the centre of Pietrasanta. It is easy going for cyclists and riders. There are numerous camp sites, hotels and restaurants beside the route.

Stage Ascent: 150m                    Stage Descent: 147m

| Waypoint | Distance between waypoints | Total km | Directions | Verification Point | Compass | Altitude m |
|---|---|---|---|---|---|---|
| 78A1.001 | 0 | 0.0 | At the T-junction, turn right on via del Parmignola | Towards Autostrada | SW | 8 |
| 78A1.002 | 1900 | 1.9 | At the crossroads, turn left towards the sea | Via della Repubblica | S | 3 |
| 78A1.003 | 120 | 2.0 | At the T-junction with the main road, turn left on the road | Cross the waterways on the SP432 and enter Marina di Carrara | SE | 3 |
| 78A1.004 | 3300 | 5.3 | After passing through Marina di Carrara, bear left to turn inland and remain on the main road | Viale delle Pinete, coast road dead ends at a boat marina | SE | 3 |
| 78A1.005 | 4000 | 9.3 | At the roundabout, turn right towards the sea | Via Casola, direction Viareggio | SW | 2 |
| 78A1.006 | 230 | 9.5 | Turn left, continue with sea on right | Pass through Marina di Massa | SE | 0 |
| 78A1.007 | 1500 | 11.0 | At the roundabout continue straight ahead. Note:- to regain the "Official Route" in Massa centre turn left and follow viale Roma | Direction Forte dei Marmi | SE | 1 |
| 78A1.012 | 1400 | 24.0 | At the traffic lights, take the pedestrian crossing and continue straight ahead on the cycle track | Tree lined road towards the hills | NE | 9 |

| Waypoint | Distance between waypoints | Total km | Directions | Verification Point | Compass | Altitude m |
|---|---|---|---|---|---|---|
| 78A1.013 | 700 | 24.7 | At the T-junction turn left on the cycle track | Direction Seravezza, pass commercial centre on the left | NW | 9 |
| 78A1.014 | 260 | 24.9 | At the roundabout take the cycle track beside the first exit and pass under the railway | Via Vincenzo Santini, direction Pietrasanta centre | N | 7 |
| 78A1.015 | 270 | 25.2 | At the T-junction turn right to join the "Official Route" | Via Marconi | | 10 |

### Accommodation & Facilities ....    Sarzana - Massa

Casa di Accoglienza Caritas,Via Godola, 5,54100 Massa(MS),Italy; Tel:+39 0585 792909; +39 3395 829566; Email:buragino@tin.it; Price:D

Parrocchia Borgo Ponte,Via San Martino, 1,54100 Massa(MS),Italy; Tel:+39 0585 42282; Email:info@sanmartinoalborgo.org; Web-site:www.sanmartinoalborgo.org

Parrocchia San Pietro Apostolo,Piazza Finelli,54033 Carrara(MS),Italy; Tel:+39 0585 857203; +39 3388 333413; Email:alpi500@interfree.it; Price:D

Convento Cappuccini,Piazza San Francesco, 3,54100 Massa(MS),Italy; Tel:+39 9058 542181; Price:D

Camping Luni,Via Luni, 16,54100 Marina-di-Massa(MS),Italy; Tel:+39 0585 869278; +39 3388 330366; Web-site:www.campingluni.com; Price:C

Centro Ippico il Falco,Viale 25 Aprile,19038 Sarzana(SP),Italy; Tel:+39 3334 703446

Comune di Massa,Piazza del Teatro, 1,54100 Massa(MS),Italy; Tel:+39 0585 8811

Banca Monte dei Paschi di Siena,Via della Chiesa, 16,19038 Sarzana(SP),Italy; Tel:+39 0187 649775

Banca di Roma,Piazza Aranci,54100 Massa(MS),Italy; Tel:+39 0585 811574

## Accommodation & Facilities  ....  Sarzana - Massa

**$** Banca Monte dei Paschi di Siena,Via Roma, 77,54038 Montignoso(MS),Italy;
Tel:+39 0585 349400

🚉 Stazione Ferrovie,Piazza 4 Novembre, 32,54100 Massa(MS),Italy;
Tel:+39 06 6847 5475; Web-site:www.renitalia.it

**H** Ospedale Generale,Via Carlo Orecchia,54100 Massa(MS),Italy;
Tel:+39 0585 4931; Web-site:www.usl1.toscana.it

**H** Ospedale,Via Aurelia Sud,54100 Montepepe(MS),Italy; Tel:+39 0585 493617;
Web-site:www.ftgm.it

➕ Beeli - Ambulatorio Medico,Piazza Mercurio,54100 Massa(MS),Italy;
Tel:+39 0585 41137

🐕 Busti - Ambulatorio Veterinari,Via dei Margini, 3,54100 Massa(MS),Italy;
Tel:+39 0585 47531

🥾 Articoli Sportivi,Via Giovanni Pascoli, 5,54100 Massa(MS),Italy;
Tel:+39 0585 40914

🚲 Brewo Srl,Via Azeglio Petracci, 13,54038 Montignoso(MS),Italy;
Tel:+39 0585 821296

📞 Andreani Massimo,Stazione Ferroviaria,54033 Carrara(MS),Italy;
Tel:+39 3292 175809

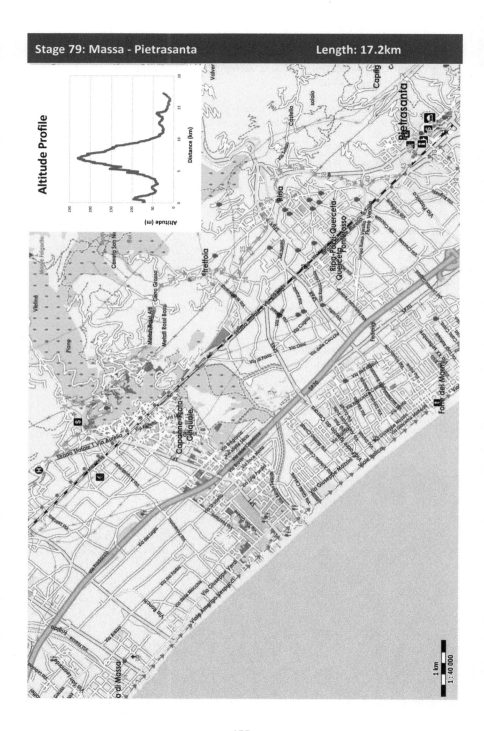

Altitude Profile

Altitude (m)

Distance (km)

1 km

1 : 40 000

Stage Summary: the route leaves Massa on the very busy via Aurelia, before returning to narrow hillside roads and then descending to the industrial zone for the entry to the attractive town of Pietrasanta.

Distance from Vercelli: 380km      Distance to St Peter's Square, Rome: 469km
Stage Ascent: 394m          Stage Descent: 444m

| Waypoint | Distance between waypoints | Total km | Directions | Verification Point | Compass | Altitude m |
|---|---|---|---|---|---|---|
| 79.001 | 0 | 0.0 | With the Duomo behind go straight ahead on via Dante Alighieri | Towards piazza Aranci | SW | 73 |
| 79.002 | 120 | 0.1 | At the entranc to piazza Aranci, turn left | Trees and obelisk on the right | SE | 69 |
| 79.003 | 90 | 0.2 | At the exit from the piazza, bear left and immediately right | Keep the palazzo immediately on you right | S | 72 |
| 79.004 | 160 | 0.4 | Keep to the left side of piazza Mercurio and turn left to climb the steps. Note:- to avoid the steps continue straight ahead on via Mario Bigini and via Prado | Via Bigini on the right | NE | 71 |
| 79.005 | 30 | 0.4 | At the T-junction with the road, turn right | Via Piastronata | SE | 74 |
| 79.006 | 160 | 0.5 | Beside Chiesa della Madonna del Carmine, bear right on via Santa Chiara | Keep Castello Malaspina high on your left | S | 93 |
| 79.007 | 500 | 1.0 | At the T-junction, turn left on the small road | Via Grondini | SE | 76 |
| 79.008 | 30 | 1.1 | At the T-junction with the larger road, turn right | Via del Bargello | SW | 76 |
| 79.009 | 190 | 1.3 | At the crossroads turn left and proceed with caution on the pavement beside the main road | Pizzeria on the left | S | 59 |

| Waypoint | Distance between waypoints | Total km | Directions | Verification Point | Compass | Altitude m |
|---|---|---|---|---|---|---|
| 79.010 | 210 | 1.5 | Take the left fork | Remain beside the main road | SE | 49 |
| 79.011 | 1500 | 3.0 | After passing the hospital on the left, bear left away from the via Aurelia | Via Carlo Sforza, No Entry | SE | 37 |
| 79.012 | 800 | 3.7 | At the end of the road, turn left | Concrete wall ahead, No Entry sign | NE | 44 |
| 79.013 | 500 | 4.2 | Turn right across the road and then left | Car park on the left, river immediately to your right | NE | 68 |
| 79.014 | 160 | 4.4 | Cross the footbridge and turn left. Note:- horse-riders should take the road bridge 150m ahead | Via Bottaccio | E | 73 |
| 79.015 | 160 | 4.5 | At the end of the road turn right up the hill on via Patatina | Pass Fortezza Aghinolfi on the hilltop | S | 87 |
| 79.016 | 2500 | 7.0 | Keep right on the road | Avoid the left fork | SE | 230 |
| 79.017 | 2500 | 9.5 | Continue straight ahead on the road | Pass the hotel on your left | SE | 83 |
| 79.018 | 130 | 9.7 | Just before the road bends to the left, turn right on the small road | Via Riccio | S | 78 |
| 79.019 | 90 | 9.8 | At the junction at the end of the road, turn right | Bar beside the junction | NW | 67 |
| 79.020 | 80 | 9.8 | Just before reaching the bridge, turn left | Via della Chiesa | S | 65 |
| 79.021 | 270 | 10.1 | Keep right | Pass the church on your left | S | 53 |
| 79.022 | 70 | 10.2 | After passing the church grounds, turn left on the small road | Via SS Ippolito e Cassiano | SE | 49 |
| 79.023 | 400 | 10.6 | At the T-junction, turn right | Via Risciolo | SW | 33 |

| Waypoint | Distance between waypoints | Total km | Directions | Verification Point | Compass | Altitude m |
|---|---|---|---|---|---|---|
| 79.024 | 500 | 11.1 | At the T-junction, turn left on via Romana | Pass a small shrine on your right | E | 25 |
| 79.025 | 600 | 11.7 | Keep right on via Romana | Avoid via del Pergolene on the left | SE | 24 |
| 79.026 | 600 | 12.3 | At the Stop sign, turn right and then immediately left at the traffic lights | Direction Seravezza | NE | 32 |
| 79.027 | 210 | 12.5 | At the crossroads, continue straight ahead | Via A. De Gaspari | NE | 34 |
| 79.028 | 50 | 12.5 | Turn right on via Rinascita | Pass gelataria on your left | SE | 35 |
| 79.029 | 60 | 12.6 | At the crossroads turn left | Towards the church | NE | 35 |
| 79.030 | 100 | 12.7 | At the crossroads beside the church, turn right | Via G. Alessandrini | S | 34 |
| 79.031 | 240 | 12.9 | At the traffic lights bear left with great care on the walled road | Keep river on your left | SE | 29 |
| 79.032 | 120 | 13.1 | Continue straight ahead | Take the bridge over the river | E | 29 |
| 79.033 | 400 | 13.5 | At the Stop sign, turn right on the road | Church on your left | SE | 28 |
| 79.034 | 70 | 13.5 | Take the next turning to the left | Direction Solaio | NE | 26 |
| 79.035 | 130 | 13.7 | At the crossroads turn right | Narrow bridge | S | 33 |
| 79.036 | 180 | 13.8 | Facing the water fountain, turn right | Via Pozzone | S | 37 |
| 79.037 | 240 | 14.1 | Take the right fork | Via Pozzone | SW | 39 |
| 79.038 | 400 | 14.4 | Cross the SP8 and take the grass track beside the river | River on the right | S | 21 |
| 79.039 | 700 | 15.1 | Bear left and descend from the river-side track | Pass beside a Marble depot | SE | 15 |

| Waypoint | Distance between waypoints | Total km | Directions | Verification Point | Compass | Altitude m |
|---|---|---|---|---|---|---|
| 79.040 | 150 | 15.2 | At the T-junction, turn right | Towards the river and electricity pylon | SW | 14 |
| 79.041 | 190 | 15.4 | Turn left on via Torraccia | Pass a wood yard on the right | SE | 12 |
| 79.042 | 400 | 15.8 | At the junction, continue straight ahead | Via Torracia | SE | 12 |
| 79.043 | 600 | 16.3 | Bear left beside the road | Away from railway | E | 9 |
| 79.044 | 110 | 16.4 | At the major junction, continue straight ahead on the cycle track beside the road. The coastal Alternate Route joins from the right | Via Marconi | E | 9 |
| 79.045 | 400 | 16.8 | Continue straight ahead | Direction Centro | E | 15 |
| 79.046 | 0 | 16.8 | In piazza Matteotti bear slightly right towards the centre of Pietrasanta | Pass gladiator sculpture on your left | SE | 15 |
| 79.047 | 80 | 16.9 | Continue straight ahead | Car park on your left | SE | 16 |
| 79.048 | 50 | 16.9 | Continue straight ahead into the pedestrian zone | Pass mirrored sculpture, via Mazzini | SE | 17 |
| 79.049 | 300 | 17.2 | Arrive at Pietrasanta centre | Piazza Duomo | | 24 |

Casa Diocesana "la Rocca",(Sour Irene),Via della Rocca,55045 Pietrasanta(LU),Italy; Tel:+39 0584 793093; +39 0584 793095; Email:casarocca@tiscali.it; Price:C

Oratorio il Colosseo,Via Pietro Tabarrani, 26,55041 Camaiore(LU),Italy; Tel:+39 3358 025290; +39 3391 832857; Price:D

Ostello Turimar,Via Bondano, 64,54100 Massa(MS),Italy; Tel:+39 0585 243282; Email:info@ostelloturimar.com; Web-site:www.ostelloturimar.com; Price:B

Locanda - le Monache,Piazza 29 Maggio, 36,55041 Camaiore(LU),Italy; Tel:+39 0584 984282; +39 0584 989258; +39 3391 976565; Email:info@lemonache.com; Web-site:www.lemonache.com; Price:A

Campeggio Citta' di Massa,Via delle Pinete, 136,54100 Massa(MS),Italy; Tel:+39 0585 869361; Email:info@cittadimassa.com; Web-site:www. cittadimassa.it; Price:C; Note:Mobile homes and bungalows also available,

Agenzia Per il Turismo,Lungomare Vespucci, 24,54100 Massa(MS),Italy; Tel:+39 0585 240063

Comune di Pietrasanta,Piazza Matteotti, 29,55045 Pietrasanta(LU),Italy; Tel:+39 0584 7951

Ufficio Turistico,Viale Achille Franceschi, 8,55042 Forte-dei-Marmi(LU),Italy; Tel:+39 0584 80091

Comune di Camaiore,Piazza San Bernardino, 1,55041 Camaiore(LU),Italy; Tel:+39 0584 9860

Cassa di Risparmio di Lucca,Piazza Betti,54100 Massa(MS),Italy; Tel:+39 0585 244045

Banca di Credito Cooperativo della Versilia,Via Giuseppe Mazzini,55045 Pietrasanta(LU),Italy; Tel:+39 0584 72110; Web-site:www.bccversilia.it

Banca Monte dei Paschi di Siena,Via Giosuè Carducci, 25,55042 Forte-dei-Marmi(LU),Italy; Tel:+39 0584 78351

Banca Versilia Lunigiana e Garfagnana,Piazza,23814 29-Maggio-27(LC),Italy; Tel:+39 0584 984857; Web-site:www.bccversilia.it

Stazione Ferrovie,Piazza Stazione Ferrovie Dello Stato, 1,55045 Pietrasanta(LU),Italy; Tel:+39 06 6847 5475; Web-site:www.renitalia.it

Ospedale Versilia,Via Aurelia, 335,55041 Camaiore(LU),Italy; Tel:+39 0584 6051; Web-site:www.usl12.toscana.it

Ceolin - Ambulatorio,Viale Guglielmo Oberdan, 59,55045 Pietrasanta(LU),Italy; Tel:+39 0584 72176

Centro Medico Campus Maior,Via Oberdan Guglielmo, 39,55041 Camaiore(LU),Italy; Tel:+39 0584 984009

Cure Primarie Versilia Societa' Cooperativa,Via Martiri di Sant'Anna, 10,55045 Pietrasanta(LU),Italy; Tel:+39 0584 71563

Dalle Luche - Medico Veterinario,Via Andreuccetti, 7,55041 Camaiore(LU),Italy; Tel:+39 0584 983560

## Accommodation & Facilities  ....  Massa - Pietrasanta

Pianeta Sport,Via Provinciale Vallecchia, 23,55045 Pietrasanta(LU),Italy;
Tel:+39 0584 71481

Sporty,Via Pietro Tabarrani, 14,55041 Camaiore(LU),Italy; Tel:+39 0584 989204

Aliverti,Via Aurelia Sud, 47,55045 Pietrasanta(LU),Italy; Tel:+39 5841 962090

Taxi,1 piazza Romboni Carlo,55041 Camaiore(LU),Italy; Tel:+39 0584 980034

Taxi,Piazza Stazione,55045 Pietrasanta(LU),Italy; Tel:+39 0584 769520

Taxi,Piazza Betti Francesco,54100 Marina-di-Massa(MS),Italy;
Tel:+39 0585 780045

Altitude Profile

1 km
1 : 40 000

Stage Summary: take care on the main road as you leave Pietrasanta. Farm tracks and very small roads cross the Monteggiori ridge to the canal-side track leading to the attractive town of Camaiore. The route then climbs on farm tracks parallel to the main road to Montemagno. The route returns to the main road before returning to farm and forest tracks at Valpromaro. The route approaches Lucca along a riverside track before finally entering historic centre of the walled city. There is the opportunity to break the journey in Camaiore, but accommodation can be expensive.

Distance from Vercelli: 397km          Distance to St Peter's Square, Rome: 452km
Stage Ascent: 709m                     Stage Descent: 708m

| Waypoint | Distance between waypoints | Total km | Directions | Verification Point | Compass | Altitude m |
|---|---|---|---|---|---|---|
| 80.001 | 0 | 0.0 | From piazza Duomo in Pietrasanta take via Giuseppe Garibaldi | Beside the Duomo | SE | 24 |
| 80.002 | 300 | 0.3 | At the junction, proceed straight ahead with care on the main road | SP439, direction Lucca | SE | 20 |
| 80.003 | 600 | 0.9 | Beside the cemetery turn left, on via Valdicastello Carducci | Signpost chiesa and VF map | E | 21 |
| 80.004 | 1300 | 2.2 | Turn right on via Regnalla | Road bends to the left in 200m | SE | 53 |
| 80.005 | 400 | 2.6 | Take the second right after the bend | Uphill | S | 61 |
| 80.006 | 90 | 2.6 | Take the right fork | Keep industrial building on your left | S | 70 |
| 80.007 | 180 | 2.8 | Pass beside the factory and a quarry and take the footpath to the right through the woods | Towards the brow of the hill | S | 96 |
| 80.008 | 280 | 3.1 | Bear right on the footpath at the end of the woods and proceed directly downhill | | S | 85 |

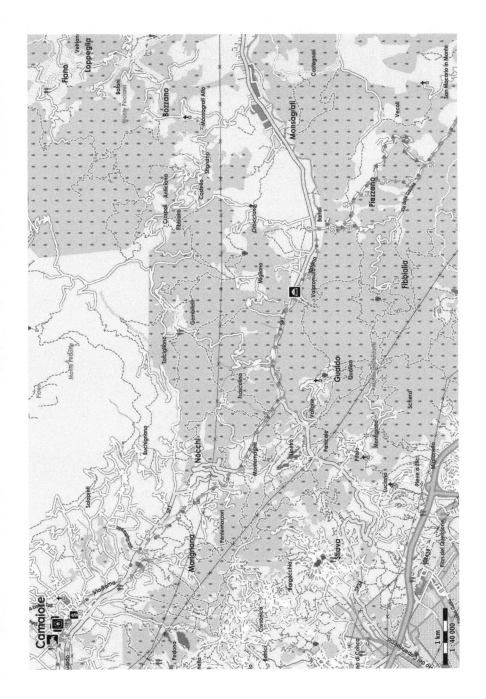

| Waypoint | Distance between waypoints | Total km | Directions | Verification Point | Compass | Altitude m |
|---|---|---|---|---|---|---|
| 80.009 | 150 | 3.3 | At the T-junction with the road, turn left and immediately right on the road | Pass the high stone wall on your left | S | 56 |
| 80.010 | 300 | 3.5 | At the T-junction, turn left | Conifers on your left | SE | 59 |
| 80.011 | 100 | 3.6 | At the junction with the main road turn left and immediately right | Strada di Monteggiori | S | 62 |
| 80.012 | 50 | 3.7 | Bear left onto a small footpath | White arrow | S | 54 |
| 80.013 | 400 | 4.1 | Bear right on the broad track | | S | 19 |
| 80.014 | 20 | 4.1 | Join the road and continue straight ahead | | S | 18 |
| 80.015 | 90 | 4.2 | At the T-junction, turn left | | SE | 11 |
| 80.016 | 60 | 4.3 | Fork left | Junction beside large ornamental gates | SE | 11 |
| 80.017 | 300 | 4.6 | At the crossroads with via Selvaiana continue straight ahead | Map on your right at the junction | SE | 12 |
| 80.018 | 600 | 5.2 | Bear left | Via Dietro Monte | SE | 17 |
| 80.019 | 230 | 5.4 | Cross the bridge and at the junction turn left | Towards the main road | E | 12 |
| 80.020 | 290 | 5.7 | Just before the traffic lights take the left fork | Initially parallel to the main road | N | 15 |
| 80.021 | 180 | 5.9 | At the Stop sign, take the first turning to the right | Take the lower road | E | 21 |
| 80.022 | 500 | 6.3 | Just before the T-junction with the main road, turn left and follow the path parallel to the busy road | Line of trees on your right | NE | 17 |

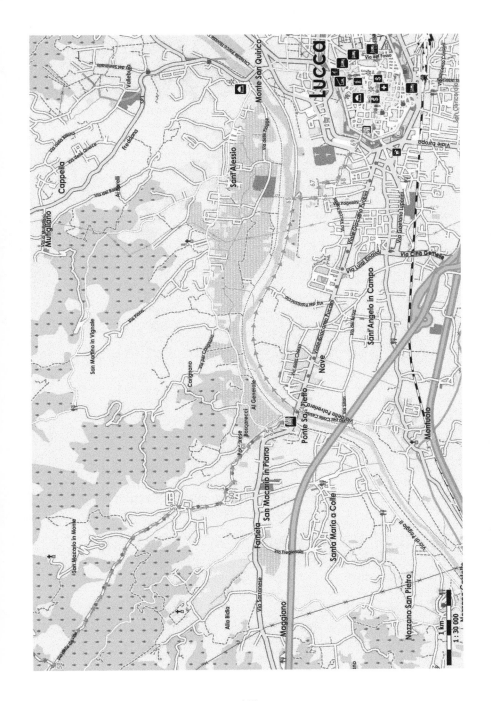

| Waypoint | Distance between waypoints | Total km | Directions | Verification Point | Compass | Altitude m |
|---|---|---|---|---|---|---|
| 80.023 | 220 | 6.5 | Beside the playground, turn right, carefully cross the road and take the bridge over the canal. Then turn left | Keep the canal close on your left | E | 20 |
| 80.024 | 1100 | 7.6 | Continue straight ahead on the road beside the canal, via Virgilio Boschi | Pass football ground on the left | E | 33 |
| 80.025 | 600 | 8.2 | Take the bridge to the left, cross the main road and continue straight ahead | Direction Centro, via Carignoni | NE | 30 |
| 80.026 | 130 | 8.3 | At the T-junction, turn left | Direction Centro | NW | 31 |
| 80.027 | 70 | 8.4 | Before reaching the petrol station turn right | Piazza 29 Maggio | NE | 30 |
| 80.028 | 40 | 8.4 | With the church directly ahead, take the first turn to the right | Via VIV Novembre | SE | 31 |
| 80.029 | 500 | 8.9 | After passing the church on your right, turn left and then take the next turning to the right | Contrada la Rocca leading to via Vittorio Emanuele | E | 35 |
| 80.030 | 110 | 9.1 | At the roundabout in piazza Carlo Romboni, continue straight ahead | Via Roma | SE | 35 |
| 80.031 | 1100 | 10.2 | At the junction with the SP1, cross over the main road and take the minor road over the bridge | Towards the sports ground "Tori" | SE | 46 |
| 80.032 | 400 | 10.5 | Continue straight ahead on the footpath | Sports ground to the left | SE | 56 |
| 80.033 | 170 | 10.7 | At the T-junction with the tarmac road turn left | Frazione Marignana | NE | 56 |
| 80.034 | 280 | 11.0 | Just before reaching the canal, turn right on the road | Keep canal to the left | SE | 54 |
| 80.035 | 400 | 11.4 | As the road enters a farm turn right on the track | Towards the woods | SW | 59 |

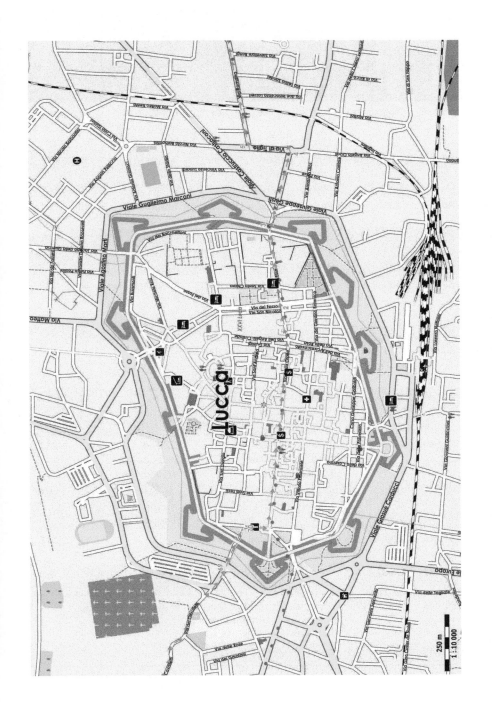

| Waypoint | Distance between waypoints | Total km | Directions | Verification Point | Compass | Altitude m |
|---|---|---|---|---|---|---|
| 80.036 | 100 | 11.5 | Turn left on the footpath | Between the woods and a field | SE | 64 |
| 80.037 | 240 | 11.7 | Beside the farm buildings, cross the tarmac driveway and bear right on the track | Beside the woods | SE | 74 |
| 80.038 | 700 | 12.4 | Turn left on the track | Towards the church | SE | 82 |
| 80.039 | 70 | 12.5 | At the T-junction with the road, turn left and immediately right | Pass the church on the right | SE | 79 |
| 80.040 | 600 | 13.0 | After passing a large country house, bear left onto the track | Keep house on right | SE | 117 |
| 80.041 | 70 | 13.1 | Turn right onto the SP1 | Uphill | SW | 128 |
| 80.042 | 130 | 13.2 | On the apex of the bend to the left, turn right up the stony track | VF sign | E | 127 |
| 80.043 | 200 | 13.4 | Continue straight on, up the narrow pathway | Beside electricity substation | SE | 167 |
| 80.044 | 200 | 13.6 | Turn right onto the main road – SP1 and enter Montemagno | Bar and restaurant on left and right | SE | 213 |
| 80.045 | 1800 | 15.5 | Bear right off the main road onto the unmade road | Pass the restaurant "Purgatorio" | E | 193 |
| 80.046 | 300 | 15.8 | Return to the main road and bear right | | E | 187 |
| 80.047 | 1300 | 17.0 | Bear right on a minor road into Valpromaro | VF sign | E | 161 |
| 80.048 | 600 | 17.6 | After passing through the village, turn right onto track between houses | VF sign | E | 139 |
| 80.049 | 1000 | 18.5 | At the T-junction, turn right onto the minor road | VF sign, direction Piazzano | S | 112 |

| Waypoint | Distance between waypoints | Total km | Directions | Verification Point | Compass | Altitude m |
|---|---|---|---|---|---|---|
| 80.050 | 200 | 18.7 | Just before the road turns to the left, turn right onto a gravel track. Note:- the off-road section is steep over rough ground. Cyclists should remain on the road to Piazzano | VF sign | S | 134 |
| 80.051 | 600 | 19.3 | At the T-junction with a minor road turn left | Via delle Gavine | NE | 189 |
| 80.052 | 110 | 19.4 | Take the right fork into Piazzano | VF sign, via della Chiesa XII | E | 197 |
| 80.053 | 600 | 20.0 | At the crossroads in centre of Piazzano turn right | VF sign | SE | 209 |
| 80.054 | 300 | 20.3 | On leaving the village, continue straight ahead on the road | Pass the church on the left | SE | 190 |
| 80.055 | 400 | 20.7 | Bear right on the track . Note:- cyclists continue straight ahead on the road to the T-junction | Pass cemetery on your right | S | 187 |
| 80.056 | 80 | 20.7 | At the junction in the tracks continue straight ahead | Downhill | S | 181 |
| 80.057 | 800 | 21.5 | At the T-junction with the road, turn left | Across the stream | SE | 70 |
| 80.058 | 300 | 21.8 | Continue straight ahead on via delle Gavine. Cyclists rejoin from the road on the left | VF sign, stream on the right | SE | 66 |
| 80.059 | 2800 | 24.6 | At the Stop sign in Alla Bidia bear right on the major road | Sign to Piazzano on your left at the junction | S | 23 |
| 80.060 | 700 | 25.3 | On entering San Macario Piano, bear left on the narrow street, in the direction of the church tower | VF sign, via della chiesa Ventitreesima | SE | 21 |
| 80.061 | 800 | 26.1 | Bear right on the road | Embankment on your left | SE | 13 |

| Waypoint | Distance between waypoints | Total km | Directions | Verification Point | Compass | Altitude m |
|---|---|---|---|---|---|---|
| 80.062 | 260 | 26.3 | At the crossroads, continue straight ahead onto a small road skirting the village | VF sign, towards church | S | 15 |
| 80.063 | 500 | 26.8 | At the crossroads, turn left over the river bridge | VF sign, Ponte San Pietro | E | 13 |
| 80.064 | 160 | 26.9 | Immediately after crossing the bridge, turn left onto a small tarmac riverside road | VF sign, keep river close on your left | E | 15 |
| 80.065 | 3200 | 30.1 | Pass under the footbridge and fork right onto the tarmac road | VF sign | S | 17 |
| 80.066 | 400 | 30.5 | At the crossroads, turn left | VF sign, keep football ground on the right | E | 13 |
| 80.067 | 200 | 30.7 | At the end of the football ground, turn right onto a small tarmac road | VF sign | S | 14 |
| 80.068 | 250 | 30.9 | At the T-junction with via dei Cavalletti, turn left | Keep the park on the right | SE | 15 |
| 80.069 | 600 | 31.5 | At the traffic lights, cross the road and pass under the arch into walled centre of Lucca | VF sign | SE | 17 |
| 80.070 | 200 | 31.7 | At the T-junction, turn right on piazza Giuseppe Verdi | Pass the ancient Porta San Donata on your right | S | 19 |
| 80.071 | 100 | 31.8 | Take the first left turn | Towards Ostello S. Frediano, No Entry | E | 18 |
| 80.072 | 400 | 32.2 | Arrive at Lucca (XXVI) centre in piazza San Michele | Church to the left | | 25 |

Parrocchia San Martino,Valpromaro,55041 Camaiore(LU),Italy; Tel:+39 0584 956028; +39 0584 956159; +39 3276 948204; Email:mario.andreozzi46@alice. it; Price:D

Convento dei Frati Cappuccini,Via della Chiesa - Monte San Quirico, 87,55100 Lucca(LU),Italy; Tel:+39 0583 341426; +39 3391 118421; Price:D

Misericordia di Lucca,2 via Battisti Cesare,55100 Lucca(LU),Italy; Tel:+39 0583 409546; Web-site:www.misericordialucca.org/web/index.php/foresteria.html; Price:D

Ostello San Frediano,Via della Cavallerizza, 12,55100 Lucca(LU),Italy; Tel:+39 0584 461007; +39 0583 469957; Email:info@ostellolucca.it; Web-site:www. ostellolucca.it; Price:B

La Gemma di Elena - B&B,Via della Zecca, 33,55100 Lucca(LU),Italy; Tel:+39 0583 496665; +39 3202 346331; Email:lagemma@interfree.it; Web-site:www. lagemmadielena.it; Price:A

Affittacamere la Camelia,Piazza San Francesco, 35,55100 Lucca(LU),Italy; +39 3394 840178; Email:info@affittacamerelacamelia.com; Web-site:www. affittacamerelacamelia.com; Price:B

Hotel Da Elisa,Via Elisa, 25 ,55100 Lucca(LU),Italy; Tel:+39 0583 494539; Email:info2@daelisa.com; Web-site:www.daelisa.com; Price:B

Guest House Casa Dini,Viale Regina Margherita, 195,55100 Lucca(LU),Italy; Tel:+39 0583 467331; +39 3343 234872; Email:post@casadini.com ; Web-site:www.casadini.com; Price:A

Azienda di Promozione Turistica,Piazzale Giuseppe Verdi,55100 Lucca(LU),Italy; Tel:+39 0583 469964

Unicredit,Piazza San Michele, 47,55100 Lucca(LU),Italy; Tel:+39 0583 4971

Stazione Ferrovie,Piazzale Bettino Ricasoli, 169,55100 Lucca(LU),Italy; Tel:+39 06 6847 5475; Web-site:www.renitalia.it

Presidio Ospedaliero,Via Dell'Ospedale, 238,55100 Lucca(LU),Italy; Tel:+39 0583 9701

Puccetti - Medico Chirurgo Studio,Via del Battistero, 18,55100 Lucca(LU),Italy; Tel:+39 0583 494139

Ambulatorio Veterinario,Viale Idelfonso Nieri, 131,55100 Lucca(LU),Italy; Tel:+39 0583 581936

Tuttosport,Via Antonio Mordini, 25,55100 Lucca(LU),Italy; Tel:+39 0583 91600

Cicli Bizzarri,Piazza Santa Maria, 32,55100 Lucca(LU),Italy; Tel:+39 0583 496682

Cure Primarie Versilia Societa' Cooperativa,Via Martiri di Sant'Anna, 10,55045 Pietrasanta(LU),Italy; Tel:+39 0584 71563

Dalle Luche - Medico Veterinario,Via Andreuccetti, 7,55041 Camaiore(LU),Italy; Tel:+39 0584 983560

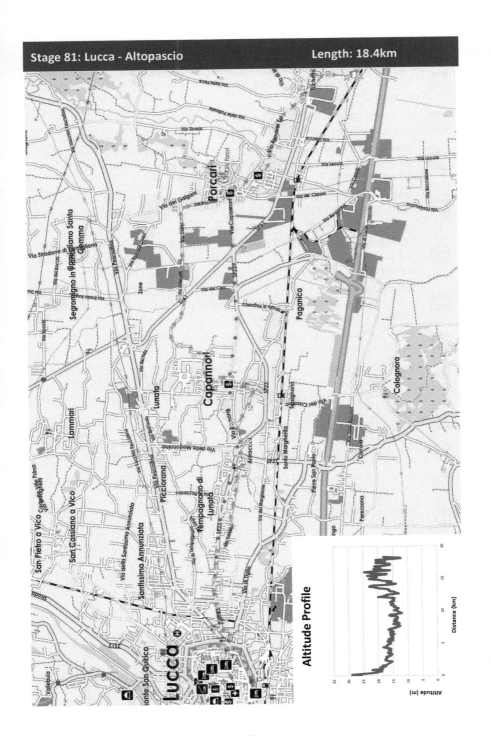

# Stage 81: Lucca - Altopascio

**Length: 18.4km**

## Altitude Profile

Distance (km)

Altitude (m)

Stage Summary: the route to the welcoming town of Altopascio is substantially undertaken on the tarmac weaving a course on minor roads to the south and north of the busy SP6.

Distance from Vercelli: 429km
Stage Ascent: 99m

Distance to St Peter's Square, Rome: 419km
Stage Descent: 107m

| Waypoint | Distance between waypoints | Total km | Directions | Verification Point | Compass | Altitude m |
|---|---|---|---|---|---|---|
| 81.001 | 0 | 0.0 | From piazza San Michele, take via Roma and then via San Croce | Keep church to the left | E | 25 |
| 81.002 | 600 | 0.6 | Go through archway, Porta San Gervasio and across the canal onto via Elisa | VF sign | E | 20 |
| 81.003 | 300 | 0.9 | After passing through the triple arched Porta Elisa, continue straight ahead across the main road onto viale Luigi Cadoma | VF sign, direction Pontedera | E | 22 |
| 81.004 | 400 | 1.3 | At the T-junction, turn left onto via di Tiglio | Towards the domed Santuario di S. Gemma | N | 19 |
| 81.005 | 180 | 1.5 | Turn right onto via Romana | Towards the hotels | E | 17 |
| 81.006 | 900 | 2.3 | Continue straight ahead at the roundabout | Petrol station on right | E | 17 |
| 81.007 | 600 | 2.9 | Turn right onto the small road, via dei Paladini | VF sign, pass doorway with crucifix on your left | E | 17 |
| 81.008 | 1500 | 4.4 | At the Stop sign, continue straight ahead on via Vecchia Romana | VF sign, pass the church of San Michele on the left | E | 17 |
| 81.009 | 400 | 4.8 | At the crossroads with the main road, continue straight ahead on the small road | VF sign, pass house n° 1241 on your left | E | 16 |

| Waypoint | Distance between waypoints | Total km | Directions | Verification Point | Compass | Altitude m |
|----------|----------|----------|-----------|-------------------|---------|-----------|
| 81.010 | 270 | 5.1 | At the next crossroads, continue straight ahead on the small road | VF sign, enter Capannori | E | 16 |
| 81.011 | 400 | 5.5 | At the junction, after passing the cemetery on the right, continue straight ahead | Pass a shrine on your left | E | 15 |
| 81.012 | 300 | 5.8 | Keep right at the junction | House n°21 on your right | SE | 15 |
| 81.013 | 400 | 6.1 | At the crossroads, turn left | Crucifix at the junction | NE | 15 |
| 81.014 | 140 | 6.3 | At the T-junction, turn left | Towards the petrol station | N | 15 |
| 81.015 | 290 | 6.6 | At the crossroads beside the church of San Quirico turn right and then take the first road to the left | Into the parking area | NE | 15 |
| 81.016 | 180 | 6.7 | At the end of the parking area, bear left, pass through a second parking area | Towards the bank | NW | 15 |
| 81.017 | 130 | 6.9 | At the junction with the road, turn right | Cycle track on the right of the road | N | 15 |
| 81.023 | 1000 | 9.3 | At the junction with the main road, SP61, turn left and immediately right | Over the bridge, towards the industrial zone | E | 16 |
| 81.024 | 700 | 10.0 | At the roundabout, turn right and then left on the road | Via Ciarpi, enter Porcari | E | 14 |
| 81.025 | 1100 | 11.1 | Just after crossing stream turn right | Via Pacconi | S | 15 |
| 81.026 | 900 | 12.0 | At the T-junction, turn left on via Capannori | Towards the post office | E | 14 |

| Waypoint | Distance between waypoints | Total km | Directions | Verification Point | Compass | Altitude m |
|---|---|---|---|---|---|---|
| 81.027 | 140 | 12.1 | In the centre of Porcari (XXV) turn right at the traffic lights | Pass church on the hill to the left | SE | 18 |
| 81.028 | 2100 | 14.2 | Immediately after entering Turchetto, bear right on the small road | Towards industrial area, VF sign | SE | 14 |
| 81.029 | 300 | 14.6 | At the junction with a major road, cross straight over onto via Pistoresi-Tappo-Turchetto | VF sign, pass supermarket on your left | SE | 15 |
| 81.030 | 400 | 14.9 | Turn right onto the track towards trees | Commercial building on left at junction | S | 22 |
| 81.031 | 260 | 15.2 | Continue straight ahead onto a gravel track | VF sign | S | 20 |
| 81.032 | 170 | 15.4 | Continue straight ahead | Pass the cemetery on the left | S | 21 |
| 81.033 | 110 | 15.5 | Turn left at the end of the wall | VF sign | SE | 22 |
| 81.034 | 20 | 15.5 | Follow the road keeping the church to your left | Via Chiesa | E | 22 |
| 81.035 | 500 | 16.0 | At the crossroads, proceed straight ahead into Badia Pozzeveri on via Catalani | VF sign, small shrine to the right | E | 24 |
| 81.036 | 1900 | 17.9 | At the T-junction with the SP3, turn right to go under the road bridge | Towards the bell-tower | SE | 20 |
| 81.037 | 500 | 18.4 | Arrive at Altopascio | Beside Chiesa di San Jacopo | | 18 |

Ostello Per Pellegrini,Office of Tourism - piazza Garibaldi, 10,55011 Altopascio(LU),Italy; Tel:+39 0583 216525; +39 0583 216280; +39 3346 821060; Email:turismo@comune.altopascio.lu.it; Web-site:www.altopasciocultura.it/lospitalit_dei_pellegrini_-124-It.html; Price:D

Affitacameret il Ponte,Via Sarzanese, 11,55056 Lucca(LU),Italy; Tel:+39 0583 329815; +39 3496 128128; Email:info@affittacamereilponte.com; Web-site:www.affittacamereilponte.com; Price:C

Albergo Cavalieri del Tau,Via Gavinana,55011 Altopascio(LU),Italy; Tel:+39 0583 25131; Email:info@cavalieridetau.it; Web-site:www.cavalieridetau.it; Price:A

Hotel Da Paola,Via Francesca Romea, 24,55011 Altopascio(LU),Italy; Tel:+39 0583 276453; +39 36 8765 0227; Email:info@hotelpaolalucca.it; Web-site:www.hotelpaolalucca.it; Price:B

Apartment,(Amelia Barbieri),Via Firenze, 55,55011 Altopascio(LU),Italy; Tel:+39 0583 25265; Price:B

Hotel Astoria,Via Roma, 86,55011 Altopascio(LU),Italy; Tel:+39 0583 264746; +39 3485 606868; Email:info.hotelastoria@gmail.com; Web-site:www.hotel-astoria-altopascio.com; Price:A

Comune di Altopascio,Piazza Vittorio Emanuele, 24,55011 Altopascio(LU),Italy; Tel:+39 0583 216455

Banca Toscana,Via Per Corte Giusti,55012 Capannori(LU),Italy; Tel:+39 0583 433050

Banca Monte dei Paschi di Siena,Viale Guglielmo Marconi, 3,55016 Porcari(LU),Italy; Tel:+39 0583 297585

Cassa di Risparmio di Lucca,Via Capannori, 79,55016 Porcari(LU),Italy; Tel:+39 0583 298531

Banca Toscana,Via Firenze, 81a,55011 Altopascio(LU),Italy; Tel:+39 0583 241105

Unicredit,Via Cavour, 1,55011 Altopascio(LU),Italy; Tel:+39 5831 797411

Gal Galilei Airport,56121 Pisa(PI),Italy; Tel:+39 0508 49111; Web-site:www.pisa-airport.com

Urbani - Medico Chirurgo,Via Roma, 5,55011 Altopascio(LU),Italy; Tel:+39 0583 25962

Bianchi - Medico Veterinario,Via Bientina, 67,55011 Altopascio(LU),Italy; Tel:+39 0583 25463

Crazy Sport,Via Cavour, 12,55011 Altopascio(LU),Italy; Tel:+39 0583 264750

Jolly Bike di Fornari Andrea,Via delle Cerbaie, 16,55011 Altopascio(LU),Italy; Tel:+39 0583 216591

Dalle Luche - Medico Veterinario,Via Andreuccetti, 7,55041 Camaiore(LU),Italy; Tel:+39 0584 983560

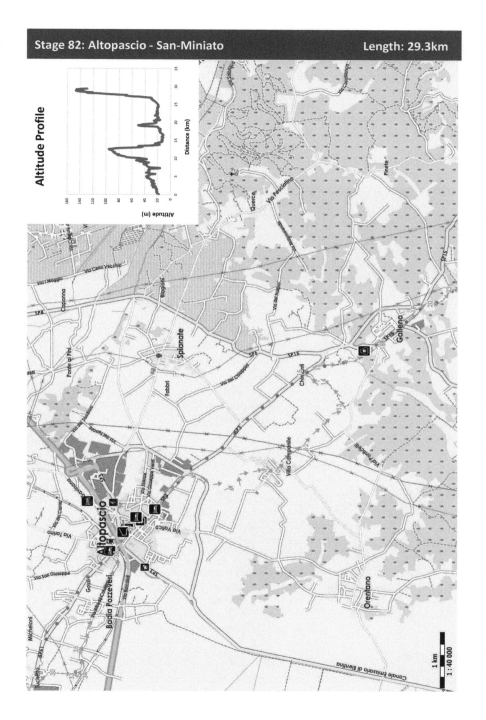

Stage Summary: the route follows the highways to Galleno before discovering an ancient stretch of the via Francigena leading to the hilltop paths of the Cerbaie.  From Ponte a Cappiano the route follows the canal to Fucecchio before crossing the valley of the river Arno and climbing to the historic hilltop town of San Miniato.  There are ample stopping places en route.

Distance from Vercelli: 447km          Distance to St Peter's Square, Rome: 401km
Stage Ascent:  431m                          Stage Descent: 320m

| Waypoint | Distance between waypoints | Total km | Directions | Verification Point | Compass | Altitude m |
|---|---|---|---|---|---|---|
| 82.001 | 0 | 0.0 | In Piazza Vittorio Emanuele with the chiesa di San Jacopo to your right, cross the piazza, turn right after passing the Municipio, cross the second square and pass through the arch | Keep the arches in front of the Municipio close on your right | E | 19 |
| 82.002 | 80 | 0.1 | Continue straight ahead on via della Dispensa and then turn right at the crossroads | Pass through a further arch | SE | 18 |
| 82.003 | 200 | 0.3 | At the junction with the main road, bear right on via Cavour, direction Fucecchio | Small building with arched portico to the left | SE | 19 |
| 82.004 | 1300 | 1.6 | At the roundabout turn right on the tarmac track beside the new road.  Note:- the route formerly continued staright ahead on the main road | Houses on the right of the track | S | 22 |
| 82.005 | 300 | 1.9 | As the road turns to the right, cross the to the left side of the road, turn right and then bear left on the track | Into the trees | SW | 23 |
| 82.006 | 500 | 2.4 | At the T-junction, turn left | Woods on your left | SE | 26 |

| Waypoint | Distance between waypoints | Total km | Directions | Verification Point | Compass | Altitude m |
|---|---|---|---|---|---|---|
| 82.007 | 270 | 2.7 | At the end of the woods, turn left and then turn right | | SE | 27 |
| 82.008 | 700 | 3.3 | At the junction with the tarmac road, bear left | Pass the parking area on your left | SE | 29 |
| 82.009 | 100 | 3.4 | At the T-junction, turn right | Towards the Tabacchi | SW | 30 |
| 82.010 | 70 | 3.5 | At the Stop sign, turn left | Direction Orentano | SE | 29 |
| 82.011 | 260 | 3.8 | At the end of the road, turn left and then right on the gravel track | | SE | 26 |
| 82.012 | 500 | 4.2 | At the junction, bear right and then left on the long straight track | Beside the copse of trees | SE | 30 |
| 82.013 | 1100 | 5.3 | At the junction in the woods, turn left | | NE | 33 |
| 82.014 | 800 | 6.1 | Turn right following the gravel road | Entrance gates on your left | NE | 38 |
| 82.015 | 280 | 6.4 | At the T-junction with the main road, turn right | Leave the region of Lucca | SE | 34 |
| 82.016 | 160 | 6.5 | Fork right onto the unmade road | The ancient via Francigena | S | 34 |
| 82.017 | 800 | 7.3 | Continue straight ahead | Cross the small bridge | SE | 16 |
| 82.018 | 400 | 7.7 | Arrive in Galleno and continue straight ahead on the main road | Via Romana Lucchese, direction Fucecchio | SE | 35 |
| 82.019 | 1000 | 8.8 | Bear right at the major road junction | Direction Fucecchio | SE | 38 |
| 82.020 | 120 | 8.9 | Shortly after crossing a bridge, turn right on the track | Pass a house on your left | S | 33 |

| Waypoint | Distance between waypoints | Total km | Directions | Verification Point | Compass | Altitude m |
|---|---|---|---|---|---|---|
| 82.021 | 60 | 8.9 | Take the left fork | Towards the woods | SE | 36 |
| 82.022 | 500 | 9.5 | Cross over the driveway and continue straight ahead | Equestrian centre on the right | SE | 53 |
| 82.023 | 50 | 9.5 | Keep left on the track into the woods | Downhill | SE | 53 |
| 82.024 | 200 | 9.7 | At the T-junction with the road, turn right | | SE | 39 |
| 82.025 | 100 | 9.8 | Shortly after passing the buildings on the left, join a white road and continue straight ahead | | SE | 37 |
| 82.026 | 130 | 9.9 | Turn left at the next junction | In the woods | SE | 41 |
| 82.027 | 170 | 10.1 | Brear right, uphill | Pond on the left | S | 47 |
| 82.028 | 220 | 10.3 | At the first junction after a short climb, continue straight ahead | | S | 67 |
| 82.029 | 40 | 10.4 | At the next junction bear left | | SE | 68 |
| 82.030 | 220 | 10.6 | Join a broader track and bear slightly left | Horse track below on the left | SE | 71 |
| 82.031 | 1600 | 12.2 | At the T-junction with a busy tarmac road, bear right on the SP 61 | Pass a grove of trees on your right | SE | 90 |
| 82.032 | 400 | 12.5 | Take the left fork on the narrow, busy road, via di Poggio Adorno | Direction Santa Croce | SE | 94 |
| 82.033 | 230 | 12.8 | After the first bend to the left, turn sharp left on the track downhill into the woods | VF sign | E | 84 |
| 82.034 | 400 | 13.1 | Take the right fork on the track | Pond on the right | SE | 47 |
| 82.035 | 280 | 13.4 | Bear left on the road | Via De Medici | E | 46 |

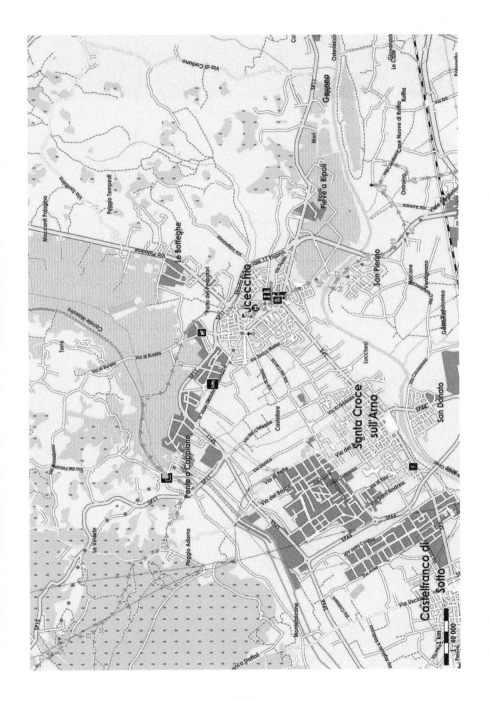

182

| Waypoint | Distance between waypoints | Total km | Directions | Verification Point | Compass | Altitude m |
|---|---|---|---|---|---|---|
| 82.036 | 500 | 13.9 | Cross the SP11 and continue straight ahead | VF sign | SE | 19 |
| 82.037 | 70 | 13.9 | Bear left | Brick garden wall on your left | NE | 21 |
| 82.038 | 500 | 14.4 | In piazza A. Donnini, turn right | Towards the covered bridge | SE | 20 |
| 82.039 | 60 | 14.4 | Cross the bridge and turn left down the steps into the car park and continue along the banks of the canal. Note:- riders should continue to the end of the bridge and then turn sharp left | Canal immediately to the left | E | 16 |
| 82.040 | 1600 | 16.1 | Shortly after the canal begins to bend to the left, turn right away from the canal-side onto another embankment | Right angle to canal | S | 14 |
| 82.041 | 400 | 16.5 | Cross the waterway and turn left - riders can continue on the left bank to the next Waypoint where they can cross on a more substantial bridge | Waterway on the left | E | 11 |
| 82.042 | 600 | 17.0 | Cross the road and continue straight ahead on the embankment | VF sign, keep waterway on your left | E | 14 |
| 82.043 | 400 | 17.4 | Cross another road and continue straight ahead on the embankment | Pass an industrial complex on the right | SE | 16 |
| 82.044 | 1000 | 18.4 | Cross the SP11 and continue on the small road opposite, via Ponte del Rio | Pass a roundabout on the left | S | 19 |
| 82.045 | 230 | 18.6 | Cross viale Napoleone Buonaparte and continue straight ahead | Via Sotto la Valle, VF sign | S | 20 |

| Waypoint | Distance between waypoints | Total km | Directions | Verification Point | Compass | Altitude m |
|---|---|---|---|---|---|---|
| 82.046 | 170 | 18.8 | Take the next turning to the right | Via Sant'Antonio, VF sign | SW | 21 |
| 82.047 | 230 | 19.0 | At the T-junction, turn left into the centre of Fucecchio (XXIII) | VF sign, pass house n° 69 on your right | SE | 46 |
| 82.048 | 180 | 19.2 | After passing piazza S Lavagnini on the left, take the next turning to the right | Via G. di San Giorgio | SW | 50 |
| 82.049 | 70 | 19.3 | Cross piazza Garibaldi and take the small road straight ahead. Note:- horse and bike riders bear left into piazza Veneto to avoid a flight of steps | Parking area on your left | S | 43 |
| 82.050 | 60 | 19.4 | Turn left | Church on the left | E | 40 |
| 82.051 | 70 | 19.4 | Go down the steps and cross piazza Vittorio Veneto and bear right down the hill | Via del Cassero | E | 44 |
| 82.052 | 90 | 19.5 | In the next square turn right | Via Donateschi | S | 40 |
| 82.053 | 210 | 19.7 | Continue straight ahead across piazza G. Montanelli and take via N. Sauro | Statue to your right, VF sign | SE | 26 |
| 82.054 | 70 | 19.8 | At the crossroads, continue straight ahead on the road | Direction San Miniato | S | 24 |
| 82.055 | 800 | 20.6 | Continue straight ahead. Note:- caution narrow pavements on the bridge | River Arno bridge | SW | 17 |
| 82.056 | 190 | 20.8 | At the end of the bridge, turn sharp left and then right through the industrial area | Trees and river on the left | SE | 21 |
| 82.057 | 400 | 21.2 | Continue straight ahead on the footpath | On the embankment beside the river | SE | 20 |

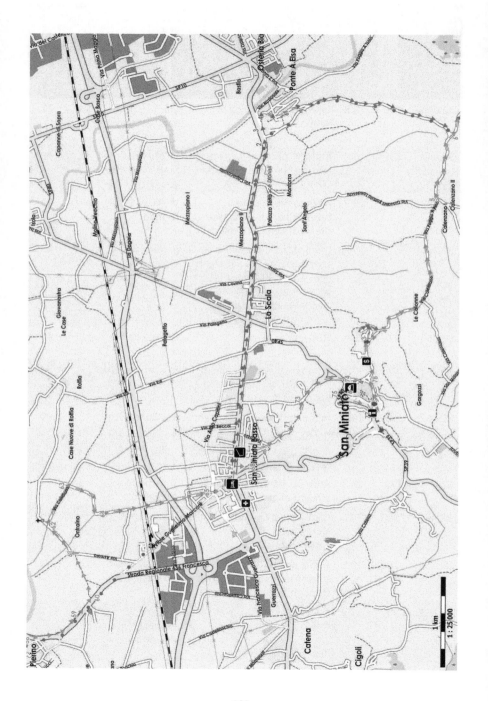

| Waypoint | Distance between waypoints | Total km | Directions | Verification Point | Compass | Altitude m |
|---|---|---|---|---|---|---|
| 82.058 | 500 | 21.6 | Bear right on the track and then turn left under the highway and then immediately right | Parallel to the main road | SE | 21 |
| 82.059 | 800 | 22.4 | Continue straight ahead between the embankment and the busy road | Main road on your right | SE | 21 |
| 82.060 | 220 | 22.6 | Turn left on the track into the fields | Garden allotments on the right | E | 20 |
| 82.061 | 500 | 23.1 | At the T-junction with a road, turn left | Road quickly bends to the right | NE | 21 |
| 82.062 | 500 | 23.6 | Pass through the hamlet of Ontraino and then turn right on the small road immediately after crossing the irrigation channel | Via Candiano | SE | 20 |
| 82.063 | 500 | 24.1 | Take the first turning to the right, gravel track | Between vines | SW | 21 |
| 82.064 | 500 | 24.6 | Bear left on the track | Towards the hilltop town of San Miniato | S | 19 |
| 82.065 | 1300 | 25.9 | At the roundabout, cross the grass and continue straight ahead | Direction San Miniato, tree lined road | SE | 24 |
| 82.066 | 280 | 26.2 | At the traffic lights turn left | Pass Tabacchi on the left | E | 28 |
| 82.067 | 130 | 26.3 | Turn right on the small road. Note:- to visit the Sigeric location – Borgo Santo Genesio (XXII) - continue straight ahead on the Alternate Route on the main road | Pass the church on your left | S | 27 |
| 82.068 | 130 | 26.4 | Bear left on the embankment | | SE | 29 |

| Waypoint | Distance between waypoints | Total km | Directions | Verification Point | Compass | Altitude m |
|---|---|---|---|---|---|---|
| 82.069 | 300 | 26.8 | Turn left down the steps | Pass between the houses | NE | 30 |
| 82.070 | 50 | 26.8 | At the junction with the road, turn right on via Pozzo | House n° 52 on your right | SE | 30 |
| 82.071 | 400 | 27.2 | At the end of via Pozzo continue straight ahead on the footpath | Pass house n° 89 on your left | SE | 57 |
| 82.072 | 190 | 27.4 | Continue straight ahead on the road | Downhill | E | 70 |
| 82.073 | 130 | 27.5 | At the junction with the main road, turn right uphill | Enter San Miniato | SE | 68 |
| 82.074 | 500 | 28.0 | Take the right fork. Note:- the "Official Route" makes a loop around the hill following the main road before arriving in the old town. Some relief from the traffic can be found by following the paths in the parks on either side of the road. The Alternate Route to the left follows a more direct but narrow road | Direction San Miniato Centre | W | 113 |
| 82.075 | 180 | 28.2 | Continue straight ahead, uphill following the road | Pass park on your left | S | 124 |
| 82.076 | 240 | 28.5 | Take the right fork, remaining on the main road | Park on the right | SW | 137 |
| 82.077 | 400 | 28.9 | In piazzetta del Fondo, turn sharp left | Towards the archway | E | 135 |
| 82.078 | 400 | 29.3 | Arrive at San-Miniato old town at the section end | Piazza Buonaparte | | 129 |

| Alternate Route #82.A1 | | | | Length: 6.2km | | |
| --- | --- | --- | --- | --- | --- | --- |

Stage Summary: route bypassing the historic centre of San Miniato to allow a visit to the location of Borgo Santo Genesio (XXII).  The route initially follows the busy road from San Miniato Basso towards Ponte a Elsa before climbing to rejoin the "Official Route" near Calenzano.

Stage Ascent: 135m                          Stage Descent: 17m

| Waypoint | Distance between waypoints | Total km | Directions | Verification Point | Compass | Altitude m |
| --- | --- | --- | --- | --- | --- | --- |
| 82A1.001 | 0 | 0.0 | Continue straight ahead on SP40 | Direction Ponte a Elsa | E | 27 |
| 82A1.002 | 3700 | 3.7 | At the entry to Ponte a Elsa bear right on via Nazionale. Note:- the chapel of San Genesio (XXII) and an archaeological dig is to the left | Towards bus stops | E | 31 |
| 82A1.003 | 180 | 3.9 | Bear right uphill on the small road | Via Poggio a Pino | E | 34 |
| 82A1.004 | 160 | 4.0 | Continue uphill on the small road | | SW | 41 |
| 82A1.005 | 120 | 4.2 | At the Stop sign, continue straight ahead | Church on the right | SE | 48 |
| 82A1.006 | 220 | 4.4 | Fork right | Uphill | S | 57 |
| 82A1.007 | 210 | 4.6 | At the Stop sign, turn left | SS67, direction Calenzano | S | 63 |
| 82A1.008 | 1700 | 6.2 | Bear left on the main road to rejoin the "Official Route" | Downhill | | 144 |

| Waypoint | Distance between waypoints | Total km | Directions | Verification Point | Compass | Altitude m |
|---|---|---|---|---|---|---|
| 82A2.001 | 0 | 0.0 | Fork left onto viale Giacomo Matteotti | Enter the historic centre | S | 115 |
| 82A2.002 | 160 | 0.2 | Bear left onto via San Francesco | Chiesa di San Francesco on your right at the junction | SE | 136 |
| 82A2.003 | 20 | 0.2 | Take the left fork | | SE | 134 |
| 82A2.004 | 70 | 0.3 | Arrive in San-Miniato old town at the section end | Piazza Buonaparte | | 122 |

**Alternate Route #82.A2**    **Length: 0.3km**

**Stage Summary: Alternate Route following the road directly to the centre of the old town**

**Stage Ascent: 21m**    **Stage Descent: 14m**

### Accommodation & Facilities ....    Altopascio - San-Miniato

Ostello Ponte dè Medici,Via Cristoforo Colombo, 237,50054 Fucecchio(FI),Italy; Tel:+39 0571 297831; +39 0571 287049; Email:pontemedici@ponteverde.it; Price:C

Misericordia San Miniato Basso,(Mario Giugni),Piazza Vincenzo Cuoco, 9,56028 San-Miniato-Basso(PI),Italy; Tel:+39 0571 419455; +39 3398 723682; Email:mario.giugni@libero.it; Web-site:www.misericordiasanminiatobasso.org; Price:D

Convento San Francesco,Piazza San Francesco, 1,56028 San-Miniato(PI),Italy; Tel:+39 0571 43051; +39 0571 43398; Price:B

San Pietro Apostolo,Via della Chiesa In Galleno,50054 Fucecchio(FI),Italy; Tel:+39 0571 299931; Email:mbroti@tin.it; Price:D

Hotel la Campagnola,Viale Cristoforo Colombo, 144,50054 Fucecchio(FI),Italy; Tel:+39 0571 260786; Email: Info@Lacampagnolahotel.Com ; Web-site:www.lacampagnolahotel.com; Price:A

Albergo Elio,Via Tosco-Romagnola Est, 485,56028 San-Miniato(PI),Italy; Tel:+39 0571 42010; Email:info@albergoelio.it; Web-site:www.albergoelio.it; Price:B

Comune di Fucecchio,Via la Marmora, 34,50054 Fucecchio(FI),Italy; Tel:+39 0571 20681

Associazione Turistica Pro Loco,Corso Giuseppe Garibaldi, 2,56028 San-Miniato(PI),Italy; Tel:+39 0571 42233

| | |
|---|---|
| 💲 | Banca Nazionale del Lavoro,Via Trieste, 19,50054 Fucecchio(FI),Italy; Tel:+39 0571 260342 |
| 💲 | Cassa di Risparmio,Piazza Giuseppe Montanelli, 27,50054 Fucecchio(FI),Italy; Tel:+39 0571 24711 |
| 💲 | Banca Cr Firenze Filiale di San Miniato Basso,Piazzale della Pace, 9,56028 San-Miniato(PI),Italy; Tel:+39 0571 419211 |
| 💲 | MPS Banca,Largo Loris Malaguzzi, 9,56028 San-Miniato(PI),Italy; Tel:+39 0571 498959 |
| 🏥 | Ospedale San Pietro Igneo,Piazza Spartaco Lavagnini,50054 Fucecchio(FI),Italy; Tel:+39 0571 7051 |
| ➕ | Mattaliano - Studio Medico,Corso Giacomo Matteotti,50054 Fucecchio(FI),Italy; Tel:+39 0571 22308 |
| ➕ | Buggiani - Studio Medico,Piazza Sandro Pertini,56028 San-Miniato(PI),Italy; Tel:+39 0571 419449 |
| 🐕 | Ambulatorio Veterinario,Via di Burello, 8,50054 Fucecchio(FI),Italy; Tel:+39 0571 242838 |
| 🚶 | Maracana' Sport,Via Roma, 7,50054 Fucecchio(FI),Italy; Tel:+39 0571 20968 |
| 🚶 | Trekking e Sport,Piazza Sandro Pertini,56028 San-Miniato(PI),Italy; Tel:+39 0571 400499 |
| 🚴 | Cicli Barone di Carmelo Barone,Via Provinciale Francesca Sud, 99,56029 Santa-Croce-Sull'Arno(PI),Italy; Tel:+39 0571 360675 |

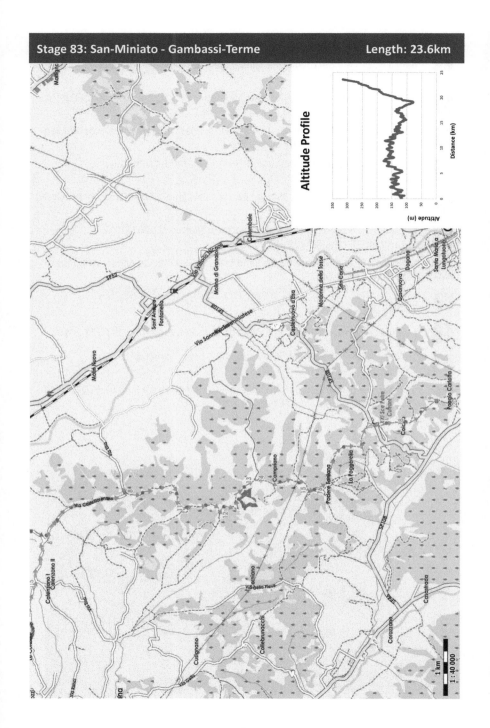

Stage Summary: the route follows a mix of country roads and broad tracks over the rolling Tuscan hills. The section can be challenging in the summer heat with few opportunities for water stops.

Distance from Vercelli: 477km      Distance to St Peter's Square, Rome: 372km
Stage Ascent: 765m           Stage Descent: 567m

| Waypoint | Distance between waypoints | Total km | Directions | Verification Point | Compass | Altitude m |
|---|---|---|---|---|---|---|
| 83.001 | 0 | 0.0 | Bear left in piazza Buonaparte and follow via Paolo Maioli | Statue of Leopold II on your right | E | 118 |
| 83.002 | 400 | 0.4 | Turn right on via Vicolo Borghizzi and almost immediately turn left through an archway. Note:- the pathway ahead involves a flight of steps - horse and bike riders are advised to remain on the road towards Calenzano | VF sign | SE | 121 |
| 83.003 | 90 | 0.5 | Turn right down a small brick passage separated by metal balustrades | VF sign | SE | 122 |
| 83.004 | 140 | 0.6 | At the T-junction with the road, turn right - riders rejoin from the left | Direction Calenzano | SE | 110 |
| 83.005 | 1900 | 2.4 | Fork left, via Castelfiorentino | VF sign, church on right | E | 150 |
| 83.006 | 800 | 3.2 | Fork right downhill | Direction Castelfiorentino, VF sign | SE | 149 |
| 83.007 | 60 | 3.3 | At the junction, turn right - Alternate Route rejoins from the left | VF sign | SE | 144 |
| 83.008 | 1800 | 5.1 | Following a sharp bend to the left, turn right and right again onto a gravel track | VF sign | S | 124 |
| 83.009 | 1100 | 6.1 | Fork right | VF sign | W | 137 |

| Waypoint | Distance between waypoints | Total km | Directions | Verification Point | Compass | Altitude m |
|---|---|---|---|---|---|---|
| 83.010 | 90 | 6.2 | Fork left up the hill towards trees | VF sign | SW | 139 |
| 83.011 | 260 | 6.5 | At the T-junction, turn left | VF sign | S | 166 |
| 83.012 | 800 | 7.2 | Turn sharp left up the hill | VF sign | SE | 157 |
| 83.013 | 1100 | 8.3 | Turn left with a house directly on the right | VF sign | SE | 155 |
| 83.014 | 30 | 8.4 | Fork right onto on via di Meleto, keep the farmhouse on the right | VF sign | S | 158 |
| 83.015 | 1100 | 9.4 | Turn onto the furthest left of the tracks via della Poggiarella | | S | 152 |
| 83.016 | 90 | 9.5 | Take the left fork | VF sign | SE | 157 |
| 83.017 | 1900 | 11.4 | At the crossroads in Coiano (XXI) continue straight ahead on the gravel road, via Coianese | VF sign | S | 172 |
| 83.018 | 400 | 11.8 | Continue straight ahead on the gravel track | VF sign | SE | 149 |
| 83.019 | 900 | 12.7 | Fork right down the hill | VF sign | S | 145 |
| 83.020 | 210 | 12.9 | Fork left up the hill | VF sign | SE | 131 |
| 83.021 | 900 | 13.7 | Continue straight ahead | VF sign | S | 138 |
| 83.022 | 1700 | 15.4 | At the T-junction, turn left between two houses | VF sign | SE | 111 |
| 83.023 | 210 | 15.6 | At the T-junction with the SP46, turn left onto the road | VF sign | NE | 104 |
| 83.024 | 150 | 15.8 | Turn sharp right onto the track | VF sign | SE | 105 |
| 83.025 | 1000 | 16.8 | After passing a house continue straight ahead onto the grass track | VF sign | S | 115 |
| 83.026 | 800 | 17.6 | At the T-junction turn left | VF sign | E | 124 |
| 83.027 | 500 | 18.0 | Keep right on the gravel road along the ridge | VF sign | E | 118 |

| Waypoint | Distance between waypoints | Total km | Directions | Verification Point | Compass | Altitude m |
|---|---|---|---|---|---|---|
| 83.028 | 700 | 18.7 | Turn right at an elevated T-junction, descend the ramp and join the main road | VF sign | SW | 92 |
| 83.029 | 210 | 18.9 | Turn left over the pedestrian crossing and continue straight ahead on an unmade road | VF sign | SE | 80 |
| 83.030 | 170 | 19.1 | Bear right after passing the house on the right | VF sign | S | 77 |
| 83.031 | 500 | 19.5 | At the T-junction, turn right with house on left | Red and white sign | SW | 114 |
| 83.032 | 230 | 19.7 | Fork left up the hill | Hedged garden on your right | S | 117 |
| 83.033 | 600 | 20.3 | Keep left, uphill on the gravel road | Shrine just before the junction | SE | 150 |
| 83.034 | 700 | 20.9 | At the T-junction, turn right onto the SP4 | VF sign | S | 184 |
| 83.035 | 1700 | 22.6 | Santa Maria a Chianni (XX) is to the left. To follow the route to Gambassi-Terme, continue uphill on the main road | VF sign | S | 252 |
| 83.036 | 800 | 23.4 | At the traffic lights, fork left direction Gambassi | Beside the church of Cristo Re in Santi Jacopo e Stefano | S | 296 |
| 83.037 | 230 | 23.6 | Arrive at Gambassi-Terme | | | 316 |

Ostello Sigerico,(Anna Giubbolini),Chiani,50050 Gambassi-Terme(FI),Italy; Tel:+39 0571 638242; +39 3247 968837; Email:ostello.sigerico@yahoo.com; Web-site:www.ostellosigerico.it; Price:C

Parrocchia Santi Jacopo e Stefano,Via Volterrana Nord, 59,50050 Gambassi-Terme(FI),Italy; Tel:+39 0571 638208; Email:parrocchia.gambassi@libero.it; Price:D

Albergo Osteria Pinchorba,Route d, 26,50050 Gambassi-Terme(FI),Italy; Tel:+39 0571 638188; Price:B

Ufficio Turistico,Via Cosimo Ridolfi,50051 Castelfiorentino(FI),Italy; Tel:+39 0571 629049

Comune di Gambassi Terme,Via Giuseppe Garibaldi, 7,50050 Gambassi-Terme(FI),Italy; Tel:+39 0571 638224

Banca di Credito Cooperativo,Via Giuseppe Garibaldi, 14,50050 Gambassi-Terme(FI),Italy; Tel:+39 0571 638644

Peretola Airport,Via del Termine, 11,50127 Firenze(FI),Italy; Tel:+39 0553 0615; Web-site:www.aeroporto.firenze.it

Ospedale Santa Verdiana,Via dei Mille,50051 Castelfiorentino(FI),Italy; Tel:+39 0571 6831

Studio Veterinario,Viale Antonio Gramsci,50050 Gambassi-Terme(FI),Italy; Tel:+39 0571 638636

Ancilotti Bike di Ancilotti Marco,Via Bruno Fanciullacci, 30,50051 Castelfiorentino(FI),Italy; Tel:+39 0571 631007

Taxi,Via della Costituente, 1,50051 Castelfiorentino(FI),Italy; Tel:+39 0571 684568

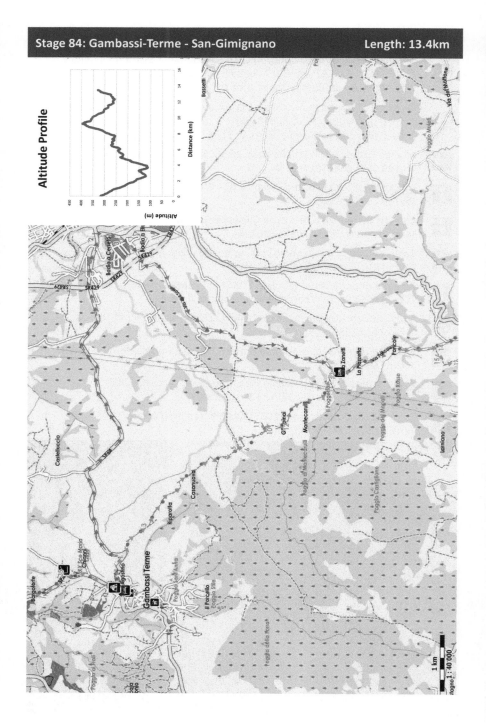

Stage Summary: the section is undertaken substantially on remote tracks winding over the Tuscan hills. Although beautiful, the section can be very tiring in the heat of summer.

Distance from Vercelli: 500km          Distance to St Peter's Square, Rome: 348km
Stage Ascent:  449m          Stage Descent: 436m

| Waypoint | Distance between waypoints | Total km | Directions | Verification Point | Compass | Altitude m |
|---|---|---|---|---|---|---|
| 84.001 | 0 | 0.7 | From the church of Cristo Re in Santi Jacopo e Stefano, take via Icilio Franchi | Direction Certaldo, VF sign | E | 316 |
| 84.002 | 700 | 1.4 | On the apex of the bend to the left, bear right onto a small road.  Note:- the route ahead is passable and generally pleasant for all groups, however there are sections where cyclists will be challenged by steep off-road climbs.  Cyclists may want to remain on the road and bear left to follow the Alternate Route to Pancole via the Elsa valley | Direction Luiano, VF sign | SE | 267 |
| 84.003 | 700 | 3.3 | Beside the small chapel, take the left fork | VF sign | SE | 210 |
| 84.004 | 1900 | 3.7 | At the junction, keep left down the hill | VF sign | SE | 149 |
| 84.005 | 400 | 3.7 | Fork right up the hill | VF sign | SW | 111 |
| 84.006 | 20 | 3.9 | Bear left onto the track in the field and skirt the field | Field on your left and trees on your right | E | 112 |
| 84.007 | 230 | 4.2 | In the opposite corner of the field, bear right through the trees and continue on the track, uphill | Trees on your left | S | 119 |
| 84.008 | 290 | 4.3 | Track enters another field, bear left | Uphill | SE | 154 |

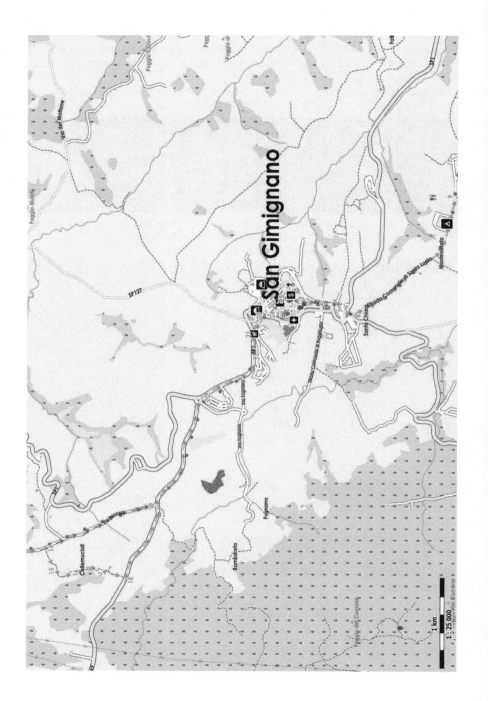

| Waypoint | Distance between waypoints | Total km | Directions | Verification Point | Compass | Altitude m |
|---|---|---|---|---|---|---|
| 84.009 | 80 | 4.4 | Bear left up the hill | VF sign | SE | 165 |
| 84.010 | 80 | 4.5 | Directly in front of a farmhouse, turn left onto a gravel track | Continuing up the hill | E | 178 |
| 84.011 | 150 | 4.9 | At the T-junction in the track, turn right up the hill | VF sign | S | 188 |
| 84.012 | 400 | 6.4 | Fork left | VF sign, via San Piero | SE | 224 |
| 84.013 | 1600 | 8.4 | At the T-junction with a tarmac road, turn right up the hill - Alternate Route rejoins from the left | Pass through Pancole | S | 268 |
| 84.014 | 1900 | 8.7 | Turn right on the gravel track. Note:- the Official Route makes a loop towards the woods and extends the distance to be covered on the busy SP69. 1km may be saved my remaining on this road and rejoining the "Official Route" at the T-junction ahead | VF sign to the right | SW | 308 |
| 84.015 | 300 | 8.9 | Take the left fork | VF sign | S | 346 |
| 84.016 | 190 | 9.3 | Continue straight ahead | Pass through the archway | S | 370 |
| 84.017 | 500 | 9.6 | Bear right across the car park | Pieve di Santa Maria Assunta on your left | SW | 387 |
| 84.018 | 240 | 10.5 | At the T-junction with the SP69, turn left and follow the main road | | SE | 361 |
| 84.019 | 900 | 11.8 | Continue straight ahead, down the hill | Direction San Gimignano | E | 324 |
| 84.020 | 1400 | 12.9 | At the roundabout, bear right, direction San Gimignano centre | Via Martiri di Citerna, VF sign | SE | 262 |

| Waypoint | Distance between waypoints | Total km | Directions | Verification Point | Compass | Altitude m |
|---|---|---|---|---|---|---|
| 84.021 | 1100 | 13.1 | Fork right up the hill on via Niccolo Cannicci | Pass crucifix on your left, VF sign | SE | 274 |
| 84.022 | 200 | 13.1 | At the junction, continue straight ahead | Uphill | SE | 301 |
| 84.023 | 50 | 13.1 | At the intersection with the main road, take the underpass to enter San-Gimignano | Pass through the arch, porta San Matteo | SE | 307 |
| 84.024 | 30 | 13.4 | Continue straight ahead on the paved road | Via San Matteo | SE | 309 |
| 84.025 | 300 | | Arrive at San-Gimignano (XIX) in piazza Duomo | Tourist offices to the right | | 329 |

| Alternate Route #84.A1 | | Length: 12.3km | | | | |
|---|---|---|---|---|---|---|

Stage Summary: a longer cyclist route to avoid tiring and difficult off-road climbs. The route descends to Certaldo in the Elsa valley before climbing to rejoin the "Official Route" in Pancole.

| Stage Ascent: 309m | | | Stage Descent: 310m | | | |
|---|---|---|---|---|---|---|
| 84A1.001 | 0 | 0.0 | Continue straight ahead on SP40 | Direction Ponte a Elsa | E | 115 |
| 84A1.002 | 6800 | 6.8 | Just before the bridge over the river Elsa, turn right | Direction San Gimignano | S | 136 |
| 84A1.003 | 500 | 7.3 | Bear right | Direction Pancole | SW | 134 |
| 84A1.004 | 5100 | 12.3 | Turn left to rejoin the "Official Route" | Enter Pancole | | 122 |

**Accommodation & Facilities  ....     Gambassi-Terme - San-Gimignano**

Convento Sant'Agostino,(Padre Brian),Piazza Sant'Agostino, 10,53037 San-Gimignano(SI),Italy; Tel:+39 0577 907012; Email:sangimignanoconvento@yahoo.it; Price:D

Monastero di San Girolamo,Via Folgore, 32,53037 San-Gimignano(SI),Italy; Tel:+39 0577 940573; Email:monasterosangimignano@gmail.com; Web-site:www.monasterosangirolamo.it; Price:B

Azienda Agricola di Cesani Vincenzo,Località Pancole 82a,53037 San-Gimignano(SI),Italy; Tel:+39 0577 955084; Email: info@agriturismocesani.it ; Web-site:www.agriturismocesani.it; Price:A

Camping Boschetto di Piemma,Località Santa Lucia,53037 San-Gimignano(SI),Italy; Tel:+39 0577 907134; Email:info@boschettodipiemma. it; Web-site:www.boschettodipiemma.it; Price:C; Note:Mobile homes also available,

Associazione Turistica Pro Loco,Via G.Boccaccio, 16,50052 Certaldo(FI),Italy; Tel:+39 0571 652730

Comune San Gimignano,Via San Matteo, 24,53037 San-Gimignano(SI),Italy; Tel:+39 0577 955604

Banca Toscana,Piazza Martiri della Liberta, 2,53037 San-Gimignano(SI),Italy; Tel:+39 0577 940329

Profeti - Medico,Localita' Camporeccia, 2,53037 San-Gimignano(SI),Italy; Tel:+39 0577 941152

Studio Veterinario,Via Nicola Cannicci, 41,53037 San-Gimignano(SI),Italy; Tel:+39 0577 941179

Dany Sport,Piazza della Cisterna,53037 San-Gimignano(SI),Italy; Tel:+39 0577 941698

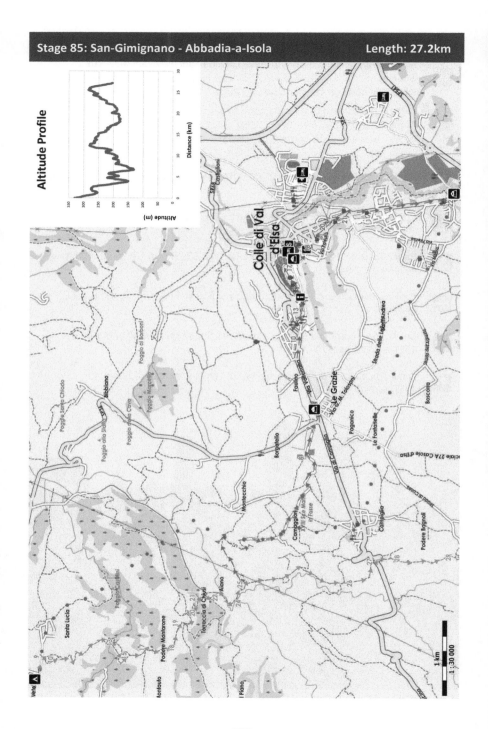

Stage Summary: this long and strenuous section leaves San Gimignano on tarmac roads before returning to the tracks through the Tuscan hills and negotiating a number of normally shallow water crossings. There are limited opportunities to break the journey on the "Official Route". An Alternate Route offers the opportunity to divert to the large town of Colle di Val d'Elsa where all facilities are available.

Distance from Vercelli: 514km          Distance to St Peter's Square, Rome: 335km
Stage Ascent: 579m                      Stage Descent: 705m

| Waypoint | Distance between waypoints | Total km | Directions | Verification Point | Compass | Altitude m |
|---|---|---|---|---|---|---|
| 85.001 | 0 | 0.0 | From piazza Duomo, continue straight ahead | Duomo and steps to the right | S | 329 |
| 85.002 | 60 | 0.1 | In piazza Cisterna, continue straight ahead down a narrow passage way, via San Giovanni | Pass through arch | SW | 323 |
| 85.003 | 30 | 0.1 | Bear left on via San Giovanni | VF sign | S | 322 |
| 85.004 | 260 | 0.3 | After passing underneath the last archway, porta San Giovanni, bear left | Keep small park to your right | S | 304 |
| 85.005 | 90 | 0.4 | Turn left and go down the steps. Note:- riders remain on the road and take the first left turn | Towards the stopping place for buses | S | 300 |
| 85.006 | 110 | 0.5 | Turn right on via Baccanella | VF sign | SW | 292 |
| 85.007 | 130 | 0.7 | At a mini roundabout, take the exit direction Montauto | Red and white VF sign | SW | 281 |
| 85.008 | 90 | 0.8 | Turn left direction Santa Lucia | VF sign | SE | 273 |
| 85.009 | 1900 | 2.6 | Shortly after passing the sports field on the left, turn right on an unmade road | Pass a small shrine on your left | SW | 268 |
| 85.010 | 50 | 2.7 | Turn right | Near to a shed | S | 267 |
| 85.011 | 240 | 2.9 | Bear right on the track | Downhill | S | 249 |

| Waypoint | Distance between waypoints | Total km | Directions | Verification Point | Compass | Altitude m |
|---|---|---|---|---|---|---|
| 85.012 | 1000 | 3.9 | Beside the house in the valley bottom turn left and ford the stream | | SW | 151 |
| 85.013 | 160 | 4.1 | Bear right around the field | Trees on your right | W | 158 |
| 85.014 | 300 | 4.4 | Turn left on the track | Keep olive trees on your right | SE | 194 |
| 85.015 | 150 | 4.6 | At the junction in the tracks, bear right on the tree lined track | Agriturismo on your left | S | 197 |
| 85.016 | 250 | 4.8 | At the junction at the top of the ridge turn left | | SE | 217 |
| 85.017 | 40 | 4.9 | Take the track to the right | Downhill | S | 215 |
| 85.018 | 300 | 5.2 | At the bottom of the hill, continue straight ahead | Cross the stream | SE | 182 |
| 85.019 | 500 | 5.6 | Turn right and then left to skirt the house | Villa della Torraccia di Chiusi | SE | 208 |
| 85.020 | 300 | 5.9 | At the intersection with the entrance to the house, turn right on the road | Downhill | SE | 209 |
| 85.021 | 400 | 6.3 | Just before the hamlet of Aiano turn right | Pass between the buildings | S | 170 |
| 85.022 | 220 | 6.5 | Take the left fork | Reservoir on the right | S | 144 |
| 85.023 | 300 | 6.8 | Continue straight ahead across the ford | | S | 132 |
| 85.024 | 100 | 6.9 | Take the left fork | | SE | 133 |
| 85.025 | 300 | 7.2 | Take the right fork. Note:- to visit Colle di Val D'Elsa and its wide range of facilities, take the left fork and follow the Alternate Route | | S | 151 |
| 85.026 | 1400 | 8.6 | At the road junction, continue straight ahead | | SE | 183 |

| Waypoint | Distance between waypoints | Total km | Directions | Verification Point | Compass | Altitude m |
|---|---|---|---|---|---|---|
| 85.027 | 600 | 9.2 | Turn right, beside the road, take the pedestrian crossing and then turn left on the track | Trees on your left | S | 200 |
| 85.028 | 300 | 9.6 | At the T-junction, turn right | Pass the farm on your right | S | 190 |
| 85.029 | 900 | 10.4 | After a section of an old paved road bear right | | S | 205 |
| 85.030 | 140 | 10.6 | Turn left, uphill | Towards the houses | S | 213 |
| 85.031 | 110 | 10.7 | At the T-junction with the road, turn right | | W | 224 |
| 85.032 | 110 | 10.8 | Take the left fork | Towards Abbazia St. Maria a Coneo | S | 215 |
| 85.033 | 180 | 11.0 | Continue straight ahead on the unmade road | Abbey on your left | S | 225 |
| 85.034 | 60 | 11.0 | Take the old paved road to the right | Downhill | SW | 225 |
| 85.035 | 700 | 11.7 | Turn left on the stony track, uphill | Between the trees | SE | 237 |
| 85.036 | 130 | 11.9 | Emerge from the woods and continue straight ahead | Pass house and swimming pool on your right | SE | 259 |
| 85.037 | 140 | 12.0 | At the T-junction at the end of the field, turn left and then right | Into the woods | SE | 266 |
| 85.038 | 170 | 12.2 | Take the right fork | | SE | 274 |
| 85.039 | 150 | 12.3 | At the crossroads continue straight ahead | | SE | 279 |
| 85.040 | 240 | 12.6 | At the T-junction, turn left on the unmade road | | E | 275 |
| 85.041 | 180 | 12.8 | At the crossroads, continue straight ahead | | SE | 277 |
| 85.042 | 600 | 13.3 | At the T-junction, turn left towards the village | San Donato | E | 263 |

| Waypoint | Distance between waypoints | Total km | Directions | Verification Point | Compass | Altitude m |
|---|---|---|---|---|---|---|
| 85.043 | 300 | 13.6 | Take the left fork on the tarmac | Towards the main road | E | 260 |
| 85.044 | 140 | 13.7 | At the T-junction with the main road (SP27), take the pedestrian crossing and turn right on the pavement | Gantry overhead | S | 255 |
| 85.045 | 180 | 13.9 | Turn left into Quartaia, on via degli Aragonesi | VF sign, pass Tabacchi on the right | E | 259 |
| 85.046 | 140 | 14.1 | Turn right | Via della Concordia | S | 261 |
| 85.047 | 130 | 14.2 | At the T-junction, turn left on the unmade road | Exit the village | NE | 261 |
| 85.048 | 1100 | 15.2 | Pass through the farm and continue on the unmade road | Road bears right | SE | 250 |
| 85.049 | 500 | 15.7 | At the T-junction at the foot of the hill, turn left and continue straight ahead | Beside the woods | E | 224 |
| 85.050 | 500 | 16.2 | Turn left on the track | Just before reaching the bridge | E | 217 |
| 85.051 | 90 | 16.3 | Take the right fork | | NE | 217 |
| 85.052 | 500 | 16.7 | Take the right fork | | NE | 212 |
| 85.053 | 260 | 17.0 | Bear right on the white road | Towards Molino le Vene | NE | 209 |
| 85.054 | 1000 | 18.0 | Join a tarmac road and bear right | Village of Onci to the left | E | 178 |
| 85.055 | 70 | 18.1 | Turn left on the road | Beside the canal | NE | 176 |
| 85.056 | 600 | 18.7 | After crossing the waterway, bear right and immediately left | Via Nino Bixio | SE | 176 |
| 85.057 | 140 | 18.8 | At the crossroads, turn right | Via Montanara | S | 180 |
| 85.058 | 200 | 19.0 | At the T-junction, turn left, right and then left again | | SE | 181 |

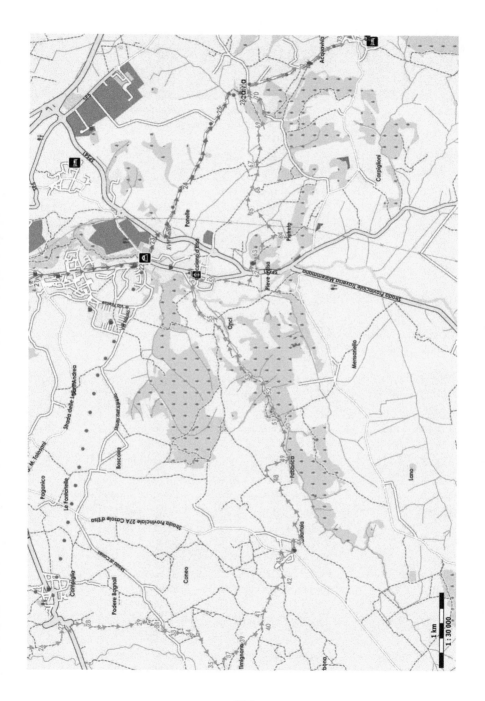

| Waypoint | Distance between waypoints | Total km | Directions | Verification Point | Compass | Altitude m |
|---|---|---|---|---|---|---|
| 85.059 | 100 | 19.1 | At the junction with the main road, turn right and take the right fork on the road | Direction Pieve a Elsa | S | 181 |
| 85.060 | 400 | 19.5 | At the crossroads, turn left on the stony track | | SE | 179 |
| 85.061 | 100 | 19.6 | Bear left at the junction | | E | 180 |
| 85.062 | 50 | 19.7 | Take the pedestrian crossing over the road and continue straight ahead on the gravel road | Towards the hotel Il Pietreto | SE | 181 |
| 85.063 | 400 | 20.0 | Take the left fork | Pass the hotel on your right | SE | 202 |
| 85.064 | 300 | 20.3 | After passing the hotel and the trees on your right, turn left on the track | | NE | 198 |
| 85.065 | 400 | 20.8 | At the T-junction, turn left and then right | Follow the line of trees | E | 189 |
| 85.066 | 400 | 21.2 | At the crossroads in the tracks, continue straight ahead | Line of trees on the right | E | 188 |
| 85.067 | 400 | 21.6 | Continue straight ahead on the path | Beside the fence | E | 194 |
| 85.068 | 500 | 22.0 | Take the right fork | Woods on the left | SE | 202 |
| 85.069 | 90 | 22.1 | Bear left and then right | Into the woods | NE | 206 |
| 85.070 | 500 | 22.6 | At the junction, continue straight ahead on the gravel road. Note:- the Alternate Route via Colle di Val D'Elsa rejoins from the left | Strada della Cerreta, VF sign | E | 222 |
| 85.071 | 130 | 22.8 | Turn right, direction Strove | Strada di Acquaviva | SE | 223 |
| 85.072 | 700 | 23.5 | Bear right on the tarmac | Stone wall on the right | SE | 244 |
| 85.073 | 800 | 24.3 | In Strove, fork left | Beside brick electricity tower | SE | 266 |

| Waypoint | Distance between waypoints | Total km | Directions | Verification Point | Compass | Altitude m |
|---|---|---|---|---|---|---|
| 85.074 | 130 | 24.4 | After passing the basketball court, bear left on strada di Strove | VF sign | E | 266 |
| 85.075 | 130 | 24.5 | At the T-junction with the main road, turn left | Gravel path beside main road | E | 257 |
| 85.076 | 180 | 24.7 | Take the pedestrian crossing and turn right | Towards Castel Pietraia | E | 256 |
| 85.077 | 170 | 24.9 | On the apex of the bend to right, turn left on the track | | NE | 265 |
| 85.078 | 250 | 25.1 | Turn right towards woods | After passing between houses | E | 269 |
| 85.079 | 300 | 25.4 | Turn right on the path into the woods and then quickly fork to the left | Ignore road on the left – leads into an industrial site | SE | 281 |
| 85.080 | 200 | 25.6 | Take the left fork | | E | 280 |
| 85.081 | 260 | 25.9 | Turn left | Remain in the woods | NE | 281 |
| 85.082 | 100 | 26.0 | Continue straight ahead and leave the woods | Cross the olive grove | NE | 279 |
| 85.083 | 170 | 26.1 | At the T-junction, turn left on the white road, strada di Certino | Between stone walls | N | 275 |
| 85.084 | 700 | 26.8 | At the T-junction, turn right | VF sign | NE | 225 |
| 85.085 | 90 | 26.9 | Take the left fork | Downhill, between houses | NE | 222 |
| 85.086 | 240 | 27.1 | Rejoin the main road and turn right | Towards bar | NE | 205 |
| 85.087 | 40 | 27.2 | Arrive at Abbadia-a-Isola (XVI) | Ancient church on the right | | 203 |

| Waypoint | Distance between waypoints | Total km | Directions | Verification Point | Compass | Altitude m |
|---|---|---|---|---|---|---|
| 85A1.001 | 0 | 0.0 | Turn left | | NE | 153 |
| 85A1.002 | 70 | 0.1 | Emerge from the woods and continue straight ahead | Between the fields | NE | 157 |
| 85A1.003 | 300 | 0.4 | Re-enter the woods and continue uphill | | E | 168 |
| 85A1.004 | 400 | 0.7 | Turn sharp right and continue uphill | On the broad track | S | 206 |
| 85A1.005 | 500 | 1.3 | Keep left and pass between the buildings | Cascina Prodeggia | S | 252 |
| 85A1.006 | 110 | 1.4 | Continue straight ahead on the tarmac road | Pass water tap on the building on the left | S | 257 |
| 85A1.007 | 110 | 1.5 | At the junction, continue straight ahead | Large metal gates on your right | SE | 257 |
| 85A1.008 | 1700 | 3.1 | Keep right | Cemetery on your right | E | 246 |
| 85A1.009 | 400 | 3.6 | At the Stop sign, turn right and then turn left beside the main road | Enter Colle di Val D'Elsa | E | 242 |
| 85A1.010 | 1300 | 4.9 | At the junction beside the turreted town gate, bear left | Porta Nova | NE | 231 |
| 85A1.011 | 150 | 5.0 | At the crossroads, turn right | Via Porta Vecchia | SE | 227 |
| 85A1.012 | 60 | 5.1 | Pass to the left of the brick turret and take the small road overlooking the valley on the left | Via Dietro le Mura | E | 226 |
| 85A1.013 | 280 | 5.3 | Bear right into piazza santa Caterina and then bear left | Via F. Campana | NE | 200 |

| Waypoint | Distance between waypoints | Total km | Directions | Verification Point | Compass | Altitude m |
|---|---|---|---|---|---|---|
| 85A1.014 | 600 | 5.9 | End of street turn right and take ramp to leave old town | | E | 189 |
| 85A1.015 | 220 | 6.2 | Turn right and right again on the street at the foot of the hill | Via Meoni | SW | 156 |
| 85A1.016 | 110 | 6.3 | Turn left on the narrow street | Continue through the archway | S | 164 |
| 85A1.017 | 50 | 6.3 | At the crossroads, continue straight ahead | Via della Pieve in Piano | SE | 156 |
| 85A1.018 | 400 | 6.7 | At the Stop sign bear right on via Armando Diaz | Pass bank on the left | SE | 152 |
| 85A1.019 | 70 | 6.8 | Turn left on the narrow street | Via Maremmana Vecchia | SE | 152 |
| 85A1.020 | 300 | 7.1 | At the junction with the main road, cross the pedestrian crossing and turn right and then bear left at the roundabout | Direction Siena | S | 161 |
| 85A1.021 | 300 | 7.4 | At the next roundabout continue straight ahead | SS541, direction Grosseto | S | 164 |
| 85A1.022 | 1400 | 8.8 | At the roundabout, after crossing the river Elsa, turn left and pass Parrocchia San Marziale on your left | Continue beside the sports field | E | 174 |
| 85A1.023 | 400 | 9.2 | Pass under the road bridge and bear right at the junction | Climb the hill to the hamlet of Ponelle | SE | 180 |
| 85A1.024 | 1100 | 10.3 | Take the left fork on the broad track | | SE | 193 |
| 85A1.025 | 1200 | 11.4 | In the centre of the village of Scarna, take the right fork, downhill | | S | 219 |
| 85A1.026 | 500 | 11.9 | At the T-junction, turn left and rejoin the "Official Route" | VF sign | | 223 |

## Accommodation & Facilities .... San-Gimignano - Abbadia-a-Isola

Casa Per Ferie Santa Maria Assunta Ospitalita Pellegrini,Piazza Roma, 23,53035 Monteriggioni(SI),Italy; Tel:+39 0577 304214; +39 3356 651581; +39 3359 009134; Email:dondoriano@interfree.it; Web-site:www. monteriggioniviafrancigena.it; Price:D; Note:15€ per person per night, credentials required,

Ospitale dei Santi Cirino e Giacomo,Località Abbadia d'Isola,53035 Monteriggioni(SI),Italy; Tel:+39 0577 304214; +39 3356 651581; +39 3270 655678; Email:casaferiesma@yahoo.it; Price:D; Note:Open Easter to October,

Comunità Salesiana Sant'Agostino,Piazza Sant'Agostino,53034 Colle-di-Val-d'Elsa(SI),Italy; Tel:+39 0577 920195; Email:sdbcolle@tin.it; Price:D

Parrocchia di Santa Maria a le Grazie,(Don Stefano Nicoletti),Via Volterrana, 55,53034 Colle-di-Val-d'Elsa(SI),Italy; Tel:+39 0577 959068; Email:gigicol64@libero.it; Price:D

Parrocchia S.Marziale,(Don Mario Costanz),Via San Marziale, 1,53034 Gracciano-di-Colle-Val-d'Elsa(SI),Italy; Tel:+39 0577 928677; Email:parrocchiasanmarziale@valdelsa.net; Price:C; Note:Credentials required,

Parrocchia di Cristo Re e Santa Maria Nascente,Piazza Cristo Re, 1,53035 Castellina-Scalo-Abate(SI),Italy; Tel:+39 0577 304214; +39 3356 651581; Email:dondoriano@interfree.it; Price:C

Albergo il Nazionale,Via Giuseppe Garibaldi, 20,53034 Colle-di-Val-d'Elsa(SI),Italy; Tel:+39 0577 920039; Price:B

Hotel Cristall,Via Liguria, 1,53034 Colle-di-Val-d'Elsa(SI),Italy; Tel:+39 0577 920361; Email:info@cristall-feri.com; Web-site:www.cristall-feri.com; Price:B

Hotel Villa Belvedere,SP5 Colligiana,53034 Colle-di-Val-d'Elsa(SI),Italy; Tel:+39 0577 920966; Email:email@villabelvedere.com; Web-site:villabelvedere.com; Price:B

B&B - Relais Castelbigozzi,Località Strove,53035 Monteriggioni(SI),Italy; Tel:+39 0577 300000; Email:info@castellobigozzi.it; Price:A

Pro Loco,Via Francesco Campana, 43,53034 Colle-di-Val-d'Elsa(SI),Italy; Tel:+39 0577 922621

Ufficio Turistico,Piazza Roma,53035 Monteriggioni(SI),Italy; Tel:+39 0577 304834

Cassa di Risparmio di Volterra,Via Guglielmo Oberdan, 33,53034 Colle-di-Val-d'Elsa(SI),Italy; Tel:+39 0577 923781; Web-site:www.crvolterra.it

Chiantibanca Credito Cooperativo,Via Fratelli Bandiera, 67,53034 Colle-di-Val-d'Elsa(SI),Italy; Tel:+39 0577 908080; Web-site:www.chiantibanca.it

## Accommodation & Facilities .... San-Gimignano - Abbadia-a-Isola

🏥 Ospedale Dell'Alta Val d'Elsa,Campostaggia,53036 Poggibonsi(SI),Italy;
Tel:+39 0577 9941

➕ Azienda Speciale Multiservizi,Via Liguria,53034 Colle-di-Val-d'Elsa(SI),Italy;
Tel:+39 0577 922569

➕ Berti,Via Fratelli Bandiera, 118,53034 Colle-di-Val-d'Elsa(SI),Italy;
Tel:+39 0577 928703

🐕 Dr Francesca Messeri,Via Teano, 7,53034 Colle-di-Val-d'Elsa(SI),Italy;
Tel:+39 0577 908145

🥾 Idea Sport,Via Guglielmo Oberdan, 27,53034 Colle-di-Val-d'Elsa(SI),Italy;
Tel:+39 0577 921993

🚲 Ciclosport di Porciatti Fabio,Via Lazio, 19,53036 Poggibonsi(SI),Italy;
Tel:+39 0577 938507

🐎 Podere Tremulini Centro di Equitazione Toscana,Loc.Tremulini,53031 Casole-
d'Elsa(SI),Italy; Tel:+39 0577 963910

☎ Bernardini Taxi Ncc Luciana,Strada di Serfignano, 6,53100 Siena(SI),Italy;
Tel:+39 0577 301199

☎ Taxi,Piazza Mazzini,53036 Poggibonsi(SI),Italy; Tel:+39 0577 934513

Altitude Profile

Monteriggioni

Montereggi

Poggiola

Colli

Cerboia

Colle Clupi

Via Cassia

La Posta

Strisennano

Abbadia Isola

XVI Bargenev

Strada del Castel

Sodo di

Cerreto

Castel Petraio

Strove

Acquaviva

Pieve di Montereggioni Grove

Via Tietto Nenni

Stage Summary: the route largely follows tracks and small roads to the edge of Siena adding a little distance to visit the unmissable Monteriggioni, but making a large loop to the west of the via Cassia.

Distance from Vercelli: 541km          Distance to St Peter's Square, Rome: 307km
Stage Ascent: 578m                     Stage Descent: 442m

| Waypoint | Distance between waypoints | Total km | Directions | Verification Point | Compass | Altitude m |
|---|---|---|---|---|---|---|
| 86.001 | 0 | 0.0 | With the church on the right, continue straight ahead beside the main road | Monteriggioni on hill-top to the right | NE | 203 |
| 86.002 | 270 | 0.3 | At the crossroads, turn right and then bear left on the track | VF sign, strada di Valmaggiore | SE | 198 |
| 86.003 | 1500 | 1.8 | At the end of the road, turn left. Note:- the turning to the right reduces the distance, but bypasses Monteriggioni and involves a steep climb | Woods close on the right | NE | 202 |
| 86.004 | 1300 | 3.1 | At the T-junction with the SP5, turn right and right again – keep to the grass verge on the right | SR2 towards Monteriggioni, café on the left at the junction | SE | 205 |
| 86.005 | 250 | 3.3 | Carefully cross the main road and turn left onto the unmade road | Uphill, towards the entrance to the walled town, VF sign | E | 214 |
| 86.006 | 280 | 3.6 | Pass through the arched Porta Fiorentina and continue straight ahead | Via Primo Maggio | SE | 251 |
| 86.007 | 240 | 3.9 | On leaving the town, turn right and then left on the tarmac road, towards the main road | Porta Senese | S | 263 |

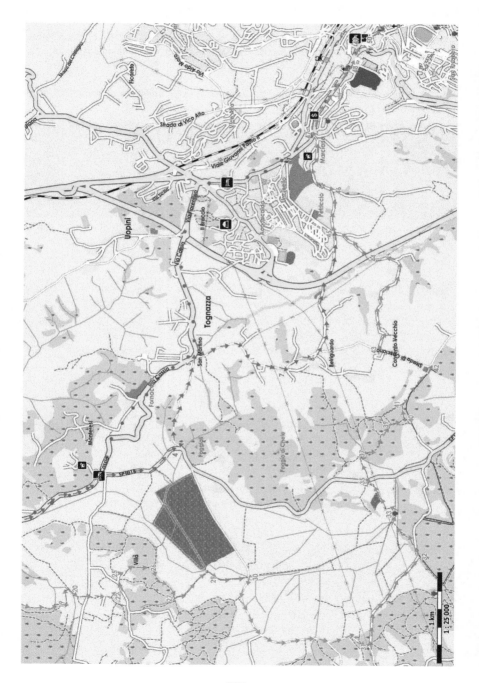

| Waypoint | Distance between waypoints | Total km | Directions | Verification Point | Compass | Altitude m |
|---|---|---|---|---|---|---|
| 86.008 | 500 | 4.3 | Turn left on the track and then bear right as the track skirts the school. Note:- in the the event that the track is blocked, continue straight ahead to the T-junction, turn left and then take the first turning to the right | Pass the school on your right | SE | 242 |
| 86.009 | 230 | 4.5 | At the junction with the main road, take the pedestrian crossing, turn right on the track and then take the first turning to the left | Towards Gallinalo | S | 242 |
| 86.010 | 210 | 4.8 | Take the right fork | VF sign, uphill | SW | 242 |
| 86.011 | 300 | 5.1 | Take the next turning to the left | White road, between trees | S | 279 |
| 86.012 | 120 | 5.2 | At the crossroads, turn left on the track | | SE | 282 |
| 86.013 | 800 | 5.9 | At the junction, take the second track from the left | Red and white VF sign | SE | 260 |
| 86.014 | 250 | 6.2 | Bear right | VF sign | SE | 274 |
| 86.015 | 280 | 6.5 | At the crossroads in the tracks, continue straight ahead on the gravel road | Stone wall on the right of the road | SE | 287 |
| 86.016 | 800 | 7.2 | At the T-junction, turn left | VF sign, large farmhouse on left | SE | 330 |
| 86.017 | 900 | 8.1 | Turn right on the track. Note:- to avoid broken ground and reduce distance by 5.5km continue ahead on the Alternate Route | Across the fields towards woods | SW | 302 |
| 86.018 | 400 | 8.5 | On the apex of the bend to the right, take the pathway to the left | Field to the left, woods to the right | S | 313 |
| 86.019 | 900 | 9.3 | Turn left on the access road to the farm | | E | 322 |
| 86.020 | 200 | 9.5 | At the T-junction, turn right | | S | 310 |

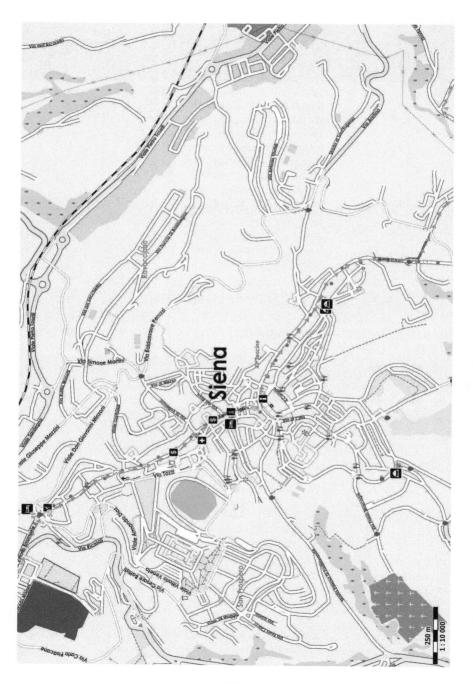

| Waypoint | Distance between waypoints | Total km | Directions | Verification Point | Compass | Altitude m |
|---|---|---|---|---|---|---|
| 86.021 | 250 | 9.8 | Cross the tarmac road and take the unmade road straight ahead | Castello della Chiocciola on the hill to the right | S | 317 |
| 86.022 | 270 | 10.1 | Bear left on the track | | SE | 318 |
| 86.023 | 120 | 10.2 | At the T-junction, turn left on the tarmac road | Towards castellated tower | NE | 318 |
| 86.024 | 100 | 10.3 | Take the right fork | Towards the Villa castello | E | 318 |
| 86.025 | 110 | 10.4 | Bear right on the track | Pass circular tower on the left | S | 317 |
| 86.026 | 400 | 10.7 | Take the right fork | Downhill and with fields on the left | SW | 283 |
| 86.027 | 500 | 11.2 | Turn left on the track between fields | Line of trees on the left of track | SE | 274 |
| 86.028 | 500 | 11.7 | Turn right on the track | Continue with a stream on your left | SW | 258 |
| 86.029 | 140 | 11.8 | At the junction, bear left | Remain beside the trees | S | 257 |
| 86.030 | 400 | 12.2 | At the T-junction with the tarmac road, SP101, turn right | Small bridge on the left at the junction | SW | 256 |
| 86.031 | 2000 | 14.1 | At the junction in the woods, turn left on the gravel road | Via dell'Osteriaccia, direction Montalbuccio | SE | 288 |
| 86.032 | 1200 | 15.4 | Bear left on the road and quickly take the pathway to the left | Beside house on the edge of the woods | NE | 267 |
| 86.033 | 600 | 15.9 | Bear right and then left on the track | Beside the monument | NE | 259 |
| 86.034 | 500 | 16.5 | At the T-junction beside the house, turn right | Towards the main road | E | 279 |

| Waypoint | Distance between waypoints | Total km | Directions | Verification Point | Compass | Altitude m |
|---|---|---|---|---|---|---|
| 86.035 | 30 | 16.5 | Take the pedestrian crossing over the main road and continue on the track straight ahead | VF signs | E | 278 |
| 86.036 | 260 | 16.7 | Take the track to the right uphill | Into the woods | SE | 273 |
| 86.037 | 140 | 16.9 | At the crossroads, turn left and then right | | SE | 282 |
| 86.038 | 280 | 17.2 | Turn right on the track | | SE | 294 |
| 86.039 | 170 | 17.3 | Keep right on the track | | SE | 304 |
| 86.040 | 160 | 17.5 | At the T-junction, turn left | | E | 308 |
| 86.041 | 160 | 17.7 | Emerge from the woods and turn right | Equestrian centre on your left | SE | 295 |
| 86.042 | 500 | 18.2 | At the junction with the tarmac road, turn left | Cemetery on your left | N | 293 |
| 86.043 | 600 | 18.8 | At the top of the hill, turn right | Strada delle Coste | E | 304 |
| 86.044 | 1500 | 20.2 | Continue straight ahead | Under the highway and then up the hill | NE | 263 |
| 86.045 | 500 | 20.7 | At the crossroads, turn right. Note:- the Alternate Route rejoins from the left | Via Gaetano Milanesi | E | 299 |
| 86.046 | 500 | 21.2 | At the T-junction, turn left on strada di Marciano | Between stone walls | E | 355 |
| 86.047 | 800 | 22.0 | At the roundabout, turn right direction Centro | Viale Camillo Benso Conte di Cavour | SE | 343 |
| 86.048 | 800 | 22.8 | Go straight ahead under the archway - Antiporto di Camollia | Direction centro | SE | 343 |
| 86.049 | 400 | 23.2 | At the traffic lights, continue straight ahead | Pass through porta Camollia | SE | 345 |
| 86.050 | 20 | 23.2 | Cross the piazza and take via Camollia straight ahead | Pass bike shop on the left | SE | 345 |

| Waypoint | Distance between waypoints | Total km | Directions | Verification Point | Compass | Altitude m |
|---|---|---|---|---|---|---|
| 86.051 | 400 | 23.6 | At the crossroads, continue straight ahead on via Camollia | Direction Porta Romana | SE | 344 |
| 86.052 | 700 | 24.3 | Arrive at Siena (XV) centre | Piazza del Campo directly ahead | | 340 |

**Alternate Route #86.A1**     **Length: 7.2km**

Stage Summary: shorter route for cyclists to bypass difficult ground in the woodland.  Initially the route follows the via Cassia (SR2) before continuing on quieter country roads and reduces the length of the section by 5.5km

**Stage Ascent: 21m**     **Stage Descent: 14m**

| Waypoint | Distance between waypoints | Total km | Directions | Verification Point | Compass | Altitude m |
|---|---|---|---|---|---|---|
| 86A1.001 | 0 | 0.0 | Continue straight ahead | Towards the main road | E | 301 |
| 86A1.002 | 290 | 0.3 | At the crossroads, turn right down the hill towards Siena on the SR2.  Walkers keep to the grass verge | Brown signpost ahead for Poggiolo | SE | 292 |
| 86A1.003 | 1800 | 2.0 | Turn right on strada del Pecorile direction Soviclle | Bar on the right at the junction | S | 276 |
| 86A1.004 | 1000 | 3.0 | Turn left and then left again on strada del Pian del Lago | Direction Siena | E | 276 |
| 86A1.005 | 1100 | 4.1 | At the T-junction, turn right direction Siena, SR2 | VF sign | E | 337 |
| 86A1.006 | 100 | 4.2 | Turn right direction Montalbuccio | Strada del Petriccio e Belriguardo | S | 338 |
| 86A1.007 | 1200 | 5.4 | Bear left at the fork in road | Strada del Petriccio e Belriguardo | SE | 323 |
| 86A1.008 | 400 | 5.8 | Take the left fork | Towards Petriccio | E | 327 |
| 86A1.009 | 1400 | 7.2 | At the crossroads, continue straight ahead and rejoin the "Official Route" | Via G. Milanese | | 299 |

Santa Caterina Dell'Acquacalda,Via Bologna, 4,53100 Siena(SI),Italy; Tel:+39 0577 52095; Email:donenricosiena@alice.it; Price:D

Casa Ritiri Santa Regina,(Maria Gasperini),Via Bianca Piccolomini Clementini,53100 Siena(SI),Italy; Tel:+39 0577 221206; +39 0577 282329; Price:B

Accoglienza Santa Luisa,Via di San Girolamo, 8,53100 Siena(SI),Italy; Tel:+39 0577 284377; Price:D

Convento Figlie della Carità San Vincenzo,Via di San Girolamo, 8,53100 Siena(SI),Italy; Tel:+39 0577 21271; +39 3408 721787; Email:casaprovinciale@ yahoo.it; Price:D

Caritas,Via della Diana, 4,53100 Siena(SI),Italy; Tel:+39 0577 280643; Email:caritas@caritas-siena.org; Web-site:www.caritas-siena.org; Price:D; Note:Men only,

Bed and Breakfast - il Ceppo,Via Cassia Nord, 3,53035 Monteriggioni(SI),Italy; Tel:+39 0577 593387; Email:info@bedandbreakfastilceppo.it; Web-site:www. bedandbreakfastilceppo.it; Price:A

Soggiorno Lo Stellino,Via Fiorentina, 89,53100 Siena(SI),Italy; Tel:+39 0577 51987; Email:info@sienaholidays.com ; Web-site:www.sienaholidays.com; Price:B

Casa di Alfredo - B&B,Via Lelio e Fausto Socino, 4,53100 Siena(SI),Italy; Tel:+39 0577 47628; +39 3398 820175; Price:B

Casa di Antonella - B&B,Via delle Terme, 72,53100 Siena(SI),Italy; +39 3393 004883; Price:B

Camping Siena Colleverde,Via Scaccapensieri, 47,53100 Siena(SI),Italy; Tel:+39 0577 334080; +39 0577 332545; Email:info@sienacamping.com; Web-site:www.sienacamping.com

Agenzia Per il Turismo,Piazza il Campo, 56,53100 Siena(SI),Italy; Tel:+39 0577 280551

Bancaetruria,Viale Camillo Benso Conte di Cavour, 202,53100 Siena(SI),Italy; Tel:+39 0577 49590; Web-site:www.bancaetruria.it

Banca Monteriggioni,Via dei Montanini,53100 Siena(SI),Italy; Tel:+39 0577 41113; Web-site:www.chiantibanca.it

Banca Monte dei Paschi di Siena,Via Banchi di Sopra, 84,53100 Siena(SI),Italy; Tel:+39 0577 294111; Web-site:www.mps.it/default.htm

Stazione Ferrovie,Piazza Carlo Rosselli, 7,53100 Siena(SI),Italy; Tel:+39 06 6847 5475; Web-site:www.renitalia.it

Ampugnano Airport,53018 Ampugnano,53018 Sovicille(SI),Italy; Tel:+39 0577 392226; Web-site:www.aeroportosiena.it

Policlinico,Viale Bracci, 16,53100 Siena(SI),Italy; Tel:+39 0577 586111

Bausani - Studio Medico,Piazza Giacomo Matteotti, 3,53100 Siena(SI),Italy; Tel:+39 0577 285508

Ciampoli - Medico Veterinario,Strada di Monteresi,53035 Monteriggioni(SI),Italy; Tel:+39 0577 319949

Clinica Veterinaria,Via Piero Strozzi,53100 Siena(SI),Italy; Tel:+39 0577 289103

In Voga,Via dei Pontani,53100 Siena(SI),Italy; Tel:+39 0577 236338

Rossi Martino di Rossi Luca & C.S.A.S.- Cicli e Ricambi Noleggio,Via Camollia, 204,53100 Siena(SI),Italy; Tel:+39 0577 249161

Ido Fantin,Via Arturo Toscanini, 19,53018 Sovicille(SI),Italy; Tel:+39 0577 345285; +39 3358 070224

La Francigena Sas,Chiantigiana, 69,53035 Monteriggioni(SI),Italy; +39 3356 677639

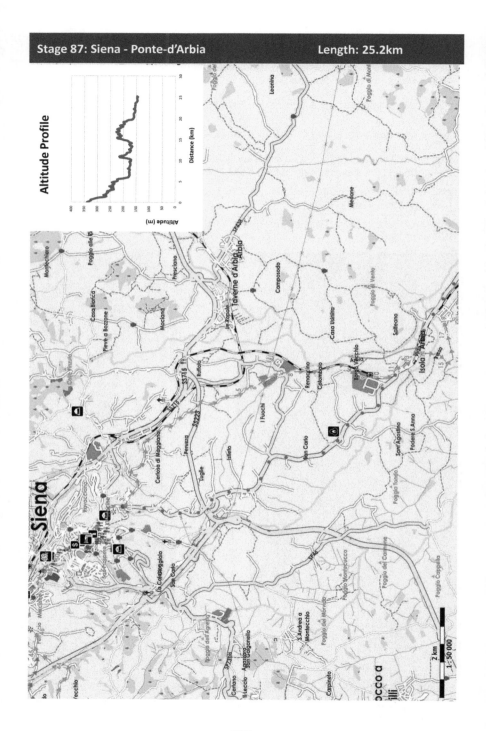

Stage Summary: the route quickly leaves the centre of Siena on a small tarmac road. After a short section on a busy road, the route returns to the tracks over the beautiful, but exposed Tuscan hills.  The route passes close to, but not through, a number of intermediate villages with a range of facilities.

Distance from Vercelli: 565km      Distance to St Peter's Square, Rome: 283km
Stage Ascent: 291m            Stage Descent: 484m

| Waypoint | Distance between waypoints | Total km | Directions | Verification Point | Compass | Altitude m |
|---|---|---|---|---|---|---|
| 87.001 | 0 | 0.0 | In via di Citta with piazza del Campo on your right, go straight ahead | Direction Porta Romana | SE | 340 |
| 87.002 | 1100 | 1.1 | After passing through the Porta Romana, immediately turn left through the archway and take the narrow road downhill | VF sign | E | 301 |
| 87.003 | 150 | 1.2 | Cross the main road (SR2) and go straight ahead | VF sign, strada di Certosa | E | 279 |
| 87.004 | 700 | 2.0 | Turn right, remain on strada di Certosa | VF sign, direction Renaccio | SE | 266 |
| 87.005 | 3600 | 5.5 | Road becomes a gravel track, continue straight ahead | VF sign, pass house on your right | SE | 222 |
| 87.006 | 90 | 5.6 | As the road bends to the left bear right across the field. Note:- in the event that the track across the field has been ploughed, follow the road to the foot of the hill and then turn right to skirt the field | Towards the industrial zone | SE | 217 |
| 87.007 | 300 | 6.0 | Continue straight ahead on the road through the industrial zone | Roundabout at the start of the road | S | 184 |
| 87.008 | 600 | 6.5 | At the roundabout with the main road, continue straight ahead on the road | | S | 176 |

| Waypoint | Distance between waypoints | Total km | Directions | Verification Point | Compass | Altitude m |
|---|---|---|---|---|---|---|
| 87.009 | 2000 | 8.5 | Immediately after passing the bar in the Isola D'Arbia industrial zone, turn left on the track. Note:- to avoid a subway ahead, remain on the road and then turn left on the main road and rejoin the "Official Route" beside the pizzaria | Narrow track between industrial buildings | SE | 175 |
| 87.010 | 70 | 8.6 | Take the subway under the railway track and turn right on the road | Pass the railway station building on your left | S | 175 |
| 87.011 | 700 | 9.3 | At the junction with the main road, bear left and turn right at the crossroads | Via della Mercanzia | S | 172 |
| 87.012 | 170 | 9.5 | Bear left on the road – via della Mercanzia | Pass the shops on your right | SE | 173 |
| 87.013 | 300 | 9.8 | At the T-junction with the SR2, turn right | | SE | 173 |
| 87.014 | 140 | 10.0 | Iimmediately after passing the restaurant, turn right | Road passes under the railway | S | 170 |
| 87.015 | 900 | 10.8 | Turn sharp left towards Ponte a Tressa | VF sign | SE | 214 |
| 87.016 | 200 | 11.0 | At the top of the ridge fork left down the hill and away from the crucifix | VF sign, via del Poggio | E | 215 |
| 87.017 | 600 | 11.6 | Continue straight ahead | Pass equestrian centre | E | 189 |
| 87.018 | 230 | 11.8 | At the entry to Ponte a Tressa turn right on the track | House n° 412 on your left | SE | 188 |
| 87.019 | 180 | 12.0 | At the road junction, turn right | Pass apartments on your left | S | 179 |

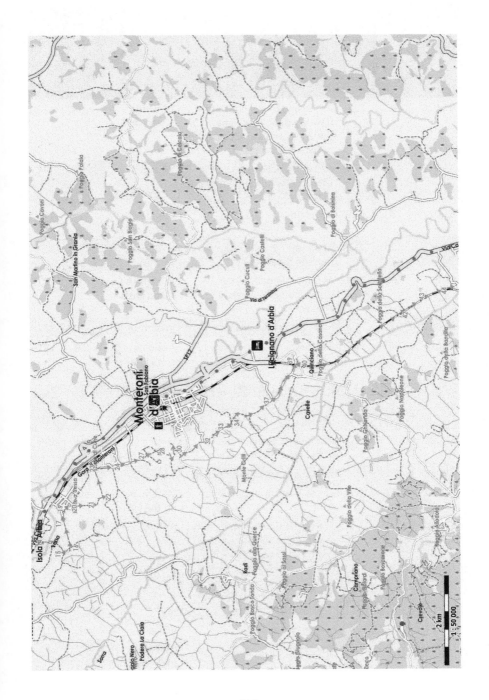

| Waypoint | Distance between waypoints | Total km | Directions | Verification Point | Compass | Altitude m |
|---|---|---|---|---|---|---|
| 87.020 | 40 | 12.0 | At the end of the housing development, fork right onto the gravel track and pass between the trees | Direction II Canto del Sole | S | 175 |
| 87.021 | 700 | 12.7 | At the T-junction on the top of the ridge, turn left on via di Villa Canina | VF sign | SE | 178 |
| 87.022 | 230 | 12.9 | Turn left | Towards the village of Cuna | E | 172 |
| 87.023 | 700 | 13.6 | At the entrance to Cuna turn right on the track | Beside the wall | S | 173 |
| 87.024 | 300 | 13.9 | At the crossroads in the tracks, continue straight ahead | VF sign and metal cross | S | 177 |
| 87.025 | 500 | 14.3 | Fork right up the hill | VF sign | S | 172 |
| 87.026 | 250 | 14.6 | Fork left | Avoiding strada della Fornacina | SE | 181 |
| 87.027 | 140 | 14.7 | Track forks in three directions take middle track straight up the hill | VF sign | SE | 181 |
| 87.028 | 230 | 15.0 | Just before reaching the top of the hill, fork right | VF sign | SW | 199 |
| 87.029 | 400 | 15.4 | Turn sharp left onto the ridge | VF sign | E | 223 |
| 87.030 | 260 | 15.6 | At the T-junction, turn sharp right | VF sign, pond on the left | SW | 211 |
| 87.031 | 250 | 15.9 | At the T-junction with a minor road, cross straight over and turn immediately left and follow the gravel track. Cyclists should turn left on the road and then bear right on the track in 70 metres | Parallel to the road | SE | 210 |
| 87.032 | 600 | 16.4 | Fork right up the hill | VF sign | SE | 218 |
| 87.033 | 700 | 17.1 | Fork left | Pass farm on the right | SE | 217 |

| Waypoint | Distance between waypoints | Total km | Directions | Verification Point | Compass | Altitude m |
|---|---|---|---|---|---|---|
| 87.034 | 150 | 17.2 | Continue straight ahead on the central track | Towards the top of ridge | SE | 218 |
| 87.035 | 280 | 17.5 | Fork right | Towards the farm on the ridge | S | 223 |
| 87.036 | 700 | 18.2 | Continue on the tarmac section and pass between two houses | White arrow | SE | 211 |
| 87.037 | 100 | 18.3 | Fork right | Direction Quinciano, VF sign | SE | 212 |
| 87.038 | 800 | 19.1 | At the junction in Quinciano bear left on the road, downhill | Pass conifers on your right | E | 200 |
| 87.039 | 300 | 19.4 | Fork right down the hill on the track and then turn right | Towards the main road | SW | 186 |
| 87.040 | 200 | 19.6 | Cross the road at the pedestrian crossing and turn right | Continue behind barrier | SW | 180 |
| 87.041 | 30 | 19.7 | Bear left down a gravel track | VF sign, continue beside railway track | SE | 176 |
| 87.042 | 2600 | 22.2 | At the crossroads, turn left, cross the bridge and then turn right | Continue with the railway on the right | SE | 158 |
| 87.043 | 800 | 23.0 | Continue straight ahead | Level crossing on your right | SE | 155 |
| 87.044 | 280 | 23.3 | After crossing small ditch, continue ahead on track | Railway on the right | SE | 153 |
| 87.045 | 1500 | 24.8 | At the junction with a tarmac road on the edge of Ponte d'Arbia, fork right on via degli Stagni towards river | VF sign, direction Piana | SE | 147 |
| 87.046 | 140 | 24.9 | At the T-junction turn left | VF sign, river on right | NE | 145 |
| 87.047 | 100 | 25.0 | At the T-junction with the main road, turn right | Pass over the river bridge | SE | 146 |

| Waypoint | Distance between waypoints | Total km | Directions | Verification Point | Compass | Altitude m |
|---|---|---|---|---|---|---|
| 87.048 | 180 | 25.2 | Arrive at Ponte-d'Arbia (XIV) | Beside the pilgrim hostel | | 147 |

## Accommodation & Facilities  ....  Siena - Ponte-d'Arbia

Centro Cresti,(Signora Lotti),Località Ponte d'Arbia ,53014 Monteroni-d'Arbia(SI),Italy; Tel:+39 0577 370096; +39 3277 197439; Email:padrinim@libero.it; Price:C

Santi Simone e Giuda,Località,Colle Malamerenda,53100 Siena(SI),Italy; Tel:+39 0577 282182

Parrocchia Santi Pietro e Paolo,Via del Sole, 13,53022 Buonconvento(SI),Italy; Tel:+39 0577 806089; +39 3489 153745; +39 36 6959 7645; Email:donclaudiorosi@libero.it; Price:D

Albergo Bella Napoli,Via Roma, 55,53014 Monteroni-d'Arbia(SI),Italy; Tel:+39 0577 375255; Price:B

Hotel Borgo Antico,Via di Lucignano, 405,53014 Monteroni-d'Arbia(SI),Italy; Tel:+39 0577 374688; Email:info@hotelborgoantico.com; Web-site:www.hotelborgoantico.com; Price:A

Affittacamere Martelli,Ss Cassia (Km204),53014 Ponte-d'Arbia(SI),Italy; Tel:+39 0577 806262; +39 3487 463634; Price:B

Albergo Roma,Via Soccini, 14,53022 Buonconvento(SI),Italy; Tel:+39 0577 806021; Price:B

Hotel Ghibellino,Via Dante Alighieri, 1,53022 Buonconvento(SI),Italy; Tel:+39 0577 809112; +39 0577 809114; Email:Info@hotelghibellino.it; Web-site:www.hotelghibellino.it; Price:A

Comune di Buonconvento,Via Soccini, 32,53022 Buonconvento(SI),Italy; Tel:+39 0577 80971

Banca Monte dei Paschi di Siena,Piazza Matteotti, 19,53022 Buonconvento(SI),Italy; Tel:+39 0577 809041

Cerruto - Studio Medico,Via del Sole, 46,53022 Buonconvento(SI),Italy; Tel:+39 0577 806070

Vittoria - Ambulatorio Veterinario,Via Siena, 23,53014 Monteroni-d'Arbia(SI),Italy; Tel:+39 0577 374723

Ambulatorio Veterinario Cereda Mulinari Dott.Vanni - Veterinari,Via Oreste Lizzadri, 27,53022 Buonconvento(SI),Italy; Tel:+39 0577 807066

Linea Sport,Circonvallazione John Kennedy,53014 Monteroni-d'Arbia(SI),Italy; Tel:+39 0577 374000

# Stage 88: Ponte-d'Arbia - San-Quirico-d'Orcia

Length: 26.1km

## Altitude Profile

1 km
1 : 30 000

Stage Summary: the route continues over the Tuscan hills interleaving long stretches on gravel tracks with shorter stretches on tarmac roads. The route passes through the bustling town of Buonconvento before passing through the village of Torrenieri (XIII) and arriving in the attractive hill top town of San Quirico (XII).

Distance from Vercelli: 591km          Distance to St Peter's Square, Rome: 258km
Stage Ascent: 723m                          Stage Descent: 456m

| Waypoint | Distance between waypoints | Total km | Directions | Verification Point | Compass | Altitude m |
|---|---|---|---|---|---|---|
| 88.001 | 0 | 0.0 | From the Centro Cresti continue beside the main road, SS2 | Enter Buonconvento | SE | 147 |
| 88.002 | 170 | 0.2 | Turn left on the road | Direction Serravalle | SE | 145 |
| 88.003 | 600 | 0.8 | Just before reaching the cemetery, turn sharp right on the stony road | Towards chiesa di San Lorenzo | W | 176 |
| 88.004 | 170 | 0.9 | As the road turns right towards the village centre, turn left on the path | Downhill and between the fields | SE | 166 |
| 88.005 | 200 | 1.1 | At the T-junction with the broad track, turn right | Downhill towards the main road | SW | 153 |
| 88.006 | 210 | 1.3 | At the T-junction with the gravel road, turn left, uphill | Main road immediately to your right | SE | 148 |
| 88.007 | 1300 | 2.6 | At the junction, turn right | Top of the hill | S | 221 |
| 88.008 | 1200 | 3.8 | At the T-junction, turn right | Pass under the railway bridge | SW | 142 |
| 88.009 | 210 | 4.0 | Pass the cemetery and at the T-junction with the SS2, turn left | Pass a petrol station on your left | SE | 142 |
| 88.010 | 270 | 4.2 | After, crossing the river bridge turn right | Direction Centro | SW | 143 |
| 88.011 | 90 | 4.3 | Turn left | Pass through the archway, Porta Senese | S | 144 |

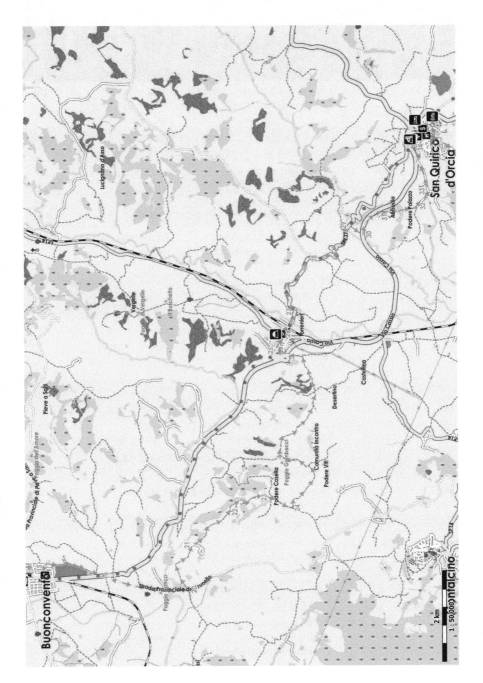

San Quirico d'Orcia

Buonconvento

Luciáno d'Asso

Vergelle
Poggio di Vergelle
Al Bolchetto

Pieve o Salti

Poggio dell'Amore
da Provinciale di Me

Torrenieri

Castellina
Desertino
Comunità incontro
Podere Villi
Poggio Gambacci
Podere Casella

Via Cassia
Via Cassia

Via Cassia

Abbadia
Podere Palazzo

Montalcino

Strada Provinciale de Brunello
Poggio

2 km

1 : 50 000

| Waypoint | Distance between waypoints | Total km | Directions | Verification Point | Compass | Altitude m |
|---|---|---|---|---|---|---|
| 88.012 | 230 | 4.5 | In piazza Matteotti, turn left on the narrow street | Pass a sign "Roma 201" on your right | E | 146 |
| 88.013 | 130 | 4.7 | Cross the main road (SR2) and continue straight ahead | Over the level crossing | E | 146 |
| 88.014 | 190 | 4.9 | Turn right on the road | Via 1 Maggio | S | 147 |
| 88.015 | 600 | 5.5 | At the crossroads with via E. Berlinger, turn left | Between apartment buildings | E | 146 |
| 88.016 | 80 | 5.5 | At the end of the street, take the track ahead and immediately bear right | Pass under the power lines | S | 150 |
| 88.017 | 1200 | 6.7 | At the T-junction with the stony road, turn right towards the main road | Row of conifers to the right | W | 150 |
| 88.018 | 70 | 6.8 | At the T-junction with the busy main road, cross over and turn left on the grass verge | Via Cassia – SR2 | S | 146 |
| 88.019 | 400 | 7.1 | Turn right on the road | Direction Montalcino | S | 142 |
| 88.020 | 1700 | 8.9 | Just before the road bends to the left, turn sharp left | Direction Castello Altesi | E | 151 |
| 88.021 | 1300 | 10.1 | After passing the castello take the left fork | Follow ridge | SE | 192 |
| 88.022 | 1100 | 11.2 | Bear left to skirt the buildings on the right | Tree lined road | S | 203 |
| 88.023 | 1200 | 12.4 | Keep left on the white road | | SW | 265 |
| 88.024 | 600 | 12.9 | Just before reaching a large farm on the right, turn left | Follow the road to Torrenieri | E | 264 |
| 88.025 | 5100 | 18.0 | At the T-junction in Torrenieri, turn right on the main street | Via Romana | E | 273 |
| 88.026 | 400 | 18.4 | At the crossroads in the centre of Torrenieri (XIII), continue straight ahead | VF sign, church directly ahead | SE | 257 |

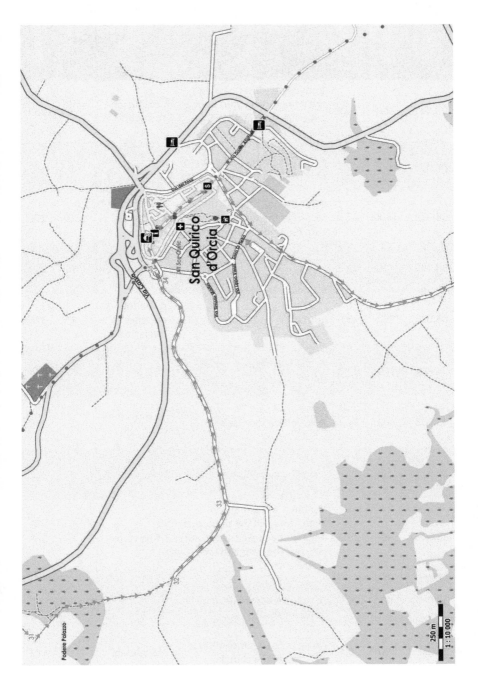

San Quirico d'Orcia

| Waypoint | Distance between waypoints | Total km | Directions | Verification Point | Compass | Altitude m |
|---|---|---|---|---|---|---|
| 88.027 | 600 | 19.0 | Immediately after passing the cemetery on your right, continue straight ahead on the road | Conifers on the right | E | 253 |
| 88.028 | 1500 | 20.5 | Fork right and continue on the main road | VF sign | SE | 333 |
| 88.029 | 1800 | 22.3 | After passing through the woods at the foot of the hill, turn right on the stony road | Towards the elevated highway | SW | 252 |
| 88.030 | 400 | 22.7 | Immediately after passing under the highway, bear left | Parallel to the highway | SE | 250 |
| 88.031 | 900 | 23.6 | Turn left | Avoid the entrance to the farm | SE | 326 |
| 88.032 | 700 | 24.3 | At the T-junction, turn left, uphill | VF sign | SE | 370 |
| 88.033 | 400 | 24.7 | Keep left on the track | Towards the town | E | 388 |
| 88.034 | 1100 | 25.8 | Continue straight ahead | Under the arch | E | 387 |
| 88.035 | 40 | 25.9 | Continue straight ahead. Note:- to avoid the steps, turn left and then take the second left over the bridge to the town centre | Climb steps | E | 392 |
| 88.036 | 50 | 25.9 | At the top of the steps, continue straight ahead on via Dante Alighieri | Towards the church | E | 399 |
| 88.037 | 130 | 26.1 | Arrive at San-Quirico-d'Orcia (XII) beside the church | Piazza Chigi | | 413 |

Parrocchia Santa Maria Maddalena,Via San Giovanni, 24,53024 Montalcino(SI),Italy; Tel:+39 0577 834138; Price:B

Collegiata dei Santi Quirico e Giulitta,(Signora Maramai Lucrezia),Via Dante Aligheri, 1,53027 San-Quirico-d'Orcia(SI),Italy; Tel:+39 0577 897278; +39 0577 897236; +39 3477 748732; Email:giorgio.maramai@teletu.it; Price:C; Note:Credentials required,

Ostello Tabor Abbazia di Sant'Antimo,Localita' S.Antimo, 222,53024 Castelnuovo-Dell'Abate(SI),Italy; Tel:+39 0577 835659; Email:foresterie@antimo.it; Web-site:www.antimo.it; Price:C

Hotel il Garibaldi,Via Cassia, 17,53027 San-Quirico-d'Orcia(SI),Italy; Tel:+39 0577 898315; +39 0577 898057; Email:ilgaribaldi@live.com; Price:B

Affittacamere l'Antica Sosta,Via Dante Alighieri, 145,53027 San-Quirico-d'Orcia(SI),Italy; Tel:+39 0577 898040; +39 3406 491216; Email:info@anticasosta.eu; Web-site:www.anticasosta.eu; Price:A

Fattoria Pieve a Salti Bio,Strada Provinciale Pieve a Salti,53022 Buonconvento(SI),Italy; Tel:+39 0577 807244; Email:info@pieveasaltibio.it; Web-site:pieveasaltibio.it

Ufficio Turistico,Piazza Chigi, 33,53027 San-Quirico-d'Orcia(SI),Italy; Tel:+39 0577 897211

Banca Monte dei Paschi di Siena,Via Romana, 28,53024 Montalcino(SI),Italy; Tel:+39 0577 832945

Banca Monte dei Paschi di Siena,Via Dante Alighieri, 32,53027 San-Quirico-d'Orcia(SI),Italy; Tel:+39 0577 897507

Bani Antonio,Via dei Canneti, 37B,53027 San-Quirico-d'Orcia(SI),Italy; Tel:+39 0577 897262

Ambulatorio Veterinario,Via dei Canneti, 45/a,53027 San-Quirico-d'Orcia(SI),Italy; +39 3393 282810

## Altitude Profile

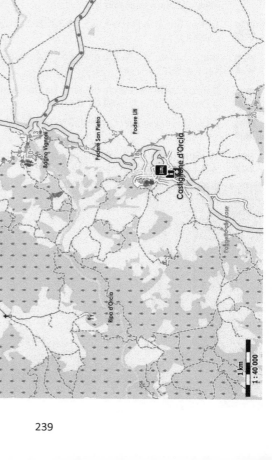

Stage Summary: a very strenuous, long and exposed uphill stage with few en route opportunities to break the journey after passing Castiglione d'Orcia.  The route is generally undertaken on quiet broad gravel roads, however there is a section of 1.5km on the via Cassia followed by several stretches on the quieter SS478.

Distance from Vercelli: 617km                Distance to St Peter's Square, Rome: 232km
Stage Ascent: 1081m                          Stage Descent: 702m

| Waypoint | Distance between waypoints | Total km | Directions | Verification Point | Compass | Altitude m |
|---|---|---|---|---|---|---|
| 89.001 | 0 | 0.0 | From the church in San-Quirico-d'Orcia on piazza Chigi continue ahead on via Dante Alighieri | Pass through piazza della Libertà | SE | 413 |
| 89.002 | 400 | 0.4 | Turn right at the crossroads on the edge of the old town | VF sign, via Giacomo Matteotti | SW | 408 |
| 89.003 | 190 | 0.6 | At the next crossroads, continue straight ahead on via Giuseppe Garibaldi | VF sign, direction Vignoni | SW | 418 |
| 89.004 | 700 | 1.2 | Take the left fork on the gravel road, towards Vignoni | VF sign | S | 424 |
| 89.005 | 1300 | 2.5 | Take the left fork | Towards Vignoni | SE | 497 |
| 89.006 | 900 | 3.4 | Take the left fork , towards the village | Direction Vignoni | E | 486 |
| 89.007 | 190 | 3.6 | Pass through the archway and then turn right | Chapel on the left | SW | 478 |
| 89.008 | 90 | 3.7 | At the T-junction with the broad track, turn left, downhill | VF sign | SE | 476 |
| 89.009 | 300 | 4.0 | Take the left fork, downhill | Agriturismo on the right | SE | 444 |
| 89.010 | 1300 | 5.3 | At the T-junction in Bagno Vignoni, turn left | VF sign | E | 301 |
| 89.011 | 400 | 5.7 | Turn right on gravel track | VF sign | SW | 267 |
| 89.012 | 120 | 5.8 | Continue straight ahead | Cross the foot-bridge | SE | 258 |

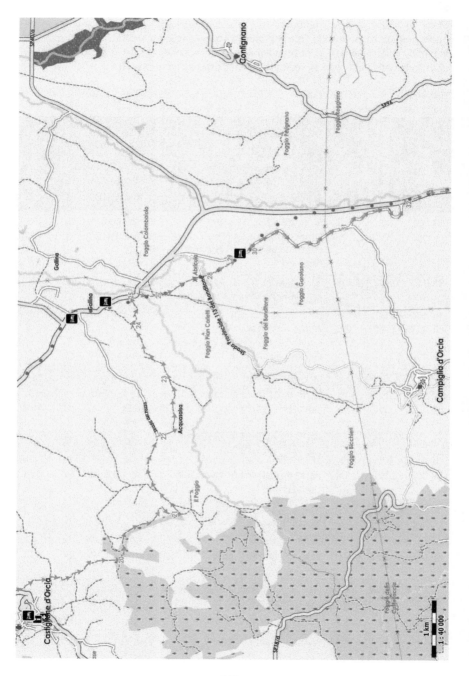

Contignano

SP40/a

Poggio Pelignano

Poggio Reggiano

SP64

Poggio Colomboiolo

Gallina

Gallina

Abituro

Poggio Garofano

29

30

28

Poggio dei Bandinone

Strada Provinciale 113 del Romitorio

Poggio Pian Caleni

24

23

Acquasola

Campiglia d'Orcia

Strada del Pozzo

22

Poggio Bicchieri

Il Poggio

Castiglione d'Orcia

20

Poggio della Colonnocie

SP18/a

1 km

1 : 40 000

| Waypoint | Distance between waypoints | Total km | Directions | Verification Point | Compass | Altitude m |
|---|---|---|---|---|---|---|
| 89.013 | 210 | 6.0 | Just after passing Osteria dell'Orcia, turn right | Keep the woods on your left | S | 272 |
| 89.014 | 900 | 6.9 | Cross the road and continue on the track with the vines on your left | Rocca d'Orcia visible on your right | S | 354 |
| 89.015 | 200 | 7.1 | At the T-junction with the gravel road, turn left | Olive trees on your left | SE | 363 |
| 89.016 | 500 | 7.6 | Take the right fork | Beside farmhouse, towards another farm | SE | 362 |
| 89.017 | 90 | 7.7 | Turn right | Beside farmhouse | SW | 367 |
| 89.018 | 600 | 8.2 | Shortly before reaching the main road, turn left on the track | Keep the road on your right | SE | 433 |
| 89.019 | 300 | 8.5 | Bear right up the the hill on the short track and then keep left on the gravel road | Pass the vines on your right | S | 442 |
| 89.020 | 2000 | 10.6 | In the valley bottom, continue straight ahead | Cross the bridge | SE | 343 |
| 89.021 | 1800 | 12.3 | At the junction, after passing the woods on the right, turn sharp left on the gravel road along the ridge | VF signs | E | 417 |
| 89.022 | 1600 | 13.9 | On the crown of the bend to the left, turn right on the track | Pass farm on the left | E | 428 |
| 89.023 | 1300 | 15.2 | At the junction, continue straight ahead on the gravel road | Farmhouse on the left | NE | 382 |
| 89.024 | 1300 | 16.4 | Turn right on the track beside the driveway | Pass Agriturismo on the left | E | 365 |
| 89.025 | 700 | 17.0 | Bear right on the track and cross the stream | Main road close on the left | S | 311 |

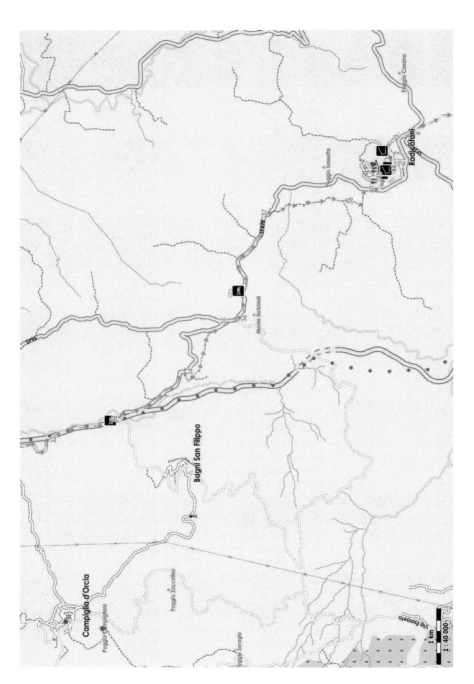

| Waypoint | Distance between waypoints | Total km | Directions | Verification Point | Compass | Altitude m |
|---|---|---|---|---|---|---|
| 89.026 | 400 | 17.5 | At the junction with the white road, bear right | Uphill between the conifers | S | 323 |
| 89.027 | 90 | 17.6 | Take the left fork beside the fencing and pass near the vestiges of Briccole (XI) | Pass farm on the left | SE | 333 |
| 89.028 | 800 | 18.3 | Take the pedestrian crossing over the main road and continue straight ahead on the track | Across the stream | SE | 336 |
| 89.029 | 700 | 19.0 | At the intersection with the old via Cassia, turn right on the road | Pass agriturismo | SE | 337 |
| 89.030 | 250 | 19.2 | Take the left fork | Tarmac road, uphill | S | 343 |
| 89.031 | 2200 | 21.4 | Take the left fork | Stone walled garden on your right | SE | 437 |
| 89.032 | 1300 | 22.7 | At the T-junction with the via Cassia (SR2), turn right and proceed with care beside the main road | Concrete wall on the right | S | 401 |
| 89.033 | 1400 | 24.1 | Shortly after passing the hotel on your left, turn left on the road across the river | Towards Radicofani, VF sign | SE | 422 |
| 89.034 | 1500 | 25.6 | At the end of the crash barriers, shortly after SP478 Km32, turn right and then bear left on the gravel road | Pass close to the farm buildings on your left | SE | 463 |
| 89.035 | 1600 | 27.1 | At the T-junction with the road, turn right | Direction Radicofani | S | 587 |
| 89.036 | 170 | 27.3 | Bear left on the road | Direction Radicofani | E | 597 |
| 89.037 | 2300 | 29.6 | After a bend to the left following SP478 Km28, turn right on the track | At the end of the the crash barrier | S | 667 |
| 89.038 | 1400 | 30.9 | At the junction with the stony road, bear left | | S | 726 |

| Waypoint | Distance between waypoints | Total km | Directions | Verification Point | Compass | Altitude m |
|---|---|---|---|---|---|---|
| 89.039 | 400 | 31.3 | At the junction, bear left and continue uphill on the stony road | | E | 752 |
| 89.040 | 280 | 31.6 | At the T-junction with the main road, turn right | | S | 772 |
| 89.041 | 220 | 31.8 | Turn left towards the centre of Radicofani | Viale Odoardo Lucchini | SE | 764 |
| 89.042 | 260 | 32.0 | At the crossroads, go straight ahead and then bear right on the ramp | Towards centre, VF signs | SE | 791 |
| 89.043 | 40 | 32.1 | Fork left, uphill | No Entry | SE | 795 |
| 89.044 | 150 | 32.2 | Arrive at Radicofani centre | Church of San Pietro to the right | | 792 |

**Accommodation & Facilities ....     San-Quirico-d'Orcia - Radicofani**

Ospitale del Comune,Via Fonte Antese,53040 Radicofani(SI),Italy; +39 3293 812742; Email:comunediradicofani@inwind.it; Price:C

Casa d'Accoglienza San Jacopo di Compostela,Via Renato Magi,53040 Radicofani(SI),Italy; Tel:+39 0578 55614; +39 3389 240307; Email:doneliasantori@libero.it; Price:D

Spedale di San Pietro e Giacomo,(Don Elia),Via Dello Spedale, 2,53040 Radicofani(SI),Italy; Tel:+39 0578 55614; +39 3387 982255; Price:D; Note:Credentials required,

Le Rocche - Ristorante Affittacamere,Via Senese, 10,53023 Castiglione-d'Orcia(SI),Italy; Tel:+39 0577 887031; Web-site:www.ristorantelerocche.it; Price:B

Osteria Gallina,Via Cassia, 5,53023 Castiglione-d'Orcia(SI),Italy; Tel:+39 0577 880113; Price:B

Agriturismo Sant' Ansano,Località Gallina,53023 Castiglione-d'Orcia(SI),Italy; Tel:+39 0578 748477; +39 3382 867369; Email:s.ansano@cretedisiena.com; Web-site:www.santansano.com; Price:B

Agriturismo - Sant'Alberto,Via Vecchia Cassia,53023 Castiglione-d'Orcia(SI),Italy; Tel:+39 0577 897227; +39 3382 988959; Email:info@santalberto.com; Web-site:www.santalberto.com; Price:A

Hotel Beyfin,Via Cassia, 161,53023 Castiglione-d'Orcia(SI),Italy; Tel:+39 0577 872877; Email:castiglionedorcia@hotelbeyfin.it; Web-site:www.hotelbeyfin.it/castiglionedorcia; Price:A

## Accommodation & Facilities ....    San-Quirico-d'Orcia - Radicofani

| | |
|---|---|
| 🛏 | La Selvella,Strada Provinciale 478-Km29,53040 Radicofani(SI),Italy; Tel:+39 0578 55555; Email: selvella@selvella.com ; Web-site:www.selvella.com; Price:A |
| ℹ | Comune di Castiglione d'Orcia,Via Aldobrandeschi, 13,53023 Castiglione-d'Orcia(SI),Italy; Tel:+39 0577 88401 |
| ℹ | Comune di Radicofani,Via Renato Magi, 59,53040 Radicofani(SI),Italy; Tel:+39 0578 55878 |
| $ | Banca Monte dei Paschi di Siena,Piazza Unità d'Italia, 15,53023 Castiglione-d'Orcia(SI),Italy; Tel:+39 0577 888929 |
| $ | Banca Monte dei Paschi di Siena,Piazza Tassi, 8,53040 Radicofani(SI),Italy; Tel:+39 0578 55907 |
| Ⓗ | Presidio Ospedaliero Amiata Senese,Via Trento,53021 Abbadia-San-Salvatore(SI),Italy; Tel:+39 0577 7731 |
| ➕ | Mengano - Studio Medico,Via Sandro Pertini, 3,53023 Castiglione-d'Orcia(SI),Italy; Tel:+39 0577 887455 |

## Altitude Profile

Trevinano

Celle sul Rigo

Radicofani

Ponte a Rigo

Viale Romio

Castagnolo

2 km

1 : 60 000

Stage Summary: this is another long section with few opportunities for intermediate stops after reaching the valley bottom at Ponte a Rigo . The descent from Radicofani on a gravel road is followed by brief stretch of main road and a longer section on a minor road . The route then follows another exposed stretch over the hills on broad country tracks. The section is easy going for cyclists and riders. Aquapendente is a bustling town offering a broad range of facilities.

Distance from Vercelli: 649km            Distance to St Peter's Square, Rome: 200km
Stage Ascent:  621m                      Stage Descent: 1024m

| Waypoint | Distance between waypoints | Total km | Directions | Verification Point | Compass | Altitude m |
|---|---|---|---|---|---|---|
| 90.001 | 0 | 0.0 | From the church of San Pietro turn right and continue along the main street | Via Roma | E | 792 |
| 90.002 | 300 | 0.3 | Pass through the archway and leave the historic centre. Continue with care straight ahead on the road downhill - no pavement and road bounded with crash barriers | Viale Giacomo Matteotti | SE | 763 |
| 90.003 | 500 | 0.8 | At the crossroads, continue straight ahead | Direction Roma | S | 719 |
| 90.004 | 200 | 1.0 | On the apex of the bend to the right, continue straight ahead on the unmade road | Old via Cassia, VF sign | S | 700 |
| 90.005 | 2000 | 3.0 | Take the right fork | Uphill | S | 562 |
| 90.006 | 900 | 3.8 | Take the left fork | Towards the "Pantano" agriturismo | SE | 591 |
| 90.007 | 1500 | 5.3 | Take the right fork | Farm on your left | S | 522 |
| 90.008 | 3000 | 8.3 | Take the right fork, remaining between the trees | Keep river Rigo to the left | SW | 310 |
| 90.009 | 2300 | 10.5 | At the T-junction with the main road, turn right, cross the road and continue to the right on the track parallel to the road | SR2, pass bar on the right | SW | 294 |

| Waypoint | Distance between waypoints | Total km | Directions | Verification Point | Compass | Altitude m |
|---|---|---|---|---|---|---|
| 90.010 | 500 | 11.0 | Leave Ponte a Rigo, and keep left on the track. In the event the track is overgrown or has been ploughed in proceed on the grass beside the road to the Sovana junction | Continue on the left side of the road towards Abbadia S.S. | SW | 295 |
| 90.011 | 500 | 11.4 | At the end of the track turn right and then left to follow the road with care - crash barriers bound the road ahead | The road crosses the river | SW | 294 |
| 90.012 | 500 | 12.0 | Take the next road to the left | Direction Sovana | S | 298 |
| 90.013 | 3700 | 15.7 | Turn left onto a gravel track, direction la Valle | VF sign | SE | 359 |
| 90.014 | 700 | 16.4 | Fork right down the hill | VF sign at end of farmyard | E | 340 |
| 90.015 | 700 | 17.1 | Continue straight ahead, over the crossroads in the track | VF sign on telegraph pole | E | 312 |
| 90.016 | 900 | 18.0 | At the T-junction in the track, shortly after crossing the river, turn right | VF sign | S | 300 |
| 90.017 | 1200 | 19.2 | Take the left fork | | E | 358 |
| 90.018 | 1300 | 20.5 | Continue straight ahead | Towards la Casina | NE | 406 |
| 90.019 | 1100 | 21.6 | At the T-junction, turn right | VF sign | SE | 400 |
| 90.020 | 3400 | 25.0 | At the T-junction beside the cemetery, turn left up the hill on the road | Direction Proceno | SE | 367 |
| 90.021 | 150 | 25.1 | Take the right fork towards the castello in Proceno | VF sign | SE | 372 |
| 90.022 | 600 | 25.7 | In the piazza in Proceno, bear left on viale Marconi | Pass palazzo Sforza on your left | NE | 413 |
| 90.023 | 90 | 25.8 | At the T-junction, turn left and continue downhill on the winding road | Skirting the village on via Belvedere | NE | 401 |

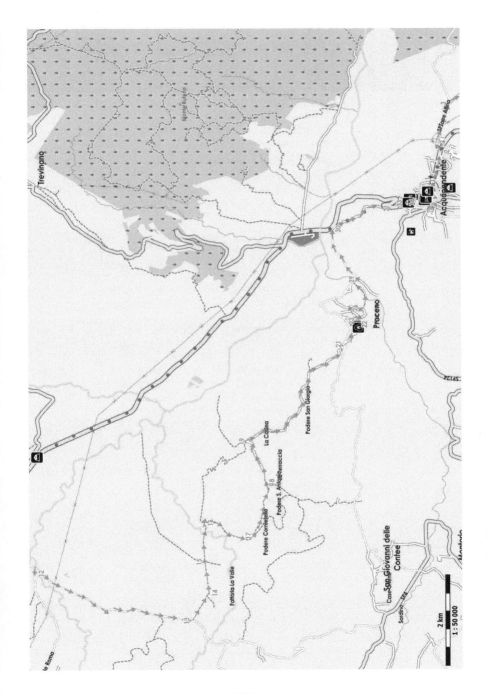

| Waypoint | Distance between waypoints | Total km | Directions | Verification Point | Compass | Altitude m |
|---|---|---|---|---|---|---|
| 90.024 | 400 | 26.2 | On the crown of the sharp bend to the left, continue straight ahead on the small road, downhill | Via della Pace | NE | 386 |
| 90.025 | 400 | 26.5 | Beside the sports ground, take the right fork, downhill | VF sign | NE | 334 |
| 90.026 | 110 | 26.6 | At the T-junction, turn right | Downhill | S | 321 |
| 90.027 | 300 | 26.9 | Just after entering the woods, turn left on the track and skirt the field | | E | 321 |
| 90.028 | 800 | 27.7 | At the T-junction with the road, turn right | Cross the river bridge | SE | 258 |
| 90.029 | 140 | 27.8 | Bear left on the strada Provinciale | After river bridge | NE | 266 |
| 90.030 | 1300 | 29.1 | At the bottom of the hill, shortly before the T-junction with the via Cassia, turn right on the small road | Strada Viccinale di San Giglio, VF sign | S | 251 |
| 90.031 | 1600 | 30.7 | At the T-junction with the via Cassia, turn right | Enter Aquapendente | S | 359 |
| 90.032 | 160 | 30.8 | Turn left, across the car park, and take the track to the left of the Albergo | "Aquila d'Oro" | SE | 367 |
| 90.033 | 170 | 31.0 | Cross the orchard and take the footpath downhill and to the left | | SE | 347 |
| 90.034 | 40 | 31.0 | At the T-junction, turn right on the stony track, uphill | Gardens below on the left | SE | 343 |
| 90.035 | 170 | 31.2 | In front of the albergo "la Ripa" turn left and then bear right | Via Cesare Battisti and via Roma | SE | 363 |
| 90.036 | 800 | 31.9 | Arrive at Aquapendente (IX), beside the church of Santo Sepulcro | Piazza del Duomo | | 389 |

Caritas Diocesana,(Leonello Toccaceli),Via Cassia (Km146),01021 Aquapendente(VT),Italy; Tel:+39 0578 53628; +39 0578 50016; Tel:+39 3398 999610; Price:D

Villa San Ermanno di Geronzi,Via Cassia Km-144,01021 Aquapendente(VT),Italy; +39 3291 644501; Email:gerokhappa@libero.it ; Web-site:www.villasermanno.altervista.org; Price:D

Monastero di Santa Chiara di Acquapendente,Via Malintoppa, 10,01021 Acquapendente(VT),Italy; Tel:+39 0763 734153; Price:C

Casa del Pellegrino San Rocco,(Don Erico Castauro),Via Roma, 51,01021 Acquapendente(VT),Italy; Tel:+39 0763 733958; +39 3454 452534; Price:C

Convento Cappuccini-Casa San Lazzaro,(Suor Amelia),Via dei Cappuccini, 21,01021 Acquapendente(VT),Italy; Tel:+39 0763 730177; +39 3394 327383; Email:cercam@libero.it; Web-site:www.casadilazzaro.org; Price:D

Parrocchia S.Salvatore,Via Sant'Agnese,01020 Proceno(VT),Italy; Tel:+39 3402 265595; Price:D

Hotel la Ripa,Via Cesare Battisti, 61,01021 Acquapendente(VT),Italy; Tel:+39 0763 730136; +39 0763 733620; Price:B

Albergo il Borgo,Via Porta Sant'Angelo, 3,01021 Acquapendente(VT),Italy; Tel:+39 0763 733971; Email:ristoranteilborgoacquapendentevt@msn.com; Web-site:ristoranteilborgo-acquapendente-vt.blogspot.fr; Price:B

Hotel Toscana,Piazza N.Sauro, 5,01021 Acquapendente(VT),Italy; Tel:+39 0763 711220; Email: info@albergotoscana.net ; Web-site:www.albergotoscana.net; Price:B

Agriturismo - Maneggio San Filippo,Strada della Falconiera,02043 San-Filippo(RI),Italy; Tel:+39 3387 524339

Comune di Proceno,Piazza della Libertà, 12,01020 Proceno(VT),Italy; Tel:+39 0763 710092

Comune di Acquapendente,Piazza Girolamo Fabrizio, 17,01021 Acquapendente(VT),Italy; Tel:+39 0763 711215

Banco di Brescia,Via del Rivo, 34,01021 Acquapendente(VT),Italy; Tel:+39 0763 711179

Cassa di Risparmio di Viterbo,Piazza Nazario Sauro, 6,01021 Acquapendente(VT),Italy; Tel:+39 0763 711223

Ospedale Civile,Via Cesare Battisti, 68,01021 Acquapendente(VT),Italy; Tel:+39 0763 731455

Menchinelli - Studio Medico,Via del Teatro, 14,01021 Acquapendente(VT),Italy; Tel:+39 0763 733337

Fratangeli - Medico Veterinario,Località Villa le Grazie, 79C,01021 Acquapendente(VT),Italy; Tel:+39 0763 733032

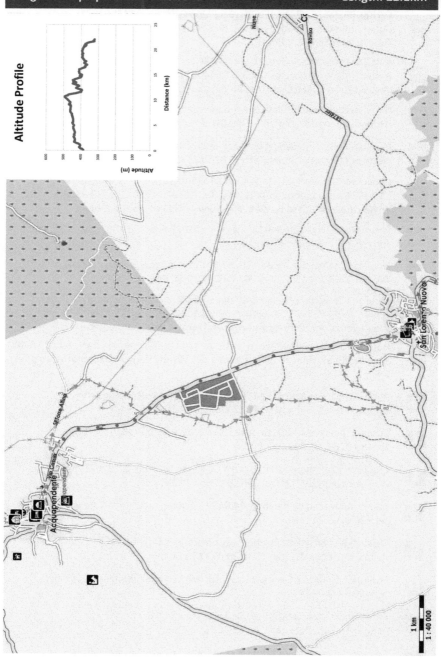

Altitude Profile

Stage Summary: after leaving Aquapendente, the route meanders on farm tracks rejoining the via Cassia to pass through the town of Saint Lorenzo Nuovo and also unfortunately for a short section to the south of the town. The route continues on the lower slopes of the hills overlooking lake Bolsena. The latter part includes paths over broken ground with some short steep ascents making for difficult progress for cyclists.

Distance from Vercelli: 681km      Distance to St Peter's Square, Rome: 168km
Stage Ascent: 384m      Stage Descent: 449m

| Waypoint | Distance between waypoints | Total km | Directions | Verification Point | Compass | Altitude m |
|---|---|---|---|---|---|---|
| 91.001 | 0 | 0.0 | From the Basilica del Santo Sepolcro, turn left on the main road | Pass Torre Giulia de Jacopo on your right | E | 389 |
| 91.002 | 600 | 0.6 | Turn left, direction Torre Alfina | VF sign, shrine on the apex of the bend | E | 410 |
| 91.003 | 1200 | 1.8 | After a large factory building, bear right onto the gravel track | VF sign, pass silos on your right | SE | 439 |
| 91.004 | 400 | 2.2 | At the fork, bear right on the gravel track | VF sign, line of trees to your left | SW | 435 |
| 91.005 | 1300 | 3.5 | At the junction with the via Cassia, cross straight over onto the small road | VF sign | S | 435 |
| 91.006 | 1800 | 5.3 | At the T-junction with a minor road, turn left and then immediately right | VF sign, farmhouse on your left | SE | 447 |
| 91.007 | 700 | 6.0 | Take the right fork | Strada del Podere del Vescovo | S | 445 |
| 91.008 | 1900 | 7.9 | At the T-junction, turn left | | E | 462 |
| 91.009 | 60 | 7.9 | At the next T-junction, turn left | VF sign on small building ahead | NE | 463 |
| 91.010 | 130 | 8.1 | Fork right on the track | | NE | 460 |

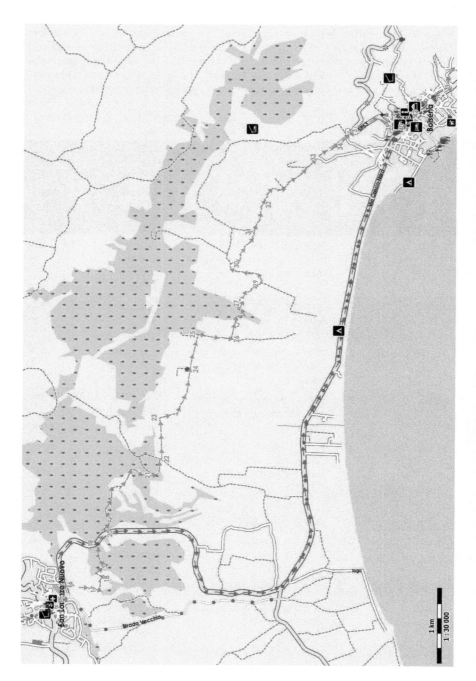

| Waypoint | Distance between waypoints | Total km | Directions | Verification Point | Compass | Altitude m |
|---|---|---|---|---|---|---|
| 91.011 | 900 | 9.0 | At the T-junction, turn sharp right | Track quickly bends to the left | E | 459 |
| 91.012 | 600 | 9.5 | At the T-junction with the main road, turn right on the via Cassia | Towards San Lorenzo Nuovo | S | 462 |
| 91.013 | 1100 | 10.6 | At the traffic lights, in the centre of San Lorenzo Nuovo, continue straight ahead | Direction Bolsena, Roma 124 | SE | 494 |
| 91.014 | 210 | 10.8 | Take the right fork down the ramp, parallel to main road | VF sign | S | 489 |
| 91.015 | 50 | 10.8 | At the next junction bear left | Return towards the main road | E | 485 |
| 91.016 | 220 | 11.1 | Bear right, parallel to the main road, and then right again on the concrete road. Note:- at the time of writing there is an unresolved dispute over rights off way ahead and as a result the track may be blocked.  If in doubt, remain on the main road and proceed with care for 1200m to the VF signed junction with the gravel road on the left | Steeply downhill, house on the right | S | 472 |
| 91.017 | 500 | 11.6 | Continue straight ahead across the clearing and then turn left to follow the track | | E | 403 |
| 91.018 | 150 | 11.7 | Skirt the house and bear left on the white road | House on your left | E | 402 |
| 91.019 | 700 | 12.4 | At the T-junction cross the road with great care and turn right | Via Cassia, stone wall on your left | SE | 429 |

| Waypoint | Distance between waypoints | Total km | Directions | Verification Point | Compass | Altitude m |
|---|---|---|---|---|---|---|
| 91.020 | 160 | 12.6 | Turn left onto a gravel track. Note:- the route ahead is generally off-road and while the conditions for walkers and horse-riders are good it is strenuous for bike riders, who can remain on the via Cassia rejoining the "Official Route" in Bolsena | Km 122,7, direction agriturismo "Pomele" | SE | 421 |
| 91.021 | 1400 | 13.9 | At the fork in the track, continue straight ahead down the hill | VF sign | SE | 447 |
| 91.022 | 270 | 14.2 | Bear right and then fork left parallel to lake-shore | VF sign, "vocabolo Pomele" | E | 426 |
| 91.023 | 600 | 14.8 | Fork right down the hill | Quarry on left | SE | 408 |
| 91.024 | 900 | 15.6 | At the fork, keep right | VF sign | E | 413 |
| 91.025 | 500 | 16.1 | At the T-junction, turn right | VF sign | S | 411 |
| 91.026 | 400 | 16.5 | Turn left | VF sign, strada della Roccaccia | E | 376 |
| 91.027 | 700 | 17.2 | Fork left up the hill | Line of posts directly on right | SE | 377 |
| 91.028 | 300 | 17.6 | At the T-junction, turn right down the hill | Entrance to a large house on left | SE | 377 |
| 91.029 | 120 | 17.7 | Take the left fork | VF sign | NE | 372 |
| 91.030 | 600 | 18.2 | Fork right onto a smaller track | VF sign | SE | 389 |
| 91.031 | 600 | 18.8 | Bear right | Parallel to lake-shore | E | 394 |
| 91.032 | 400 | 19.2 | Fork left | Between a line of trees | SE | 389 |
| 91.033 | 1100 | 20.3 | Keep left on the track | Between olive groves | SE | 390 |
| 91.034 | 250 | 20.5 | Continue straight ahead onto a minor tarmac road | Pass house and parking area on your right | SE | 387 |

| Waypoint | Distance between waypoints | Total km | Directions | Verification Point | Compass | Altitude m |
|---|---|---|---|---|---|---|
| 91.035 | 210 | 20.7 | At the T-junction, turn left | VF sign | E | 376 |
| 91.036 | 20 | 20.8 | Continue straight ahead at the junction | Ostello to the left | S | 379 |
| 91.037 | 290 | 21.1 | At the Stop sign turn right down the hill | VF sign | S | 377 |
| 91.038 | 500 | 21.5 | Bear right on the small road | Pass castello close on your left | SW | 348 |
| 91.039 | 40 | 21.6 | At the T-junction, turn left | Under the arch | S | 338 |
| 91.040 | 30 | 21.6 | Turn right | Via delle Piagge | SW | 336 |
| 91.041 | 70 | 21.7 | At the end of the road, in piazza Primo Maggio, turn left | Corso Cavour | SE | 325 |
| 91.042 | 260 | 21.9 | Pass under the archway, cross piazza Guglielmo Matteotti and continue straight ahead on Corso della Repubblica | Pedestrian zone | SE | 325 |
| 91.043 | 150 | 22.1 | Arrive at Bolsena (VIII) centre in piazza Santa Cristina | The Basilica of Santa Cristina ahead | | 324 |

## Accommodation & Facilities .... Aquapendente - Bolsena

La Francigena Ristorante - Affittacamere,Via Paese Vecchio,01020 San-Lorenzo-Nuovo(VT),Italy; Tel:+39 0763 727936; Email:info@ristorantelafrancigena.it; Web-site:www.ristorantelafrancigena.it; Price:B

Convento Santa Maria del Giglio,Via Madonna del Giglio,01023 Bolsena(VT),Italy; Tel:+39 0761 799066; +39 3335 710464; +39 3479 955683; Email:puntidivista@pelagus.it; Web-site:www.conventobolsena.org; Price:C

Istituto Suore Ss.Sacramento,Piazza Santa Cristina, 4,01023 Bolsena(VT),Italy; Tel:+39 0761 799058; Email:rsssbolsena@libero.it; Web-site:www.rsssacramento.it; Price:C

Ostello Gazzetta,(Mauro),Strada di Gazzetta le Valli,01023 Bolsena(VT),Italy; Tel:+39 0761 798753; +39 3357 383702; +39 3334 375473; Email:ostellogazzetta@gmail.com; Web-site:www.ostellogazzetta.it ; Price:B

Albergo Italia,Corso Cavour, 53,01023 Bolsena(VT),Italy; Tel:+39 0761 799193; +39 0761 798026; +39 3387 732831; Email:pensioneitalia@libero.it; Web-site:www.pensioneitalia.it; Price:B

Hotel Columbus,Viale Colesanti, 27 ,01023 Bolsena(VT),Italy; Tel:+39 0761 799009; Email: info@hotelcolumbusbolsena.it ; Web-site:www.hotelcolumbusbolsena.it; Price:B

Camping la Cappelletta,Via Cassia Nord,01023 Bolsena(VT),Italy; Tel:+39 0761 799543

Camping Pineta,Viale Diaz,01023 Bolsena(VT),Italy; Tel:+39 0761 796905; Web-site:www.campingpinetabolsena.it; Price:C

Comune di Bolsena,Via Guglielmo Marconi,01023 Bolsena(VT),Italy; Tel:+39 0761 799601

Banca di Roma,Piazza Europa, 1,01020 San-Lorenzo-Nuovo(VT),Italy; Tel:+39 0763 727014

Cassa di Risparmio di Orvieto,Piazza Guglielmo Matteotti, 22,01023 Bolsena(VT),Italy; Tel:+39 0761 799004

Banco di Brescia,Via A.Gramsci, 28,01023 Bolsena(VT),Italy; Tel:+39 0761 799014

Zanoni - Studio Medico,Via Dell'Ospedale, 17,01020 San-Lorenzo-Nuovo(VT),Italy; Tel:+39 0763 727774

Studio Medico Veterinario,Viale Santa Maria,01023 Bolsena(VT),Italy; Tel:+39 3386 116903

Taxi,15 piazza Matteotti,05018 Orvieto-Scalo(TR),Italy; Tel:+39 0763 301903

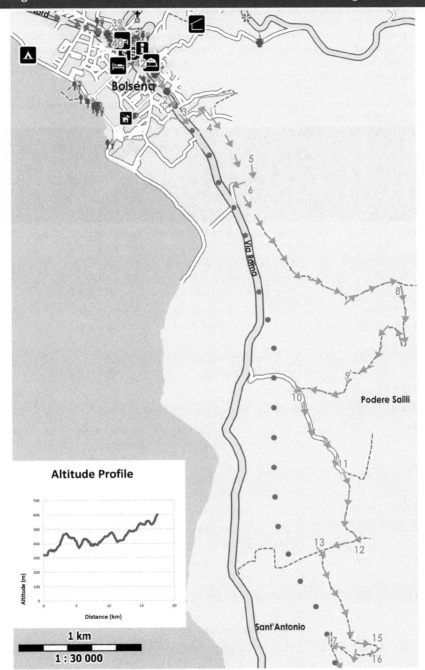

Bolsena

Via Roma

Podere Sailli

Sant'Antonio

**Altitude Profile**

1 km

1 : 30 000

## Stage 92: Bolsena - Montefiascone — Length: 17.5km

Stage Summary: the "Official Route" climbs back into the hills overlooking the lake and progresses on farm and forest tracks before following a section of Roman road. The "Official Route" makes a loop including a short section of via Cassia before the final approach to the hilltop town of Montefiscone. A slightly more direct Alternate Route using a small road will avoid the loop.

Distance from Vercelli: 703km
Stage Ascent: 605m

Distance to St Peter's Square, Rome: 146km
Stage Descent: 329m

| Waypoint | Distance between waypoints | Total km | Directions | Verification Point | Compass | Altitude m |
|---|---|---|---|---|---|---|
| 92.001 | 0 | 0.0 | Leave piazza Santa Cristina by Porta Romana | Basilica and café on the left | SE | 324 |
| 92.002 | 210 | 0.2 | At the crossroads with trees in the traffic island, continue straight ahead and join the via Cassia | Towards the petrol station | SE | 319 |
| 92.003 | 300 | 0.5 | Turn left on the small road | Località Poggio Sala | E | 319 |
| 92.004 | 280 | 0.8 | At the junction at the top of the hill, keep right | | SE | 348 |
| 92.005 | 600 | 1.4 | Turn right | | S | 351 |
| 92.006 | 120 | 1.5 | At the T-junction, turn right | | W | 355 |
| 92.007 | 110 | 1.6 | Turn left, uphill on the long straight tarmac road | Pass between gardens and olive groves | SE | 347 |
| 92.008 | 1900 | 3.5 | Beside two pine trees, turn right onto a track | Downhill between fields | SW | 472 |
| 92.009 | 1500 | 5.0 | Continue straight ahead | Across barrier | W | 420 |
| 92.010 | 500 | 5.5 | At the T-junction with the tarmac road turn left, uphill | Parallel to the lake-shore | SE | 370 |
| 92.011 | 900 | 6.3 | Fork right on the gravel track, direction Parco di Turona | VF sign | S | 434 |
| 92.012 | 600 | 7.0 | Fork right, down the hill | VF sign | W | 416 |
| 92.013 | 300 | 7.3 | Turn left on a gravel track, just before a small white chapel | VF sign | SE | 386 |
| 92.014 | 1000 | 8.3 | Fork right through a band of trees | Into the clearing | E | 394 |

| Waypoint | Distance between waypoints | Total km | Directions | Verification Point | Compass | Altitude m |
|---|---|---|---|---|---|---|
| 92.015 | 90 | 8.3 | After crossing the stream bear right | Derelict house to your left | S | 396 |
| 92.016 | 20 | 8.4 | At a junction of three tracks take the furthest right up the hill | Towards the house on the ridge | W | 398 |
| 92.017 | 500 | 8.8 | Turn left on to a paved road | The ancient via Cassia | S | 419 |
| 92.018 | 800 | 9.6 | Fork left | VF milestone | SE | 449 |
| 92.019 | 700 | 10.3 | At the crossroads, turn right on the track. Note:- the "Official Route" makes a loop descending again towards the the lake before remounting the ridge. The Alternate Route proceeds directly to Montefiascone on a normally quiet road | VF sign | SW | 473 |
| 92.020 | 400 | 10.6 | Continue straight ahead on the path between the fields | Large farm building on your right | S | 468 |
| 92.021 | 600 | 11.2 | At the junction with the road, turn right and carefully cross the SR-2 and take the track slightly to the right of the junction and bear left on the track | Pass through a gap in the crash barriers | S | 417 |
| 92.022 | 300 | 11.6 | Rejoin the SR-2 and continue straight ahead with care | | S | 420 |
| 92.023 | 500 | 12.0 | Bear left on the small road | VF milestone on the right | SE | 423 |
| 92.024 | 2500 | 14.5 | At the road junction, bear left, uphill | Large modern house to the right of the junction | SE | 524 |
| 92.025 | 500 | 15.0 | At the Stop sign bear right. Note:- the Alternate Route rejoins from the left | Stone VF sign on the left of the road | S | 534 |

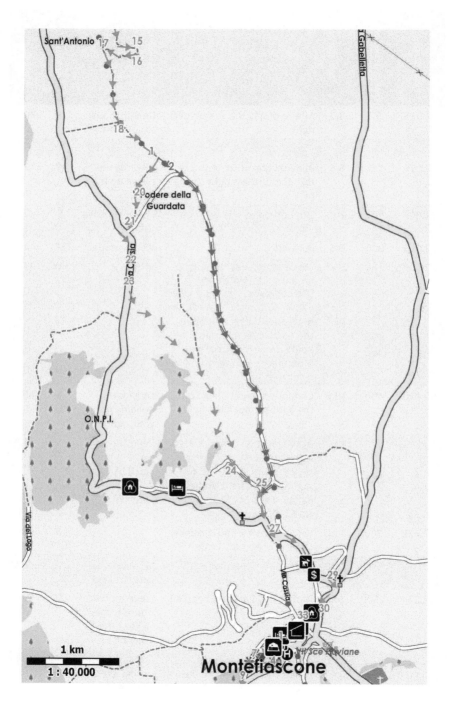

Sant'Antonio

odere della
Guardata

O.N.P.I.

Montefiascone

1 km
1 : 40.000

| Waypoint | Distance between waypoints | Total km | Directions | Verification Point | Compass | Altitude m |
|---|---|---|---|---|---|---|
| 92.026 | 400 | 15.4 | Turn left at the T-junction with the major road, direction Viterbo | Hotel on the left at the junction | SE | 530 |
| 92.027 | 210 | 15.6 | Turn left beside the modern office building on via Cardinal Salotti | Towards Orvieto | SE | 533 |
| 92.028 | 700 | 16.3 | Bear left on via Santa Maria delle Grazie | Towards Orvieto | E | 544 |
| 92.029 | 230 | 16.5 | At the junction with the SS71, turn right | Direction Viterbo | SW | 531 |
| 92.030 | 210 | 16.7 | Take the left fork | Trees lining the left side of the road | S | 534 |
| 92.031 | 230 | 17.0 | Turn right, uphill onto via San Flaviano | Keep the church on your right | W | 554 |
| 92.032 | 60 | 17.0 | Bear left continuing uphill | High stone wall on your right | SW | 557 |
| 92.033 | 160 | 17.2 | Continue straight ahead across the road and up the ramp to enter the historic centre on Corso Cavour | Pass through the archway | SW | 577 |
| 92.034 | 290 | 17.5 | Arrive at Montefiascone (VII) centre | In piazza Vittorio Emanuele | | 601 |

| Alternate Route #92.A1 | | | Length: 4.2km | | | |
|---|---|---|---|---|---|---|
| Stage Summary: direct route to Montefiascone using a generally quiet minor road | | | | | | |
| Stage Ascent: 95m | | | Stage Descent: 35m | | | |
| 92A1.001 | 0 | 0.0 | Continue straight ahead on the ancient via Cassia | | SE | 472 |
| 92A1.002 | 280 | 0.3 | At the junction with road, continue straight ahead | Pilgrim milestone | S | 466 |
| 92A1.003 | 3900 | 4.2 | Keep left at the junction. Note:- the Official Route joins from the right | Stone VF sign | | 532 |

Monastero di San Pietro,(Suor Clara),Via Garibaldi, 31,01027 Montefiascone(VT),Italy; Tel:+39 0761 826066; Email:benedettineap.mf@gmail.com; Web-site:www.monasterosanpietromontefiascone.com; Price:D

Monastero di San Pietro,(Suor Clara),Via Garibaldi, 31,01027 Montefiascone(VT),Italy; Tel:+39 0761 826066; Email:benedettineap.mf@gmail.com; Web-site:www.monasterosanpietromontefiascone.com; Price:D

Centro di Spiritualità Santa Lucia Filippini,Via Santa Maria, 11,01027 Montefiascone(VT),Italy; Tel:+39 0761 826088; Price:D; Note:Open April to October,

Accoglienza Raggio di Sole,(Signora Edy Bertolo),Via San Francesco, 3,01027 Montefiascone(VT),Italy; Tel:+39 0761 820340; +39 0761 826098; +39 3475 900953; Email:edybertolo@libero.it; Web-site:www.cappuccinilazio.com; Price:C

Parrocchia Corpus Domini,(Don Giuseppe Fucili),Coste,01027 Montefiascone(VT),Italy; Tel:+39 0761 826567; Price:D

San Flaviano,(Don Luciano Trapè),01027 Montefiascone(VT),Italy; Tel:+39 0761 826198; Email:sanflavianom.mf@alice.it

B&B Francigena Arcobaleno,Via Pelucche, 10,01027 Montefiascone(VT),Italy; +39 3400 770081; Email:bbfrancigena@yahoo.it; Price:B

Albergo Dante,Via Nazionale, 2,01027 Montefiascone (VT),Italy; Tel:+39 0761 826015; Email:info@ristorantealbergodante.it; Web-site:www.ristorantealbergodante.it; Price:B

B&B - Cassia Antica,Via Paoletti, 12,01027 Montefiascone(VT),Italy; Tel:+39 3282 444427; +39 3493 408642; Email:info@cassiantica.it; Web-site:www.cassiantica.com; Price:B

Camping Amalasunta,Via del Lago, 77,01027 Montefiascone(VT),Italy; Tel:+39 0761 825294; Email:info@campingamalasunta.it; Web-site:www.campingamalasunta.it; Price:C

Ufficio Turistico,Largo Plebiscito,01027 Montefiascone(VT),Italy; Tel:+39 0761 820884

Banca di Roma,Via Cardinal Salotti, 76,01027 Montefiascone(VT),Italy; Tel:+39 0761 825798

Banca Cooperativa Cattolica,Via Indipendenza, 4,01027 Montefiascone(VT),Italy; Tel:+39 0761 824524

Ospedale di Montefiascone,Via Donatori di Sangue,01027 Montefiascone(VT),Italy; Tel:+39 0761 8331

Minciotti - Studio Medico,Via Verentana,01027 Montefiascone(VT),Italy; Tel:+39 0761 824167

Roncella - Medico Veterinario,Via Aldo Moro, 28,01027 Montefiascone(VT),Italy; Tel:+39 0761 823056

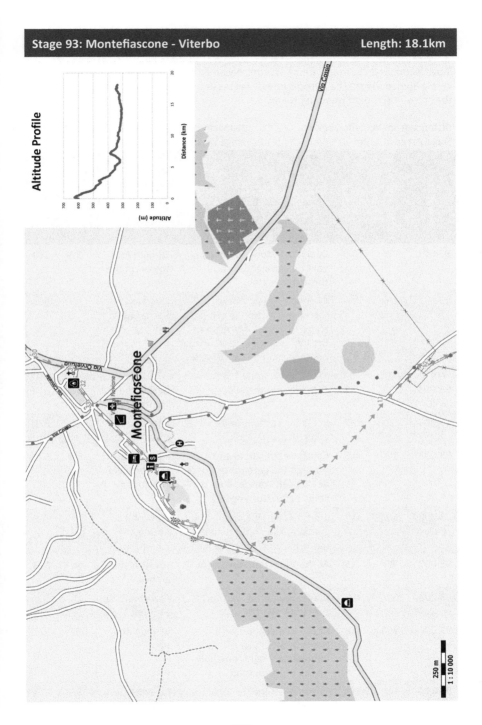

Altitude Profile

Montefiascone

250 m
1 : 10 000

Stage Summary: the route descends and becomes easier on farm tracks and clearly visible Roman roads. The "Official Route" passes beside thermal springs before entering the city of Viterbo on very busy roads.

Distance from Vercelli: 720km   Distance to St Peter's Square, Rome: 128km
Stage Ascent: 179m      Stage Descent: 445m

| Waypoint | Distance between waypoints | Total km | Directions | Verification Point | Compass | Altitude m |
|---|---|---|---|---|---|---|
| 93.001 | 0 | 0.0 | In piazza Vittorio Emanuele, continue straight ahead through the arch | Uphill, clock tower on the left | SW | 601 |
| 93.002 | 70 | 0.1 | Continue straight ahead up the steps. Note: - to avoid the steps, take via 24 Maggio to the left and rejoin the "Official Route" just before exiting the old town | Direction Rocca dei Papi | W | 608 |
| 93.003 | 20 | 0.1 | Turn left into the alley | Beside the Tourist Office | SW | 612 |
| 93.004 | 70 | 0.2 | Enter the gardens and go straight ahead | Between the trees | W | 620 |
| 93.005 | 120 | 0.3 | Continue straight ahead through the gardens of Rocca dei Papi and descend on the steps before turning left | Pass beside the Torre del Pellegrino | SW | 621 |
| 93.006 | 100 | 0.4 | From the parking area behind la Rocca, keep right in the narrow street - via della Rocca | View of lake Bolsena to your right | S | 619 |
| 93.007 | 80 | 0.5 | At the T-junction, turn right | Towards the archway | W | 613 |
| 93.008 | 60 | 0.5 | Pass through the arch and turn left downhill | Town walls on your left | S | 601 |
| 93.009 | 260 | 0.8 | At the intersection with the busy SP8, turn left and immediately right, downhill on the unmade road | VF map and sign | SE | 577 |
| 93.010 | 110 | 0.9 | Take the left fork on the unmade road | Downhill | SE | 571 |

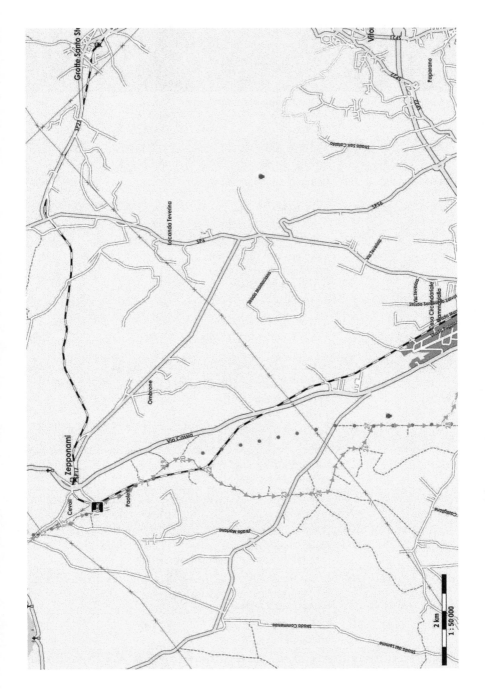

| Waypoint | Distance between waypoints | Total km | Directions | Verification Point | Compass | Altitude m |
|---|---|---|---|---|---|---|
| 93.011 | 800 | 1.7 | At the crossroads, continue straight ahead, direction Viterbo | VF sign, towards pylons | SE | 486 |
| 93.012 | 210 | 1.9 | Just after power substation, fork right onto a dirt track | VF milestone and VF sign | S | 482 |
| 93.013 | 300 | 2.3 | Bear left on the paved section | VF sign | S | 466 |
| 93.014 | 250 | 2.5 | Bear right | VF sign, olive grove on the left | S | 453 |
| 93.015 | 210 | 2.7 | Bear left onto the ancient paved road with a shrine directly to your right | VF sign | SE | 451 |
| 93.016 | 500 | 3.2 | Fork left down the hill | VF sign, via Paoletti | SE | 436 |
| 93.017 | 1400 | 4.6 | Turn left under the railway | VF sign | E | 355 |
| 93.018 | 30 | 4.7 | At the exit from the tunnel, turn right | Between the trees | SE | 354 |
| 93.019 | 600 | 5.3 | At the junction, continue straight ahead | VF signs | SE | 346 |
| 93.020 | 200 | 5.5 | Bear right to continue on the main track | VF signs | SW | 337 |
| 93.021 | 700 | 6.1 | Turn left after going under second railway tunnel | VF sign | S | 321 |
| 93.022 | 30 | 6.1 | Fork right remaining on the main track | VF sign painted on the electricity pole | S | 320 |
| 93.023 | 2100 | 8.3 | At crossroads with the major road (SP7), go straight ahead | VF sign, strada Casetta | S | 340 |
| 93.024 | 500 | 8.8 | At the crossroads in the track, continue straight ahead with farms on both sides | VF sign | S | 339 |
| 93.025 | 400 | 9.1 | Fork left after passing the house on the right | VF sign | SE | 331 |
| 93.026 | 1300 | 10.5 | Fork left beside a fence and a line of trees | VF sign | SE | 331 |

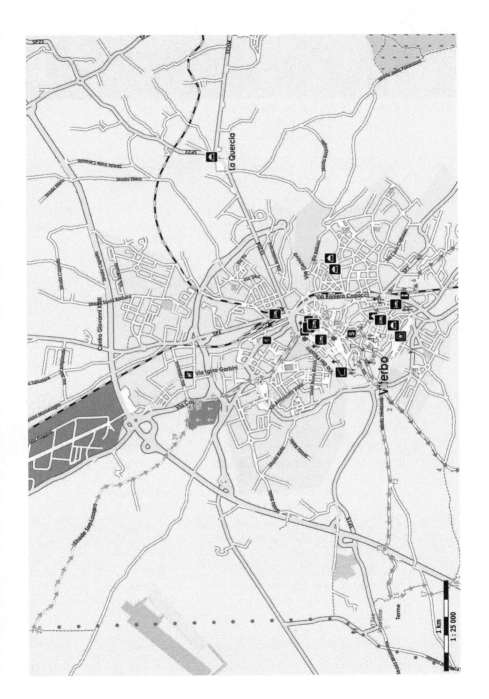

| Waypoint | Distance between waypoints | Total km | Directions | Verification Point | Compass | Altitude m |
|---|---|---|---|---|---|---|
| 93.027 | 600 | 11.1 | At the T-junction in the tracks, turn right towards the thermal ponds | VF sign | S | 320 |
| 93.028 | 1500 | 12.6 | With metal gates to your right, turn left | VF sign | SE | 311 |
| 93.029 | 2900 | 15.4 | Track joins a tarmac road, continue straight ahead | VF sign, factory buildings on your right | E | 318 |
| 93.030 | 400 | 15.9 | At the T-junction, turn right onto strada Cassia Nord | VF sign and large cemetery on your right | S | 323 |
| 93.031 | 400 | 16.2 | Pass under the fly-over and continue straight ahead | No Entry, towards petrol station | SE | 324 |
| 93.032 | 400 | 16.6 | At the roundabout, continue straight ahead, towards Viterbo centre | Via della Palazzina, pass bank offices on the left | SE | 321 |
| 93.033 | 800 | 17.3 | Pass through the arched Porta Fiorentina into the old town of Viterbo and continue straight ahead | Via Matteotti, pass piazza della Rocca on the right | SE | 342 |
| 93.034 | 400 | 17.7 | Cross piazza Verdi and take the second right | Corso Italia, pass Banca di Roma on the right | SW | 337 |
| 93.035 | 300 | 18.0 | In piazza delle Erbe continue straight ahead | Via Roma, pass fountain on your left | SW | 337 |
| 93.036 | 130 | 18.1 | Arrive at Viterbo (VI) centre | Piazza del Plebiscito, beneath bell tower | | 335 |

## Accommodation & Facilities  ....     Montefiascone - Viterbo

Ospitale Torretta Pio Vi,Via San Giovanni Decollato, 1,01100 Viterbo(VT),Italy; +39 3351 621652; Email:graziaand@libero.it; Price:C; Note:Beside chiesa della Trinità. Opening hours from 15.00, closed November to mid-March, ; PR

Complesso Santa Maria della Quercia,Viale Fiume, 112,01100 Viterbo(VT),Italy; Tel:+39 0761 321322; Email:progettualita@pronet.it; Web-site:www.madonnadellaquercia.it; Price:B

Convento Cappuccini,6 via Crispino Beato,01100 Viterbo(VT),Italy; Tel:+39 0761 220761; +39 3475 900953; Email:edybertolo@libero.it; Price:C

Il Villino - Casa Per Ferie,Viale 4 Novembre, 25,01100 Viterbo(VT),Italy; Tel:+39 0761 341900; +39 3395 687389; Web-site:www.ilvillinodiviterbo.it; Price:B

Casa Per Ferie Residenza Nazareth,Via San Tommaso, 26,01100 Viterbo(VT),Italy; Tel:+39 76 1132 1525; Email:info@residenzanazareth.it; Web-site:www.residenzanazareth.it; Price:B

Parrocchia Sant'Andrea Apostolo,Via della Fontana,01100 Viterbo(VT),Italy; Tel:+39 0761 347334; +39 3398 783818; Price:D

Hotel Trieste,Via Nazario Sauro, 32,01100 Viterbo(VT),Italy; Tel:+39 0761 341882; Price:B

Albergo Roma,Via della Cava, 26,01100 Viterbo(VT),Italy; Tel:+39 0761 227274; +39 0761 226474; Email:info@albergoromavt.com; Web-site:albergoromavt.it; Price:B

Albergo Viterbo Inn,Via San Luca, 17,01100 Viterbo(VT),Italy; Tel:+39 0761 326643; +39 3384 290639; Email:info@viterboinn.com; Web-site:www.viterboinn.com; Price:B

Tuscia Hotel,Via Cairoli 41 ,01100 Viterbo(VT),Italy; Tel:+39 0761 345976; Email:info@tusciahotel.com; Web-site:www.tusciahotel.com; Price:A

Bed & Breakfast Orchard,(Valter Labate),Via Ortaccio,01100 Viterbo(VT),Italy; +39 3400 664177; Email:info@bborchard.it; Web-site:bborchard.it; Price:B; Note:Discount with credentials, free breakfast, wifi, dryer, ; PR

B&B - Torre Medievale,Via delle Fortezze, 27,01100 Viterbo(VT),Italy; +39 3388 358534; +39 3476 762363; Email:torremedievale@torremedievale.com; Web-site:www.torremedievale.com; Price:B

Azienda di Promozione Turistica,Via Maresciallo Mariano Romiti,01100 Viterbo(VT),Italy; Tel:+39 0761 304795

Cassa Risparmio di Civitavecchia,Via S.Bonaventura, 4,01100 Viterbo(VT),Italy; Tel:+39 0761 30391

Cassa di Risparmio di Viterbo,Piazza del Plebiscito, 1,01100 Viterbo(VT),Italy; Tel:+39 0761 324848

Stazione Ferrovie,Viale Trieste,01100 Viterbo(VT),Italy; Tel:+39 06 6847 5475; Web-site:www.renitalia.it

Ospedale di Belcolle,Strada Sammartinese,01100 Viterbo(VT),Italy; Tel:+39 0761 3391

## Accommodation & Facilities  ....  Montefiascone - Viterbo

**H** Ospedale di Belcolle,Strada Sammartinese,01100 Viterbo(VT),Italy;
Tel:+39 0761 3391

**+** Meschini - Studio Medico,Via delle Fabbriche,01100 Viterbo(VT),Italy;
Tel:+39 0761 223449

**🐕** Ambulatorio Veterinario,Via Igino Garbini, 81,01100 Viterbo(VT),Italy;
Tel:+39 0761 354581

**🚶** Di Marco Sport,Piazza della Rocca,01100 Viterbo(VT),Italy;
Tel:+39 0761 220197

**🚲** Ranaldi Moto e Cicli,Via Igino Garbini, 66,01100 Viterbo(VT),Italy;
Tel:+39 0761 340865

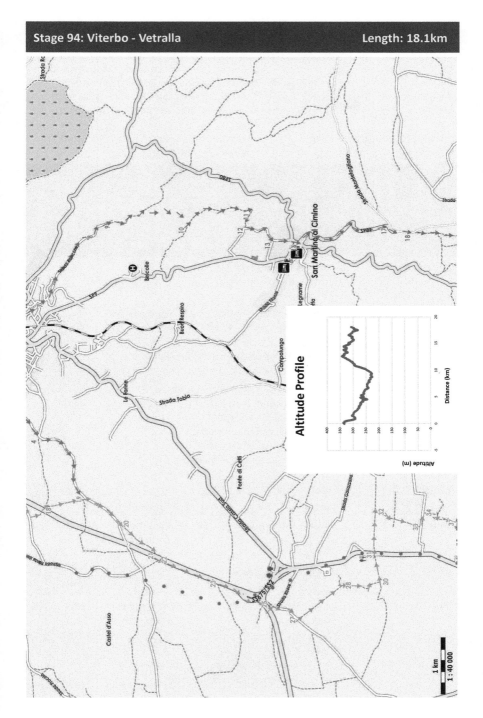

Stage Summary: the "Official Route" route quickly leaves Viterbo and takes again to the country lanes avoiding the main roads. The Alternate Route, also chosen by pilgrims in the middle ages, is more direct (8km shorter) and passes the Cistercian Abbazia di San Martino al Cimino before following the rim of the volcano surrounding Lago di Vico.

Distance from Vercelli: 738km    Distance to St Peter's Square, Rome: 110km
Stage Ascent: 284m       Stage Descent: 311m

| Waypoint | Distance between waypoints | Total km | Directions | Verification Point | Compass | Altitude m |
|---|---|---|---|---|---|---|
| 94.001 | 0 | 0.0 | From the piazza del Plebiscito continue straight ahead | Keep the square on your right | S | 335 |
| 94.002 | 30 | 0.0 | Continue straight ahead on the left hand side of the piazza. Note:- the Alternate Route via San Martino al Cimino leaves to the left on via Cavour | Tabacchi on your left. Enter via San Lorenzo | SW | 335 |
| 94.003 | 90 | 0.1 | At the junction, bear left Note:- to avoid a flight of steps, riders should turn right on via Chigi and follow the Alternate Route to the edge of the old town | Via San Lorenzo | SW | 336 |
| 94.004 | 80 | 0.2 | Bear right across piazza del Gesù | Towards chiesa di San Silvestro | W | 338 |
| 94.005 | 60 | 0.3 | Turn left on via dei Pellegrini | Pass the church on your right | SW | 334 |
| 94.006 | 100 | 0.4 | At the crossroads, turn right | Over the stone bridge | W | 334 |
| 94.007 | 110 | 0.5 | Bear right and cross piazza San Lorenzo | Towards the large arch | N | 329 |
| 94.008 | 70 | 0.5 | Pass through the arch, descend the steps and turn right. Note:- the Alternate Route for riders joins from the right | Keep the metal fence on your right | SW | 324 |

| Waypoint | Distance between waypoints | Total km | Directions | Verification Point | Compass | Altitude m |
|---|---|---|---|---|---|---|
| 94.009 | 260 | 0.8 | At the T-junction, turn left and on the crown of the bend, turn right through the arch | Porta de Valle | W | 297 |
| 94.010 | 90 | 0.9 | Cross the main road and take the small road ahead | Strada Signorino | SW | 293 |
| 94.011 | 40 | 0.9 | Take the right fork. Note:- the "Official Route" makes a wide loop passing beside the site of an Etruscan tomb before returning to this road. 1.5km may be saved by continuing straight ahead on the Alternate Route following arts of a Roman road | Stone wall on your left at the junction | W | 293 |
| 94.012 | 1000 | 1.9 | Take the right fork | Strada s. Ilario e Valentino | W | 299 |
| 94.013 | 800 | 2.7 | Take the bridge over the motorway and continue as the road bears to the left | | W | 282 |
| 94.014 | 600 | 3.3 | Continue straight ahead and follow the road as it turns to the left | Shrine to the martyrdom of Saints Hilary and Valantine on your right | S | 274 |
| 94.015 | 150 | 3.5 | Continue straight ahead on the track. The track will turn to the left and then the right before passing the site of an Etruscan tomb | Road, turns right towards the farm | SE | 273 |
| 94.016 | 400 | 3.8 | At the T-junction, turn right on the road | Embankments on both sides of the road | SW | 272 |
| 94.017 | 110 | 3.9 | Turn left on the stony road, strada San Nicolao | VF signs on the left | SE | 270 |
| 94.018 | 270 | 4.2 | Pass under the motorway and bear right on the broad track | | S | 263 |
| 94.019 | 800 | 5.0 | At the junction, bear right. Note:- the Alternate Route joins from the left | VF sign on the crash barrier | SW | 261 |

| Waypoint | Distance between waypoints | Total km | Directions | Verification Point | Compass | Altitude m |
|---|---|---|---|---|---|---|
| 94.020 | 800 | 5.7 | Fork left onto the gravel track, strada Risiere | VF sign, shrine on the corner | SW | 260 |
| 94.021 | 900 | 6.6 | Take the right fork under the highway | VF sign painted on the concrete | W | 243 |
| 94.022 | 80 | 6.7 | Take the left fork | Parallel to the main road | S | 241 |
| 94.023 | 1100 | 7.8 | At crossroads in track continue straight ahead with the main road remaining on your left. Note:- there are red and white signs that lead under the road and on towards the thermal ponds of Paliano. However, the signs quickly peter out. We advise those visiting the ponds to return here | | SW | 238 |
| 94.024 | 1100 | 8.9 | After skirting the loop of the main road intersection, turn left to go under the road | Red and white VF sign painted on wall | E | 227 |
| 94.025 | 140 | 9.0 | At the T-junction in the track, turn right | Strada Primomo | SW | 231 |
| 94.026 | 140 | 9.1 | At the junction, continue straight ahead on the tarmac | Multiple VF signs | SW | 232 |
| 94.027 | 500 | 9.6 | Turn left on the grassy track | VF sign | SE | 232 |
| 94.028 | 1000 | 10.6 | Bear right on the track | Uphill | S | 276 |
| 94.029 | 400 | 11.0 | Bear right | Pass the trees on your left | S | 296 |
| 94.030 | 400 | 11.3 | At the T-junction, turn left | Strada Quartuccio | E | 302 |
| 94.031 | 500 | 11.8 | At the junction, take the road bridge over the via Cassia and continue straight ahead | Strada Sasso San Pellegrino | E | 313 |
| 94.032 | 800 | 12.6 | Take the next turning to the right | | S | 343 |

| Waypoint | Distance between waypoints | Total km | Directions | Verification Point | Compass | Altitude m |
|---|---|---|---|---|---|---|
| 94.033 | 900 | 13.4 | At the T-junction, turn left on the road | Tree lined driveway ahead at the junction | E | 325 |
| 94.034 | 260 | 13.7 | Turn right on the track | Beside the olive grove | S | 335 |
| 94.035 | 280 | 14.0 | Shortly after the track bends to the left turn sharp right on the path | Into the trees | W | 326 |
| 94.036 | 130 | 14.1 | Turn left on the track | Uphill | S | 325 |
| 94.037 | 400 | 14.5 | At the T-junction, turn right | Via Doganella | S | 332 |
| 94.038 | 600 | 15.1 | At the T-junction, turn right on the white road | Via Doganella | SW | 318 |
| 94.039 | 280 | 15.3 | At the junction, bear right | Via Doganella | SW | 305 |
| 94.040 | 260 | 15.6 | At the junction bear left on the road | Walled gardens on both sides at the junction | S | 297 |
| 94.041 | 500 | 16.1 | Turn left on the grass track | House on the hilltop on the right just before the junction | SE | 303 |
| 94.042 | 140 | 16.2 | Continue straight ahead on the broad track | | S | 305 |
| 94.043 | 400 | 16.6 | At the T-junction with the tarmac road, turn right on the pavement beside the road | | SW | 317 |
| 94.044 | 700 | 17.2 | Take the left fork | Lower road between the trees | SW | 302 |
| 94.045 | 500 | 17.7 | At the crossroads, continue straight ahead into Vetralla (V) | Pass elevated road on left | S | 297 |
| 94.046 | 130 | 17.8 | Bear left and then right | Cross piazza del Mattatoio | SE | 298 |

| Waypoint | Distance between waypoints | Total km | Directions | Verification Point | Compass | Altitude m |
|---|---|---|---|---|---|---|
| 94.047 | 60 | 17.9 | At the traffic lights, continue straight ahead | Via della Pietà, town walls to the right | S | 297 |
| 94.048 | 210 | 18.1 | Arrive at Vetralla (V) centre | T-junction with the via Roma | | 308 |

| Alternate Route #94.A1 | | Length: 19.8km | | | | |
|---|---|---|---|---|---|---|

Stage Summary: the medieval pilgrim route via the abbey of San Martino al Cimino and Lago di Vico follows minor roads and woodland tracks to reach the rim of the Lago di Vico volcano, before returning to the "Official Route" on a quiet minor road. Accommodation is available in San Martino al Cimino.

Stage Ascent: 736m          Stage Descent: 589m

| Waypoint | Distance between waypoints | Total km | Directions | Verification Point | Compass | Altitude m |
|---|---|---|---|---|---|---|
| 94A1.001 | 0 | 0.0 | From the piazza del Plebiscito take via Cavour | No Entry | SE | 336 |
| 94A1.002 | 240 | 0.2 | In piazza Fontana Grande, bear left on via Garibaldi | Pass to the left of the fountain | E | 348 |
| 94A1.003 | 190 | 0.4 | Cross piazza S. Sisto and exit the old town through the archway | Porta Romana | SE | 357 |
| 94A1.004 | 50 | 0.5 | At the traffic lights cross the main road and then bear right on the small road, via San Biele | Railway on your right | S | 357 |
| 94A1.005 | 500 | 0.9 | Continue straight ahead up the hill | Pass through the archway of Torre di S. Biele | E | 358 |
| 94A1.006 | 150 | 1.1 | At the Stop sign, take the pedestrian crossing, turn right and follow the pavement beside the main road | Tree lined road | SE | 371 |
| 94A1.007 | 500 | 1.6 | As the main road bears right, keep left on strada Roncone | Map on the left | SE | 382 |
| 94A1.008 | 1600 | 3.1 | Continue straight ahead, avoid left fork | Fence and metal gate on the right | SE | 471 |

| Waypoint | Distance between waypoints | Total km | Directions | Verification Point | Compass | Altitude m |
|---|---|---|---|---|---|---|
| 94A1.009 | 400 | 3.5 | At the end of the road, bear right on the pathway into the woods | VF sign | S | 487 |
| 94A1.010 | 1600 | 5.1 | At the crossroads, turn left | Clearing on the right | S | 536 |
| 94A1.011 | 1300 | 6.4 | Bear right on the track | | W | 614 |
| 94A1.012 | 300 | 6.7 | At the junction with the tarmac road, take the middle road, straight ahead | Yellow arrow on electricity pole to the right | SW | 583 |
| 94A1.013 | 700 | 7.4 | At the T-junction, turn left | Uphill into San Martino al Cimino | S | 574 |
| 94A1.014 | 300 | 7.7 | Take the right fork | Strada Montagna on the left | SW | 584 |
| 94A1.015 | 100 | 7.8 | Bear left | Direction Roma | S | 576 |
| 94A1.016 | 80 | 7.9 | Turn left.  Note:- archway to Abbazia di San Martino al Cimino on the right | Direction Riserva Naturale Lago di Vico | S | 575 |
| 94A1.017 | 2000 | 9.9 | At the T-junction, turn right | Direction Ronciglione, shrine on the left | S | 741 |
| 94A1.018 | 500 | 10.4 | As the road bends to the left, bear right on the unmade road | Milestone at the junction | S | 740 |
| 94A1.019 | 3100 | 13.5 | At the crossroads, continue straight ahead | Continue through woodland on volcano rim | S | 920 |
| 94A1.020 | 3900 | 17.3 | At the junction with the tarmac road, turn right | Farm ahead | SW | 621 |
| 94A1.021 | 2400 | 19.7 | At the T-junction with the via Cassia, turn left and immediately right, then bear left on the unmade road.  Rejoin "Official Route" | Signpost Vico Matrino, VF signs | | 483 |

| Alternate Route #94.A2 | | | | Length: 0.3km | | |
|---|---|---|---|---|---|---|
| Stage Summary: route for riders avoiding the steps | | | | | | |
| Stage Ascent: 10m | | | | Stage Descent: 24m | | |

| Waypoint | Distance between waypoints | Total km | Directions | Verification Point | Compass | Altitude m |
|---|---|---|---|---|---|---|
| 94A2.001 | 0 | 0.0 | Turn right | Via Chigi | W | 336 |
| 94A2.002 | 140 | 0.1 | At the junction, bear left and then take the first turn on the right | Avoid the ramp on the left | W | 321 |
| 94A2.003 | 190 | 0.3 | Continue straight ahead. Note:- the "Official Route" joins from the steps on the left | Pass under a series of arches | | 322 |

| Alternate Route #94.A3 | | | | Length: 2.6km | | |
|---|---|---|---|---|---|---|
| Stage Summary: direct route following the old Roman road and saving 1.5km | | | | | | |
| Stage Ascent: 40m | | | | Stage Descent: 69m | | |

| Waypoint | Distance between waypoints | Total km | Directions | Verification Point | Compass | Altitude m |
|---|---|---|---|---|---|---|
| 94A3.001 | 0 | 0.0 | Take the left fork | Strada Signorino | SW | 293 |
| 94A3.002 | 210 | 0.2 | At the fork in the road keep to the right | VF sign, road continues between rock faces | SW | 309 |
| 94A3.003 | 140 | 0.4 | Take right fork | Strada Signorino | SW | 311 |
| 94A3.004 | 800 | 1.1 | At the crossroads, continue straight ahead | Between rock faces | SW | 294 |
| 94A3.005 | 1500 | 2.6 | Continue straight ahead and rejoin the "Official Route" | VF sign on the crash barrier | | 265 |

Monastero delle Benedettine Regina Pacis,Via del Giardino, 4,01019 Vetralla(VT),Italy; Tel:+39 0761 481519; Email:accoglienza@casareginapacis.com; Price:B

Albergo Doria,Via Abate Lamberto, 4,01100 Viterbo(VT),Italy; Tel:+39 0761 379924; +39 0761 379221; Email:info@albergodoria.it; Web-site:www.albergodoria.it; Price:B

La Torre di Luca B&B,Via del Monte, 28,01100 Viterbo(VT),Italy; Tel:+39 0360 912988; Email:latorrediluca@alice.it; Web-site:www.latorrediluca.it; Price:B

Albergo Da Benedetta,Via Francesco Petrarca, 3,01019 Vetralla(VT),Italy; Tel:+39 0761 460093; +39 3386 417767; Email:albergodabenedetta@gmail.com; Web-site:www.albergodabenedetta.it; Price:B; Note:Discount with pilgrim credentials,

Albergo Pino Solitario,Via Cassia, 299,01019 Vetralla(VT),Italy; Tel:+39 0761 481045; Email:alpinosolitario@libero.it; Web-site:www.pinosolitario.it; Price:A

Locanda Dal Sor Francesco,Via Blera, 28,01019 Cura(VT),Italy; Tel:+39 0761 481185; +39 3495 155719; Email:dalsorfrancesco@yahoo.it ; Web-site:www.dalsorfrancesco.it; Price:A

Azienda di Promozione Turistica,Piazza Dell'Oratorio,01100 Viterbo(VT),Italy; Tel:+39 0761 379233

Ufficio Turistico,Via Cassia Sutrina,01019 Vetralla(VT),Italy; Tel:+39 0761 460475

Cassa di Risparmio di Viterbo,San Martino al Cimino,01100 Viterbo(VT),Italy; Tel:+39 0761 379911

Banco di Brescia,Via Roma, 21,01019 Vetralla(VT),Italy; Tel:+39 0761 477025; Web-site:www.bancodibrescia.it

Guardia Medica,Via Cassia Interna, 153,01019 Vetralla(VT),Italy; Tel:+39 0761 461242; Web-site:www.asl.vt.it

Servizio Veterinario,Via Etruria, 2,01019 Vetralla(VT),Italy; Tel:+39 0761 477742

Vittorio Bike di Principi Vittorio,Via Cassia In frazione la Botte,01019 Vetralla(VT),Italy; Tel:+39 0761 480002

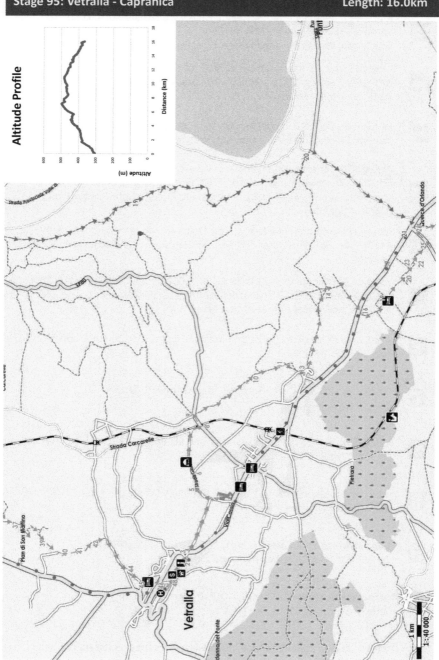

Stage Summary: the route leaves Vetralla on a small tarmac road before rejoining woodland tracks on the lower slopes of the Lago di Vico volcano and intersecting with the route from San Martino al Cimino. The route then winds through hazel nut groves to the outskirts of Capranica.

Distance from Vercelli: 757km          Distance to St Peter's Square, Rome: 92km
Stage Ascent: 291m                     Stage Descent: 231m

| Waypoint | Distance between waypoints | Total km | Directions | Verification Point | Compass | Altitude m |
|---|---|---|---|---|---|---|
| 95.001 | 0 | 0.0 | From the T-junction, turn left | Via Roma, cobbled street, uphill | SE | 306 |
| 95.002 | 400 | 0.4 | Shortly after the road bears right through piazza Marconi, take the left fork on the narrow road | Via San Michele, crucifix at the junction | SE | 319 |
| 95.003 | 250 | 0.6 | Take the subway to cross the via Cassia and continue straight ahead. Note:- to avoid the steps, turn right and then take the first turning to the left, via Dante Alighieri. Rejoin the "Official Route" by turning right at the crossroads | Via dei Cappuccini | E | 321 |
| 95.004 | 1100 | 1.7 | At the T-junction, turn left on via del Giardino | VF signs, Benedictine Monastery | NE | 383 |
| 95.005 | 290 | 2.0 | Bear right on the road | Pass an olive grove on the left | E | 381 |
| 95.006 | 300 | 2.3 | At the junction, continue straight ahead on strada del Giardino | VF sign | E | 386 |
| 95.007 | 800 | 3.1 | At the T-junction turn right on the road | Railway track on your left | S | 392 |
| 95.008 | 170 | 3.2 | At the T-junction, turn left | Over the railway crossing | NE | 392 |

| Waypoint | Distance between waypoints | Total km | Directions | Verification Point | Compass | Altitude m |
|---|---|---|---|---|---|---|
| 95.009 | 230 | 3.5 | At the crossroads turn right across the car park onto the track towards the woods | Follow the edge of the woods with fields on the right | SE | 400 |
| 95.010 | 1200 | 4.7 | At the crossroads, continue straight ahead | | SE | 436 |
| 95.011 | 700 | 5.3 | Turn right on the track towards Botte | Strada Pian della Botte | SW | 437 |
| 95.012 | 270 | 5.6 | Turn left uphill on the road | VF sign | S | 428 |
| 95.013 | 160 | 5.8 | At the top of the hill and before entering Botte, turn left onto a gravelled track into the woods | White arrow on a tree further along the track | E | 439 |
| 95.014 | 1400 | 7.2 | Take the right fork, down the hill | VF sign on tree | SE | 495 |
| 95.015 | 400 | 7.6 | At the T-junction turn right | VF sign | SW | 485 |
| 95.016 | 600 | 8.2 | At the intersection with the via Cassia, turn right and immediately left down a small track. Note:- the path ahead crosses cultivated hazel nut groves and may make for difficult going for cyclists who can turn left on the via Cassia to rejoin the "Official Route" at the Vico Marino junction | VF signs, pass disused chapel on your left | S | 468 |
| 95.017 | 400 | 8.5 | At a large stone go straight ahead between the trees | Broken fence to the right | S | 461 |
| 95.018 | 100 | 8.6 | At the end of the fence, turn left and immediately right | Parallel to the via Cassia | SE | 465 |
| 95.019 | 270 | 8.9 | At the T-junction turn left on the unmade road and immediately right through the gate | Continue across the fields parallel to the main road | SE | 469 |
| 95.020 | 500 | 9.3 | Turn left on the track and then immediately right | Grass track beside a fence | SE | 470 |

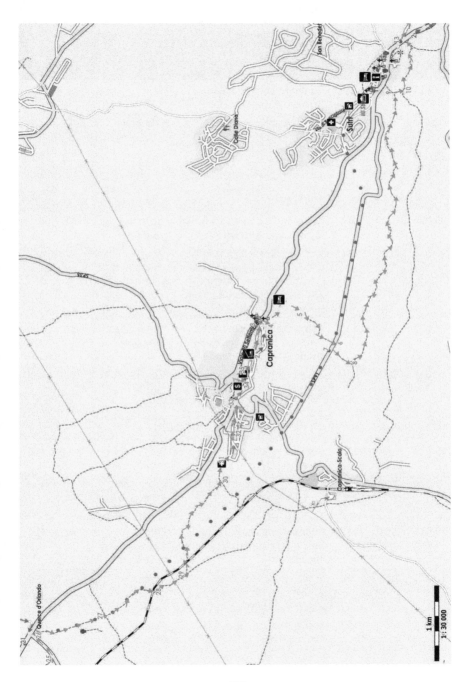

| Waypoint | Distance between waypoints | Total km | Directions | Verification Point | Compass | Altitude m |
|---|---|---|---|---|---|---|
| 95.021 | 240 | 9.6 | Continue straight ahead across the track | | SE | 470 |
| 95.022 | 120 | 9.7 | Turn left and then right | Beside the hazel grove | NE | 466 |
| 95.023 | 50 | 9.7 | Turn right | | SE | 467 |
| 95.024 | 110 | 9.8 | Turn sharp left and then right and right again beside the earthworks | Continue parallel to the main road | SE | 468 |
| 95.025 | 400 | 10.2 | At the T-junction with a broad tarmac road turn left | Open field on your right | NE | 477 |
| 95.026 | 400 | 10.7 | Just before reaching the via Cassia turn sharp right onto the unmade road. Note:- Alternate Route rejoins from the via Cassia ahead | Carved wooden VF sign | S | 483 |
| 95.027 | 1000 | 11.7 | At the crossroads in track continue straight ahead on strada Doganale Oriolese | Metal gates to the right | SE | 466 |
| 95.028 | 800 | 12.4 | Cross over the railway and continue straight ahead | Wire fencing beside the hazel nut grove on the left | SE | 448 |
| 95.029 | 600 | 12.9 | At the junction, bear left, downhill | Pass under railway track | E | 446 |
| 95.030 | 1500 | 14.5 | At the T-junction in the tracks, turn left | VF sign and crash barriers to your right | E | 404 |
| 95.031 | 290 | 14.8 | After passing again under the railway, continue straight ahead | Enter Capranica, via Valle Santi | E | 401 |
| 95.032 | 400 | 15.1 | At the crossroads, continue straight ahead on the Antica strada della Valle Santi | VF sign | E | 390 |
| 95.033 | 400 | 15.6 | At the Stop sign, turn left down the hill | High wall to the left | E | 380 |

| Waypoint | Distance between waypoints | Total km | Directions | Verification Point | Compass | Altitude m |
|---|---|---|---|---|---|---|
| 95.034 | 250 | 15.8 | At the T-junction, turn right on via Nardini | Elevated road on the left | SE | 385 |
| 95.035 | 230 | 16.0 | Arrive at Capranica | Archway ahead | | 367 |

**Accommodation & Facilities .... Vetralla - Capranica**

Monastero Santissima Concezione,Via Garibaldi, 1,01015 Sutri(VT),Italy; Tel:+39 0761 609082; Email:carmelo.s.concezione@libero.it; Web-site:www.carmelitane.org; Price:B

Sala Nardini,Piazzetta Corte Degli Anguillara,01012 Capranica(VT),Italy; Tel:+39 0761 66791; Price:D; Note:Reservation required,

Bed and Breakfast "al Casale Giallo",Località Campo Spinella,01012 Capranica(VT),Italy; Tel:+39 0761 660480; +39 3381 099072; Web-site:www.alcasalegiallo.it; Price:B

B&B - Monticelli,Località Monticelli, 1,01012 Capranica(VT),Italy; Tel:+39 0761 669692; +39 3892 399340; +39 3883 213569; Email:info@monticelli-bed-and-breakfast.it; Web-site:www.monticelli-bed-and-breakfast.it; Price:B; Note:Discounted price for pilgrims with credentials,

Hotel Sutrium,Piazza San Francesco, 1,01015 Sutri(VT),Italy; Tel:+39 0761 600468; Email:info@sutriumhotel.it; Web-site:www.sutriumhotel.it; Price:B

Centro Equitazione di Campagna le Valli,Strada Orto Rosato,01019 Vetralla(VT),Italy; +39 3313 685178

Ufficio Turistico,Piazzale delle Rimembranze, 1,01012 Capranica(VT),Italy; Tel:+39 0761 669364

Comune di Sutri,Piazza del Comune, 34,01015 Sutri(VT),Italy; Tel:+39 0761 609368

Cassa di Risparmio di Viterbo,Viale Nardini,01012 Capranica(VT),Italy; Tel:+39 0761 669004

Salza - Studio Medico,Via Cassia,01012 Capranica(VT),Italy; Tel:+39 0761 669083

Fontana - Studio Medico,Via Orazio Morone,01015 Sutri(VT),Italy; Tel:+39 0761 608616

Piferi - Studio Veterinario,Viale Laura, 75,01012 Capranica(VT),Italy; Tel:+39 0761 669922

Ambulatorio Veterinario,Via di Ronciglione, 23,01015 Sutri(VT),Italy; Tel:+39 3394 632429

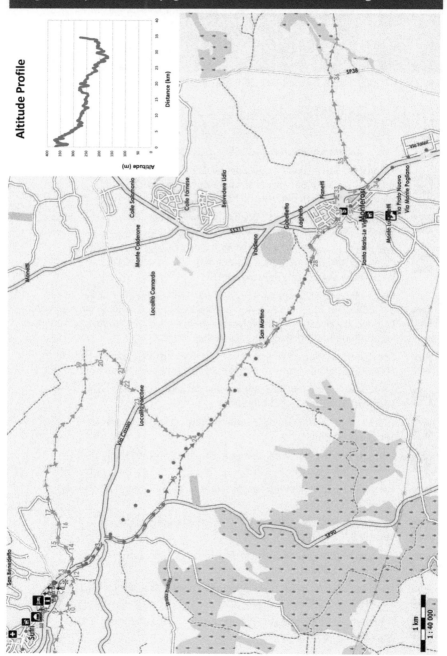

Stage Summary: the long section continues on farm tracks and minor roads making wide loops to avoid the increasingly busy via Cassia. The route passes through the park surrounding the archaeological site at Sutri and approaches Campagnano through the Parco del Treja. It is possible to shorten the section by 4km by using the Alternate Route.

Distance from Vercelli: 773km              Distance to St Peter's Square, Rome: 76km
Stage Ascent: 605m                         Stage Descent: 697m

| Waypoint | Distance between waypoints | Total km | Directions | Verification Point | Compass | Altitude m |
|---|---|---|---|---|---|---|
| 96.001 | 0 | 0.0 | Go straight ahead through the archway into the old town | Towards clock tower | E | 367 |
| 96.002 | 180 | 0.2 | Continue straight ahead. Note:- the route ahead involves a flight of steps, cyclists and riders should turn left and follow via Romana under the bridge to just before the T-junction | Ponte dell'Orolgio | E | 367 |
| 96.003 | 600 | 0.7 | After passing through the centro historico, descend on the steps and turn right | Beside the town wall | S | 332 |
| 96.004 | 130 | 0.8 | At the junction with the via Romana at the bottom of the steps turn left and immediately right on the gravel road, strade Pogliere | VF sign, factory on your left as you turn right | S | 329 |
| 96.005 | 800 | 1.6 | Just before a bend to the left, fork right on the track | | SW | 360 |
| 96.006 | 600 | 2.2 | At the T-junction with the SP91, turn right | Hazelnut grove on the right | W | 374 |
| 96.007 | 80 | 2.3 | Turn left on the track | Fencing on the left and right | SW | 372 |
| 96.008 | 300 | 2.6 | Take the left fork | Proceed in the valley bottom | E | 347 |
| 96.009 | 4100 | 6.7 | At the T-junction, turn right on the road. Note:- for Sutri centre, turn left here and cross the main road | Pass a water trough on your right | S | 268 |

| Waypoint | Distance between waypoints | Total km | Directions | Verification Point | Compass | Altitude m |
|---|---|---|---|---|---|---|
| 96.010 | 120 | 6.8 | Just before the road turns to the right, bear left on the track | Keep the woods to your right and the town on your left | E | 279 |
| 96.011 | 700 | 7.5 | At the junction with the road, turn left | Pass a metal gate and a brick wall on your right | NE | 273 |
| 96.012 | 50 | 7.6 | Take the left fork, cross the bridge and bear right to follow the subway under the main road. Note:- to follow the more direct Alternate Route bear right | Pass circular seating area on your right | NE | 266 |
| 96.013 | 90 | 7.7 | Emerge from the subway and turn right on the small tarmac road | Cross the bridge over a stream | E | 269 |
| 96.014 | 500 | 8.2 | Take the left fork | VF sign | N | 283 |
| 96.015 | 110 | 8.3 | Bear right on the tarmac road | Hazel nut grove on the left | E | 285 |
| 96.016 | 300 | 8.6 | Take the right fork | Remain on the tarmac road | E | 280 |
| 96.017 | 240 | 8.8 | Take the left fork and remain on the tarmac road | VF sign | NE | 275 |
| 96.018 | 250 | 9.1 | Fork right on an unmade road | VF sign | E | 277 |
| 96.019 | 2700 | 11.8 | At the crossroads beside the metal gates, turn right | Towards the houses | S | 256 |
| 96.020 | 180 | 12.0 | Continue straight ahead on the tarmac | Between the houses | S | 256 |
| 96.021 | 800 | 12.8 | At the T-junction with the SP Sutrina, turn right | Pass kilometre mark 4 | W | 263 |
| 96.022 | 220 | 13.1 | Take the next turning to the left, downhill on the unmade road | Large industrial buildings on your right | SW | 264 |

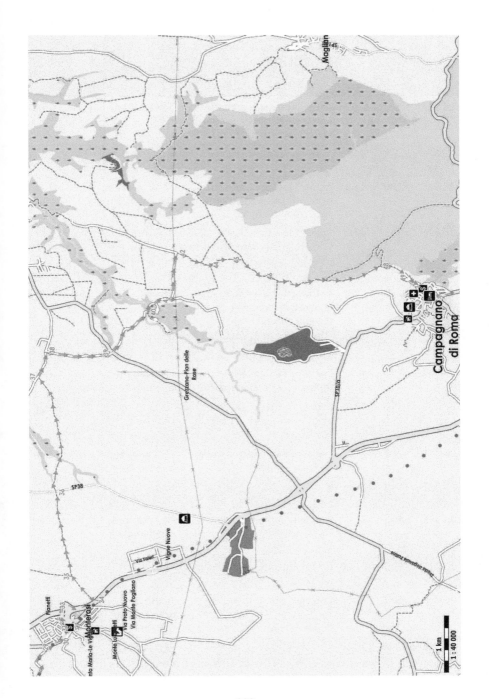

| Waypoint | Distance between waypoints | Total km | Directions | Verification Point | Compass | Altitude m |
|---|---|---|---|---|---|---|
| 96.023 | 500 | 13.6 | At the crossroads with the via Cassia (SS2), continue straight ahead on an unmade road | Towards the hill | SW | 257 |
| 96.024 | 1200 | 14.7 | At the junction, turn left | Entrance gates to the right | S | 255 |
| 96.025 | 180 | 14.9 | At the T-junction, turn left. Note:- the Alternate Route joins from the right | Metal gates on the left of the junction | SE | 256 |
| 96.026 | 2000 | 16.9 | At the T-junction, turn right to skirt the golf course on strada per Monterosi | Pass the golf academy entrance on your left | SE | 248 |
| 96.027 | 700 | 17.6 | At the fork, bear left on the unmade road, remain beside the golf course | VF sign | SE | 270 |
| 96.028 | 1200 | 18.8 | At the crossroads, continue straight ahead | Via strada Sutri Vecchia | SE | 275 |
| 96.029 | 800 | 19.6 | Continue straight ahead through car park and up hill | Elevated road on the left | SE | 252 |
| 96.030 | 190 | 19.8 | Continue straight ahead on the main road, via XIII Settembre | Towards the centre of Monterosi | SE | 265 |
| 96.031 | 290 | 20.0 | In piazza Garibaldi, turn left | Pass fountain on your right | NE | 274 |
| 96.032 | 180 | 20.2 | Bear right with care on the main road | Bridge over the highway | E | 264 |
| 96.033 | 400 | 20.6 | Bear left on the footpath | Highway and small road on the right | S | 256 |
| 96.034 | 600 | 21.2 | Turn sharp left on the small road | Via della Salivotta | NE | 255 |
| 96.035 | 600 | 21.8 | Take the right fork | House driveway on the right | E | 246 |
| 96.036 | 1600 | 23.3 | Cross over the road (SP38) and continue straight ahead on via Cascinone | Pass wire fence on the left | E | 230 |

| Waypoint | Distance between waypoints | Total km | Directions | Verification Point | Compass | Altitude m |
|---|---|---|---|---|---|---|
| 96.037 | 2200 | 25.5 | At the T-junction with the tarmac road, turn right | Via Ronci | E | 209 |
| 96.038 | 500 | 26.0 | At the junction, turn sharp right | Field visible through the trees on the left | S | 218 |
| 96.039 | 1200 | 27.2 | At the crossroads with the SP37, continue straight ahead into Parco Regionale Valle del Treja | Strada Monte Gelato | SE | 182 |
| 96.040 | 1100 | 28.2 | Shortly after crossing the bridge turn left on strada Monte Gelato | Cascate Monte Gelato on the left | SE | 175 |
| 96.041 | 600 | 28.8 | Take the left fork on strada Monte Gelato | Exposed rock face on the left | E | 177 |
| 96.042 | 900 | 29.6 | At the T-junction, turn right | Direction strada vicinale Bottagone | SW | 212 |
| 96.043 | 500 | 30.1 | Take the right fork | Strada vicinale Bottagone | S | 186 |
| 96.044 | 170 | 30.2 | Take the left fork remaining on the tarmac | Towards the houses | S | 185 |
| 96.045 | 600 | 30.8 | At the T-junction, turn right | | SW | 197 |
| 96.046 | 500 | 31.4 | Take the right fork | Beside farm building | S | 208 |
| 96.047 | 220 | 31.6 | Bear left and continue straight ahead | Towards Parci di Veio | S | 207 |
| 96.048 | 1900 | 33.5 | Bear right towards the town | Via Santa Lucia | SW | 213 |
| 96.049 | 600 | 34.1 | Bear right onto the ramp leading up to the town | | NW | 241 |
| 96.050 | 150 | 34.2 | At the T-junction, turn left on the main street through the high town - via Sant'Andrea | Pass the bell tower on the left | SW | 248 |
| 96.051 | 300 | 34.6 | Arrive at Campagno-di-Roma in piazza Cesare Leonelli | Beside the church | | 276 |

Stage Summary: the more direct and former "Official Route" route initially passes beside the via Cassia and then follows smaller roads and farm tracks saving 4km

Stage Ascent: 40m                    Stage Descent: 53m

| Waypoint | Distance between waypoints | Total km | Directions | Verification Point | Compass | Altitude m |
|---|---|---|---|---|---|---|
| 96A1.001 | 0 | 0.0 | Fork right on the track | Pass the metal barrier | SE | 268 |
| 96A1.002 | 230 | 0.2 | At junction with via Cassia, bear right and proceed straight ahead with care | Pass cemetery sign on left | SE | 277 |
| 96A1.003 | 600 | 0.9 | Take the second turning to the right | SP90, direction Bracciano | SE | 267 |
| 96A1.004 | 1400 | 2.3 | On the apex of a bend to the right, turn left on broad track | Strada Campo la Pera | SE | 274 |
| 96A1.005 | 600 | 2.9 | At the T-junction, turn left on the gravel road | Hazel nut grove on your left and right | SE | 264 |
| 96A1.006 | 700 | 3.5 | At the junction continue straight ahead and rejoin the "Official Route" | Metal gates to the left | | 256 |

**Accommodation & Facilities  ....      Capranica - Campagno-di-Roma**

Suore Francescane "oasi di Pace",Via delle Viole, 15,01015 Sutri(VT),Italy; Tel:+39 0761 659175; Email:info@oasidipace.it; Web-site:www.oasidipace.it; Price:B

Convento Suore Missionarie della Consolata - Sette Vene,Via Cassia Km.37 Località Settevene,01036 Nepi(VT),Italy; Tel:+39 0761 527253; Email:fulviarob@tiscali.it ; Web-site:www.consolazione.org; Price:C

Oratorio San Giovanni Battista,Via Dante Alighieri, 7,00063 Campagnano-di-Roma(RM),Italy; Tel:+39 06 9041 094; +39 3339 381576; Email:donrenzotanturli@virgilio.it; Price:D

Hotel Ristorante Benigni,Via della Vittoria, 13,00063 Campagnano-di-Roma(RM),Italy; Tel:+39 06 9042 671; Email: info@hotelbenigni.it ; Web-site:www.hotelbenigni.it; Price:B

Poscolieri - Agriturismo Centro Ippico,Via del Fontanile,01030 Monterosi(VT),Italy; Tel:+39 0761 699431

Banca di Formello,Via Roma, 50,01030 Monterosi(VT),Italy; Tel:+39 0761 698012

Picalarga - Studio Medico,Via Salvo d'Acquisto, 3,00063 Campagnano-di-Roma(RM),Italy; Tel:+39 06 9042 281

Limonta Fabio,Via strada Nuova, 2,01030 Monterosi(VT),Italy; Tel:+39 0761 699703

Nori - Ambulatorio Veterinario,Via del Pavone, 139a,00063 Campagnano-di-Roma(RM),Italy; Tel:+39 06 9042 867

Clinica Veterinaria Cavalli,Strada Valle di Baccano, 80,00063 Campagnano-di-Roma(RM),Italy; Tel:+39 06 9015 4681

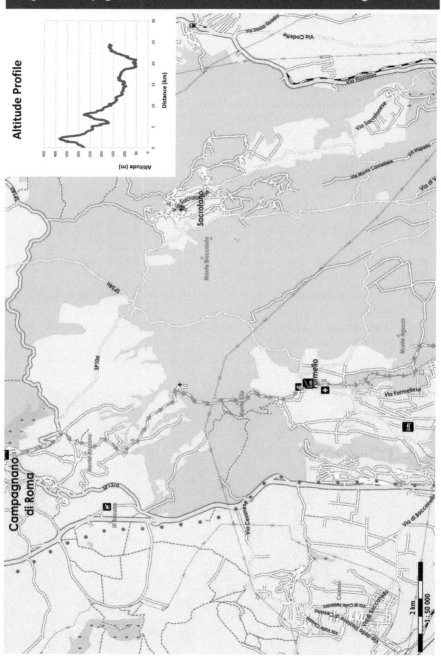

Altitude Profile

Stage Summary: despite the proximity to Rome this section remains surprisingly rural on farm and woodland tracks and small roads.  There are some tricky descents and climbs between Monte Michele and Isola Farnese and a potentially dangerous river crossing.

Distance from Vercelli: 807km
Stage Ascent: 554m

Distance to St Peter's Square, Rome: 41km
Stage Descent: 662m

| Waypoint | Distance between waypoint | Total km | Directions | Verification Point | Compass | Altitude m |
|---|---|---|---|---|---|---|
| 97.001 | 0 | 0.0 | From the church in piazza Cesare Leonelli, continue straight ahead on the main street | Towards the arch, Corso Vittorio Emanuele | SW | 276 |
| 97.002 | 290 | 0.3 | Pass through the arch and turn left in piazza Regina Elena | Towards Formello, via San Sebastiano | S | 281 |
| 97.003 | 900 | 1.2 | On the apex of a sharp bend to the left, continue straight ahead on the more minor road - via di Maria Bona | Sports ground on the right | SE | 312 |
| 97.004 | 300 | 1.5 | Turn right up the hill on strada di Follettino | Painted sign on kerb | SE | 346 |
| 97.005 | 180 | 1.7 | Turn sharp right up the hill on via di Monte Razzano | Woodland on the right | SW | 362 |
| 97.006 | 240 | 2.0 | Take the left fork - strada delle Piane | House with roof terrace on the left at the junction | S | 379 |
| 97.007 | 230 | 2.2 | Take the right fork on the unmade road - strada delle Piane | VF sign | S | 378 |
| 97.008 | 1100 | 3.3 | At the T-junction, turn left - strada delle Pastine | VF sign | SE | 281 |
| 97.009 | 500 | 3.8 | Take the left fork on the tarmac road - strada del Sorbo | VF sign painted on electricity pole | SE | 267 |

| Waypoint | Distance between waypoint | Total km | Directions | Verification Point | Compass | Altitude m |
|---|---|---|---|---|---|---|
| 97.010 | 1600 | 5.4 | Continue straight ahead on the road into the Valle del Sorbo | Pass the Santuario della Madonna del Sorbo on the left | S | 205 |
| 97.011 | 1100 | 6.5 | Cross the bridge and continue straight ahead | Uphill, towards the trees | S | 185 |
| 97.012 | 1300 | 7.8 | On entering Formello, bear right and right again | VF sign, via Antonio Angelozzi | S | 277 |
| 97.013 | 170 | 8.0 | Take the left fork on the narrow road - via Enrico Bellomi | Downhill, No Entry | SE | 274 |
| 97.014 | 400 | 8.4 | At the crossroads, continue straight ahead | Pass house n° 132 on the left | SE | 234 |
| 97.015 | 300 | 8.7 | In the centre of Formello, bear right across the piazza | Pass through archway | SE | 221 |
| 97.016 | 70 | 8.8 | On entering the historical centre of Formello, bear left and then turn right on via 20 Settembre | Pass church of San Lorenzo on your left | S | 221 |
| 97.017 | 190 | 9.0 | At the end of the road, bear left down the cobbled street | | E | 201 |
| 97.018 | 70 | 9.0 | At the T-junction with the main road, turn right downhill | Viale Regina Elena | S | 205 |
| 97.019 | 60 | 9.1 | At the foot of the hill, bear left on the small road | Pass car park on your right | S | 198 |
| 97.020 | 400 | 9.5 | Take the right fork on the unmade road | Follow valley | S | 192 |
| 97.021 | 600 | 10.1 | Turn left, through the trees | Pass an open field on the right | S | 158 |
| 97.022 | 1300 | 11.4 | At the T-junction with the gravel road, turn left | Rock outcrop across the field on the left | E | 134 |
| 97.023 | 600 | 12.0 | At the crossroads, turn right | Between the fields | S | 140 |

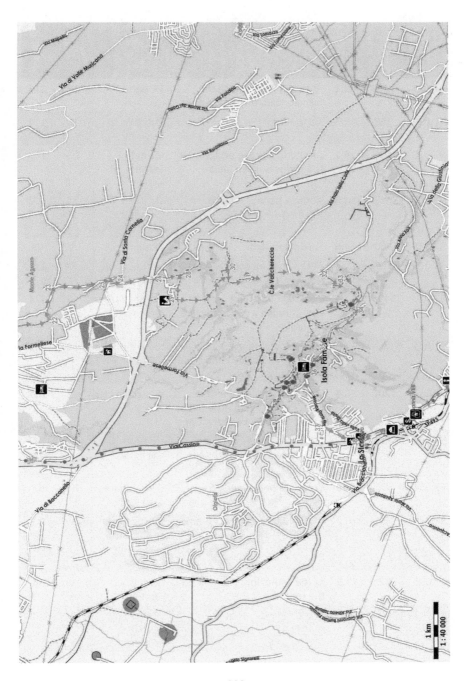

300

| Waypoint | Distance between waypoint | Total km | Directions | Verification Point | Compass | Altitude m |
|---|---|---|---|---|---|---|
| 97.024 | 1100 | 13.1 | At the T-junction with the tarmac road, turn sharp right | VF sign | NW | 116 |
| 97.025 | 160 | 13.3 | Turn left | Via del Selvotta | S | 113 |
| 97.026 | 800 | 14.1 | After crossing the bridge over the highway, keep right | Via del Selvotta, VF sign | S | 107 |
| 97.027 | 210 | 14.3 | At the junction, keep left on the road | The road becomes a track | S | 106 |
| 97.028 | 300 | 14.6 | Turn sharp right | VF sign | W | 98 |
| 97.029 | 500 | 15.1 | At the crossroads, turn left on via Monte Michele | Between the fields | SE | 111 |
| 97.030 | 1400 | 16.4 | Turn right and right again to pass through a gap in the line of trees | Keep the trees on the right | S | 124 |
| 97.031 | 900 | 17.3 | Pass through the gate and bear left on via del Prato delle Cotte | Hamlet on the right | S | 122 |
| 97.032 | 1200 | 18.4 | Take the right fork on the track through gate.  The track winds downhill between trees | VF sign on tree | S | 105 |
| 97.033 | 800 | 19.2 | Bear right to ford the river with care and bear right again on the far side | Torrente Valchetta | W | 55 |
| 97.034 | 800 | 20.0 | Cross the bridge and turn right | Via del Prato della Corte | NW | 52 |
| 97.035 | 900 | 20.9 | At the junction bear right up the hill | Football field on the left before the junction | NW | 58 |
| 97.036 | 600 | 21.5 | At the T-junction, bear left on the road | Enter Isola Farnese | W | 96 |
| 97.037 | 1100 | 22.6 | At the junction, bear left up the hill | VF sign, via dell'Isola Farnese | SW | 142 |

| Waypoint | Distance between waypoint | Total km | Directions | Verification Point | Compass | Altitude m |
|---|---|---|---|---|---|---|
| 97.038 | 500 | 23.1 | At the T-junction on the brow of the hill, turn left on the via Cassia | Roma 17km | SE | 157 |
| 97.039 | 1400 | 24.5 | Arrive at La-Storta (II) centre | Beside the elevated church on the right | | 168 |

### Accommodation & Facilities ....    Campagno-di-Roma - La-Storta

Istituto Palazzo Suore Poverelle,Via Baccarica, 5,00135 Roma(RM),Italy; Tel:+39 06 3089 0495; +39 0335 274645; Email:lastorta@istitutopalazzolo.it; Price:C

Parrocchia Sacri Cuori di Gesù e Maria,Via del Cenacolo, 43,00135 Roma(RM),Italy; Tel:+39 06 3089 0267; +39 06 3098 3136; Email:parrocchia@sacricuorilastorta.org; Web-site:www.sacricuorilastorta.org

Hostel "maripara",Piazza S.Lorenzo, 3,00060 Formello(RM),Italy; +39 3342 925118; Email:hostelmaripara@gmail.com; Price:B

Da Giovanni,Via delle Rubbia,00060 Formello(RM),Italy; Tel:+39 06 9040 0004; +39 06 9088 410; Price:B

Tempio di Apollo,Piazza della Colonnetta, 8 ,00123 Isola-Farnese(RM),Italy; Tel:+39 06 9171 2163; Email: info@tempiodiapollo.com ; Web-site:www. tempiodiapollo.com; Price:A

Seven Hills Camping Village,Via Vittorio Trucchi, 10,00189 Roma(RM),Italy; Tel:+39 06 3036 2751; +39 06 3031 0826; Email:info@sevenhills.it; Web-site:www.sevenhills.it; Price:C; Note:Chalets and apartments also available,

C.P.R.Quarter Horses Srl,Via della Vaccareccia,00060 Formello(RM),Italy; Tel:+39 06 9075 443

Comune di Formello,Piazza San Lorenzo,00060 Formello(RM),Italy; Tel:+39 06 9019 41

Comune di Roma Municipio Ufficio la Storta,Via Domenico Falcioni, 12,00123 Roma(RM),Italy; Tel:+39 06 3089 0461

Banca di Formello,Viale Umberto Primo, 4,00060 Formello(RM),Italy; Tel:+39 06 9014 301; Web-site:www.bccformello.com

Banca di Roma,Via della Storta, 926,00123 Roma(RM),Italy; Tel:+39 06 3386 741

Stazione Ferrovie,Via della Storta, 27,00123 Roma(RM),Italy; Tel:+39 06 6847 5475; Web-site:www.renitalia.it

Saccomando - Studio Medico,Via Roma,00060 Formello(RM),Italy; Tel:+39 06 9088 600

D'Ammando - Studio Medico,Via Valle della Storta, 7,00123 Roma(RM),Italy; Tel:+39 06 3089 1543

Clinica Veterinaria Parco di Veio,Via Formellese Km,00060 Formello(RM),Italy; Tel:+39 06 8982 3139

Dottor Puntieri,Via Cassia, 1819,00123 Roma(RM),Italy; Tel:+39 06 3089 1939

Cicli Magni di Stefano Magni,Via Roma,00060 Formello(RM),Italy; Tel:+39 06 9014 6048

Alltransfersinrome,Via Cesare Meano,00123 Roma(RM),Italy; +39 3472 700100

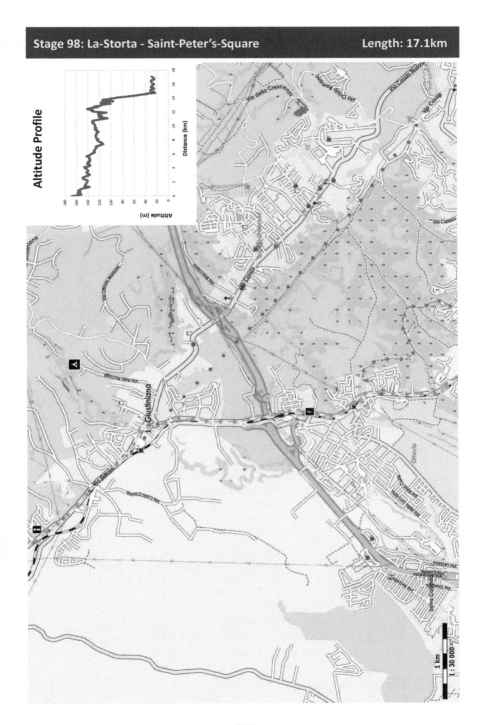

Altitude Profile

Stage Summary: the route into Rome initially uses the very busy via Cassia and via Trionfale. Relief is possible on the pathways through the Reserva Naturale della Insugherata and the Monte Mario park, where you have magnificent views of the city before returning to the broad boulevards for the final approach to the Vatican. Parts of the via Trionfiale do not have pavements/sidewalks. It is possible to continue on the via Cassia and enter the Reserva Naturale immediately after crossing the bridge over the ring road. However, the gates to the reserve may be locked. For those not wishing to deal with the Rome traffic there is a frequent and inexpensive train service from La Storta.

Distance from Vercelli: 832km          Distance to St Peter's Square, Rome: 17km
Stage Ascent: 228m                     Stage Descent: 367m

| Waypoint | Distance between waypoint | Total km | Directions | Verification Point | Compass | Altitude m |
|---|---|---|---|---|---|---|
| 98.001 | 0 | 0.0 | On the via Cassia, below the church in La-Storta, continue with great care on the road towards Roma | Church on the right and petrol station on the left | SE | 168 |
| 98.002 | 2700 | 2.7 | Take the right fork, following the flow of traffic on via Trionfale | Pass motor car sales on the right | S | 148 |
| 98.003 | 3200 | 5.9 | Pass under the flyover and continue straight ahead. Note:- some relief from the traffic may be achieved by turning left on via Silvio Antoniano and following the Alternate Route through the nature reserve | Remain on via Trionfale | S | 136 |
| 98.004 | 1500 | 7.4 | At the traffic lights following the San Filippo railway station, turn right, pass under the railway and then turn left and remain on the road, parallel to the railway | Via Giuseppe Barellai | S | 116 |
| 98.005 | 600 | 8.0 | At the mini-roundabout, turn left | Via Vincenzo Chiarugi | NE | 124 |
| 98.006 | 70 | 8.1 | Bear right | Via Franco Basaglia | E | 123 |

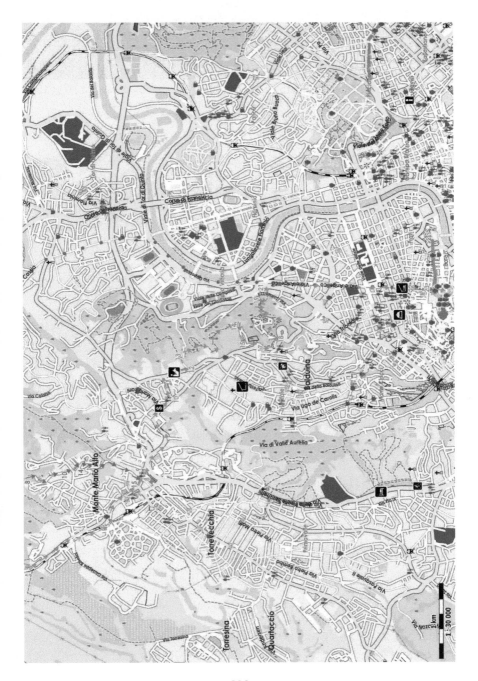

| Waypoint | Distance between waypoint | Total km | Directions | Verification Point | Compass | Altitude m |
|---|---|---|---|---|---|---|
| 98.007 | 140 | 8.2 | Return to via Trionfale and take the pedestrian crossing. Continue straight ahead on the pavement on the left side of the road | The road will divide ahead | SE | 123 |
| 98.008 | 600 | 8.8 | At the junction beside the Tabacchi, continue straight ahead on via Trionfale. Note:- the Alternate Route joins from the left | Continue between shops | E | 125 |
| 98.009 | 130 | 8.9 | Take the pedestrian crossing and cross to the extreme right hand side of the complex junction, and then continue straight ahead, remaining on via Tirionfale | Pass the entrance to the university on your right | E | 125 |
| 98.010 | 1200 | 10.2 | At the traffic lights shortly after passing the playground on your left, turn left on the broad street | Echography clinic to the right at the junction | E | 127 |
| 98.011 | 260 | 10.4 | In piazza Walter Rossi, turn right, left and then right again on via della Camilluccia | Metal railings to the left of the pavement | SE | 132 |
| 98.012 | 400 | 10.8 | Turn left on via Edmondo de Amicis | Pass olive trees on your right | E | 131 |
| 98.013 | 250 | 11.0 | On the crown of the sharp bend to the left, turn right on the path and continue to keep right at the junction in the path | Pass through the metal gates in the the Monte Mario park | SE | 112 |
| 98.014 | 1200 | 12.2 | Join the road and skirt the sports field on your right | Views of the Tiber on your left | SW | 133 |
| 98.015 | 500 | 12.7 | Join a broader road and bear right | Metal gates on your left | S | 126 |
| 98.016 | 220 | 12.9 | Exit from the park and turn left | Via Trionfale | S | 118 |

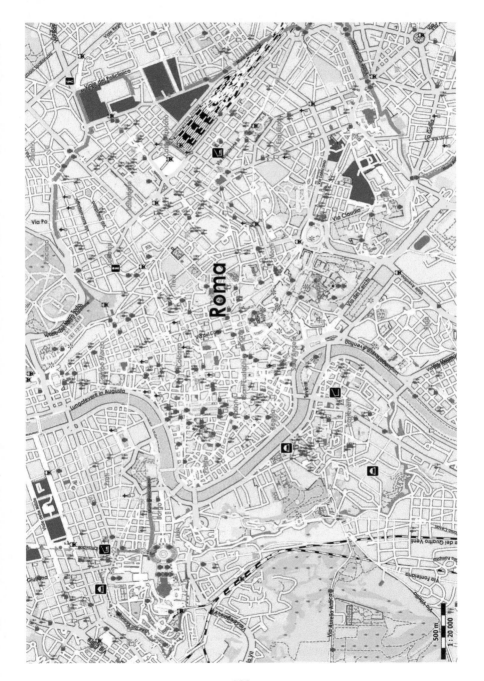

| Waypoint | Distance between waypoint | Total km | Directions | Verification Point | Compass | Altitude m |
|---|---|---|---|---|---|---|
| 98.017 | 50 | 13.0 | Turn left up the steps and through the archway into the walled Monte Mario park. Note:- to avoid the obstacles in the park remain on via Trionfale to the crossroads with the tree lined via Andrea Doria, where you should bear right on via Leone IV to rejoin the "Official Route" in piazza del Risorgimento | | SE | 116 |
| 98.018 | 170 | 13.2 | Cross the road and continue on the path | Pass the observatory on the left, views of the city to the right | E | 104 |
| 98.019 | 1500 | 14.6 | At the bottom of the hill pass through the gate and continue straight ahead | | SE | 39 |
| 98.020 | 150 | 14.8 | After leaving the park, take the pedestrian crossing over the road and continue straight ahead | Via Novenio Bucchi | E | 23 |
| 98.021 | 80 | 14.9 | At the T-junction, cross the broad road and go straight ahead through the gardens in piazza Maresciallo and turn right | Viale Angelico | S | 24 |
| 98.022 | 1900 | 16.7 | Continue straight ahead across piazza Risorgimento towards the Vatican on via di Porta Angelica | Dome of St Peter's to the right | S | 24 |
| 98.023 | 400 | 17.1 | Arrive at Saint-Peter's-Square (I) | | | 29 |

| Alternate Route #98.A1 | | | | Length: 4.1km | | |
| --- | --- | --- | --- | --- | --- | --- |

**Stage Summary:** diversion through the nature reserve avoiding parts of the via Trionfale

**Stage Ascent: 110m**      **Stage Descent: 122m**

| Waypoint | Distance between waypoints | Total km | Directions | Verification Point | Compass | Altitude m |
| --- | --- | --- | --- | --- | --- | --- |
| 98A1.001 | 0 | 0.0 | Shortly after passing under the flyover, turn left | Via Silvio Antoniano | E | 136 |
| 98A1.002 | 170 | 0.2 | Immediately after passing the garage compound, turn left on the track | Pass apartment block on your right | N | 136 |
| 98A1.003 | 70 | 0.2 | Bear right on the track | | E | 132 |
| 98A1.004 | 160 | 0.4 | In the clearing, bear right on the track | | S | 116 |
| 98A1.005 | 700 | 1.1 | Turn left on the broad track between the trees | | E | 86 |
| 98A1.006 | 700 | 1.8 | Take the right fork | | S | 75 |
| 98A1.007 | 160 | 1.9 | Take the left fork | In the valley between the buildings | S | 71 |
| 98A1.008 | 290 | 2.2 | Join the tarmac road and turn right up the hill | | SW | 94 |
| 98A1.009 | 200 | 2.4 | Turn left on via della Rimessola. Note:- there are steps on the route ahead, riders should continue straight ahead to via Trionfale, turn left and rejoin the "Official Route" | High walls on the right side of the road | SE | 122 |
| 98A1.010 | 400 | 2.8 | At the T-junction, turn right | Pass house N° 7 on the right | SW | 130 |

| Waypoint | Distance between waypoints | Total km | Directions | Verification Point | Compass | Altitude m |
|---|---|---|---|---|---|---|
| 98A1.011 | 50 | 2.9 | At the T-junction, turn left | Hotel ahead at the junction | SE | 131 |
| 98A1.012 | 200 | 3.1 | Turn right | Via Siro Corti | SW | 126 |
| 98A1.013 | 50 | 3.1 | Keep right on via Siro Corti | No Through Road | W | 123 |
| 98A1.014 | 170 | 3.3 | At the foot of the steps, turn left | House N° 56 ahead | S | 116 |
| 98A1.015 | 800 | 4.1 | At the crossroads between via Giuseppe Taverna and via Trionfale, turn left and rejoin the "Official Route" | Against the flow of traffic | | 125 |

**Accommodation & Facilities ....    La-Storta - Saint-Peter's-Square**

Centro Pellegrini S.Teresa Couderc,Largo Vincenzo Ambrosio, 9,00136 Roma(RM),Italy; Tel:+39 06 3540 1142; +39 3457 413484; Email:reservation@cenacolopellegrini.it; Web-site:www.cenacolopellegrini.it; Price:A; Note:Credentials required,

Spedale della Provvidenza,(Signora Lucia Colarusso),Via dei Genovesi 11B,00153 Roma(RM),Italy; Tel:+39 06 4959 590; +39 3272 319312; Email:info@pellegriniaroma.it; Web-site:www.pellegriniaroma.it; Price:D; Note:Credentials required,

Casa Accoglieza Paolo Vi,Viale Vaticano, 92,00165 Roma(RM),Italy; Tel:+39 06 3909 141; Email:info@casapaolosesto.it; Web-site:www.ospitiamoconcuore.it; Price:A

Casa Figlie di S.Giuseppe,Vicolo Moroni, 22,00153 Roma(RM),Italy; Tel:+39 06 5833 3490; Email:info@casasangiuseppe.it; Web-site:www.casasangiuseppe.it; Price:A

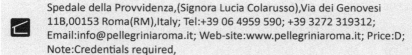

Suore Marcelline,(Suor Maria Raffaella),Via Dandolo, 59,00153 Roma(RM),Italy; Tel:+39 06 5812 443; Price:B

Pensione Ottaviano Hostel,Via Ottaviano, 6,00192 Roma(RM),Italy; Tel:+39 06 3973 8138; Email:info@pensioneottaviano.com; Web-site:pensioneottaviano.com; Price:B

Alessandro Downtown Hostel,Via Carlo Cattaneo, 23,00185 Roma(RM),Italy; Tel:+39 06 4434 0147; Email:downtown@hostelsalessandro.com; Web-site:www.hostelsalessandro.com; Price:B

Foyer Phat Diem - Pensione,Via della Pineta Sacchetti, 45,00167 Roma(RM),Italy; Tel:+39 06 6638 826; Email:foyerpdr@gmail.com; Web-site:oyerphatdiem.com; Price:B

Camping Village Roma,Via Aurelia, 831,00163 Roma(RM),Italy; Tel:+39 0291 483658; Web-site:camping-village-roma.hotel-rn.com; Price:C; Note:Chalets and apartments also available.  English language service +44 (0)203 564 2773,

Centro Ippico Montemario,Via della Camilluccia, 120,00135 Roma(RM),Italy; Tel:+39 3398 144440

Ufficio Turistico Polacco,Via Vittorio Veneto, 54,00187 Roma(RM),Italy; Tel:+39 06 4827 060

Unicredit,Via Trionfale, 7110,00135 Roma(RM),Italy; Tel:+39 06 3386 741; Web-site:www.unicreditbanca.it

Fiumicino Airport,Via Portuense, 2365,00054 Fiumicino(RM),Italy; Tel:+39 06 6595 1000; Web-site:www.adr.it

Azienda Ospedaliera Sant'Andrea,Via di Grottarossa, 1035,00189 Roma(RM),Italy; Tel:+39 06 3315 109; Web-site:www.ospedalesantandrea.it

Ospedale San Carlo,Via Aurelia, 275,00165 Roma(RM),Italy; Tel:+39 06 3975 1937

Veterinaria Medaglie d'Oro,Viale delle Medaglie d'Oro, 374,00136 Roma(RM),Italy; Tel:+39 06 3534 7397

Tutto Sport,10, via G.B.Morgagni 8 /,00161 Roma(RM),Italy; Tel:+39 06 4423 0421

Cicli Rossi,Via Trionfale,00135 Roma(RM),Italy; Tel:+39 06 3081 8820

Cicli Fatato,Via F.Albergotti, 14/e,00167 Roma(RM),Italy; Tel:+39 06 6635 440

313

## Books published by LightFoot Guides

All LightFoot Publications are also available in ebook and kindle and can be ordered directly from www.pilgrimagepublications.com

The complete 2014 LightFoot Guide to the via Francigena consists of 4 books: Canterbury to Besançon, Besançon to Vercelli, Vercelli to Rome, Companion to the Via Francigena

### LightFoot Guide to the via Domitia - Arles to Vercelli

 Even with the wealth of historical data available to us today, we can only offer an approximate version of yesterday's reality and we claim to do nothing more in this book. The route described runs roughly parallel with a section of the via Domitia between Arles and Montgenévre (a large portion of the original route having been subsumed by the A51), continues along a variety of roads and tracks that together form a modern-day branch of the via Francigena and rejoins the official main route (to Rome) in Vercelli.

### The LightFoot Companion to the via Domitia

 An optional partner to the guide, providing the additional historical and cultural information that will enhance your experience of the via Domitia and via Francigena

### The LightFoot Guide to the Three Saints' Way

  The name, Three Saint's Way, has been created by the authors of the LightFoot guide, but is based on the three saints associated with this pilgrimage: St Swithin, St Michael and St James. Far from being a single route, it is in fact a collection of intersecting routes: The Millenium Footpath Trail starting in Winchester and ending in Portsmouth, England. The Chemin Anglais to Mont St Michel and the Plantagenet Way to St Jean d'Angely, where it intersects with the St James Way (starting from Paris).

**LightFoot Guide to Foraging**
Heiko Vermeulen
"Nowadays if I look at a meadow I think lunch."

A guide to over 130 of the most common edible and medicinal plants in Western Europe, aimed at the long-distance or casual hiker along the main pilgrim routes through Western Europe. The author has had some 40 years of experience in foraging and though a Dutchman by birth, has been at home all over Europe including Germany, Ireland, England and for the last 8 years in Italy along the Via Francigena pilgrim route, where he feeds his family as a subsistence farmer, cultivating a small piece of Ligurian hillside along permaculture principles, and by gathering food from the wild.

Sylvia Nilsen is a South African freelance writer who has been published in numerous local and international publications. She worked as a research agent and editor for a UK-based travel guide publisher and produced several African city and country guides. Sylvia has walked over 5 000 km of Camino trails in France and Spain, as well as from Switzerland to Rome on the Via Francigena pilgrimage. She has served as a volunteer hospitalero in Spain and is a Spanish accredited hospitalero volunteer trainer in South Africa having trained 42 new volunteers. With amaWalkers Camino (Pty) Ltd she leads small groups of pilgrims on slackpacking trails on the Camino Frances.

**YOUR CAMINO on foot, bicycle or horseback in France and Spain**
A comprehensive Camino planning guide off ering advice to ilgrims on choosing a route, how to get to the start, info for people with disabilities, cyclists, walking with children, with a dog, a donkey or doing the Camino on horseback, with 300 pages of advice and information.

**CAMINO LINGO**
English-Spanish Words and Phrases for Pilgrims on el Camino de Santiago. Compiled by Sylvia Nilsen and her Spanish teacher Reinett e Novóa, this is a cheat's guide to speaking Spanish on the Camino. No complicated verb conjugations or rules on grammar, this book offers over 650 words and phrases just for pilgrims.

**SLACKPACKING the Camino Frances**
When and where to start walking and how to get there. Three suggested itineraries for hiking daily stages of 10km to 15km: 15km to 20km and 20km to 25km. A 17-day, 5km to 8km per day itinerary for the not-so-able pilgrim wanting to walk the last 100km to Santiago in order to earn a Compostela. A list of Camino Tour Companies and Luggage Transfer services. Contact details for buses, trains and taxis along the route.

### Riding the Milky Way

The story of Babette and Paul's journey, but it is not bout hardships and heroes. In fact it was a motley and uninspiring crew that left Le Puy en Velay, France, in July 2005. The humans, broke, burnt-out and vaguely hoping that early retirement would save their health and sanity. The horses, plucked off the equine scrapheap in France and still grappling with their new roles as something between mount and mountain goat. The dog, doing his best to understand why he was there. But 75 days later they reached their destination, overcoming the challenges, and most importantly, finding that they had become an inseparable team. Packed with sketches and photographs, this book will inspire even the most timid traveller, while also giving practical guidelines for someone wanting to do the same or a similar journey. And finally, it is quite simply an excellent, sometimes irreverent, guide to the St James Way. Much more than just a good read.

### Riding the Roman Way

"We have good equipment, our horses are fit and we are fully prepared, so why this feeling of dread? Perhaps it has something to do with knowing what to expect." Babette and Paul have come a long way since their first horseback pilgrimage and not just in kilometres. They have learnt a great deal about themselves, their animals and some of the practicalities of long distance riding, but they continue to regard themselves as incompetent amateurs and are still in search of a rationale for their insatiable wanderlust.

Common sense and the deteriorating east-west political situation put an end to their original plan, riding on from Santiago de Compostela to Jerusalem in 2006, but Paul has found an equally exciting alternative: the via Francigena pilgrimage to Rome. The good news is that there will be no war zones to contend with, but the bad news is that they will be travelling 2000 kilometres along a relatively unknown route, with a 2,469 metre climb over the Swiss Alps, often under snow, even in August. Riding the Roman Way takes you alongside this intrepid team every step of the way and shares the highs and lows with disarming honesty. It also provides a detailed account of the via Francigena and offers practical guidance for someone wanting to embark on a similar journey. But be warned, this book book will inspire even the most timid traveller and you read it at your own risk.

CPSIA information can be obtained
at www.ICGtesting.com
Printed in the USA
BVHW01s0733281117
501439BV00005B/21/P